Through a Woman's Eye

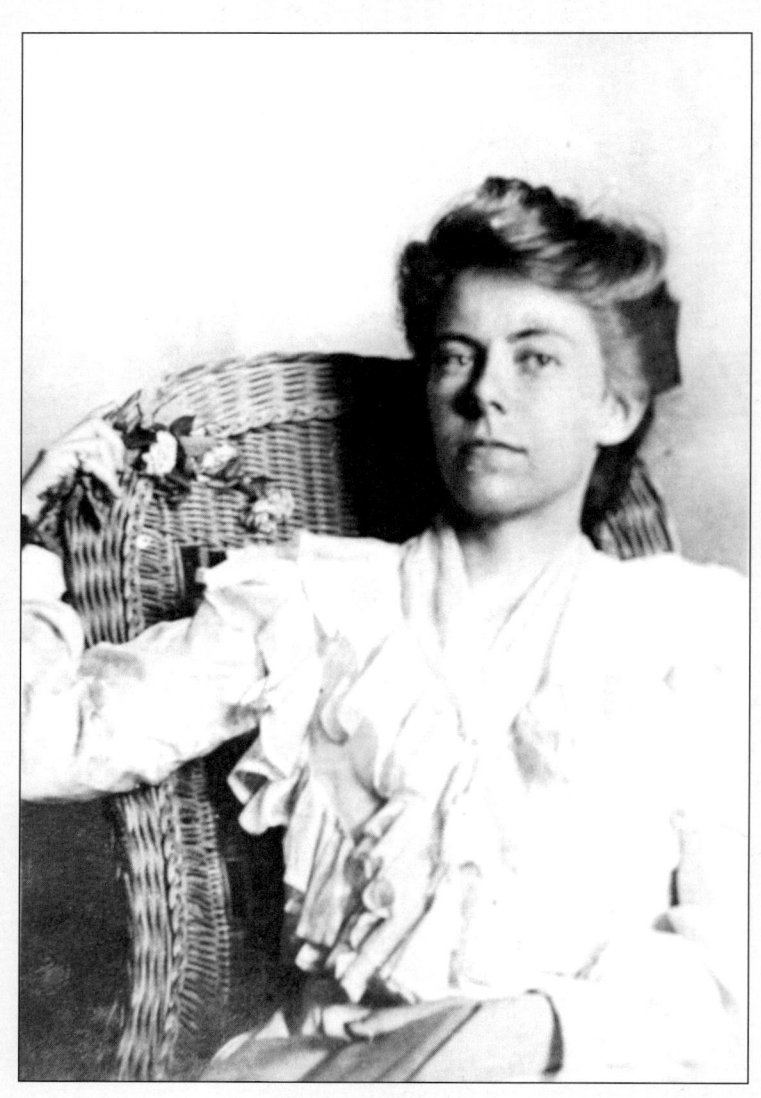

Through a Woman's Eye

The Early 20th Century Photography of Alabama's Edith Morgan

PREFACE BY MARIAN PERDUE FURMAN

ESSAYS BY MARIAN PERDUE FURMAN AND MATTHEW DANIEL MASON

FOREWORD BY HARVEY H. JACKSON III

NewSouth Books

Montgomery

NewSouth Books
105 S. Court Street
Montgomery, AL 36104

Publisher's Cataloging-in-Publication data

Through a woman's eye : the early 20th century photography of Alabama's Edith Morgan /
preface and essay by Marian Perdue Furman ; essay by Matthew Daniel Mason ;
foreword by Harvey H. Jackson III.
p. cm.
Includes index.

ISBN 978-1-58838-263-4 (hardcover)

1. Photography—History—20th century. 2. Morgan, Edith, 1875–1939. I. Title.

2015935072

Edited by Jeff Benton
Design by Randall Williams

Printed in the United States of America
by Thomson-Shore, Inc.

Contents

Foreword / VII

Preface / XI

Acknowledgments / XIII

Sources of Illustrations / XIII

Part I—Essays

Edith Morgan and Her World / 3

Maps / 13

More than Black and White / 15

Part II—Photographs

The Album / 37

Index / 139

Contributors / 143

Foreword

A Personal Memory

HARVEY H. JACKSON III

I first heard of Edith Morgan on an afternoon in the early fall of 1992. I had recently returned to teach in Alabama and had made contact with my cousin-in-law Kathryn Tucker Windham. Cuddn' Kathryn knew I was working on a history of the Alabama River System, so she promised that if I would drive down to her home in Selma, she would take me on a tour of the Black Belt, through which the Alabama River flows. I arrived early, and after a snack of pimento cheese on graham crackers we hit the road.

After wandering around Dallas and Wilcox counties, we arrived in Camden, a jewel of a Black Belt town. There Kathryn insisted we visit the Liddell house—houses down there have names, just like people—because she knew that I had a by-marriage connection to the Liddells and because she wanted to see the mistress of the house, who was an old friend. We were ushered in, and as we sat in the parlor drinking iced tea, I noticed a photo album, laid open. It was the sort of album you don't see much anymore—black pages, lick-and-stick corner clips to hold the photographs in place, captions written in white ink. Whoever went to all this trouble obviously meant for the collection to be kept and loved. When I looked closely I could see why. There, in black and white, were slices of life in the late nineteenth- and early twentieth-century small-town and rural South. Although the album contained pictures of whites, the most impressive photographs were of African Americans—some posed, some candid. I had never seen so many studies of black life in one place outside of a library or archives.

Naturally I asked, and the answer was as surprising as the photographs themselves. They were taken by Edith Morgan, a young woman whose place in Camden, Black Belt, and Alabama history is, if nothing else, unique.

In the first place, Edith Morgan and her family were outsiders, which anyone living in the Black Belt then and now will tell you was and is an obstacle to overcome. It is not that Black Belt natives are unfriendly; it is just that history has taught them to be a little wary of newcomers. Especially newcomers like the Morgans, who were Yankees, from Chautauqua County, New York, to be precise, which added to the problem of "fitting in." Making their acceptance even more unlikely was that the family arrived in 1866, not the best year for Northerners to show up in Wilcox County. And to make matters even worse, the father, Albion LeBat Morgan, seemed to many then and to many now, to be the epitome of the carpetbagger Radical Republican.

It must have been particularly galling to the citizens in and around Camden that Mr. Morgan was appointed clerk of county court and county commissioner by federal authorities, offices of critical importance that up until the end of the Civil War had filled by local, native whites. Being the choice of the county's newly enfranchised blacks and their white allies to attend the constitutional convention that wrote the Constitution of 1868, also did little to endear Morgan to the whites who had formerly occupied the courthouse. That constitution's emphasis on education and the rights of women and blacks, was not a high priority among the planters who had controlled things before the war and intended to control them again.

Because the plantation gentry of Wilcox County were and would remain bitter over the defeat of the Confederacy, Reconstruction was and would long continue to be a thorn in their flesh. Even today descendants of the vanquished speak derisively about the way the victors came in and took over. Talking with members of old families you will hear disparaging references to the great-grandchildren of carpetbaggers who still live on land and in houses they "stole" from the true owners. So it followed that the Morgans kept largely to their own kind—a handful of other Northern families who came south after the war—and it was into this insular world that Edith Morgan was born on July 28, 1875.

Not much is known about her childhood. Later one of her contemporaries told her great-niece that she "was not allowed to play with her," and likely the children of other longtime Camden residents were told the same. This left Edith Morgan with a sister, nine years her senior, a few playmates from other carpetbagger families, and her imagination for companions. And a vivid imagination it was. Early displaying an artistic talent, her parents encouraged her efforts and eventually sent her to the Art Institute of Chicago where she developed the interest in photography that led to the photographs in this book.

Returning to Camden, she organized and taught art classes for daughters of the local gentry who came to her to learn how to work in pastels, watercolors, and, of course, photography. Many of these girls were the subjects in Morgan's photographs. Her "art receptions," where student work was exhibited, became part of the Camden cultural scene and added a touch of big city sophistication to the little west Alabama Black Belt town.

Art was not Morgan's only contribution to life and learning in Camden. After returning from her studies, she began to reveal a concern for the education of black children—a concern one might find natural considering her family's politics and her father's efforts at the constitutional convention. However, as her father settled into the community, he became more comfortable with local political leanings, became a Democrat, and found a way to accommodate his Republican inclinations with those of the party of segregation and white supremacy. So when his daughter set aside a corner of the kitchen as a schoolroom where the children of the retainers of family and friends could be taught, there was apparently no uproar. Still, some might have frowned on tutoring black children were it not for the fact that in addition to this enterprise Edith Morgan took it upon herself to launch a Bible ministry.

This began with her efforts to teach her black cook to read from the Bible, but quickly expanded into Bible classes for other black women. As word of this spread, white women began seeking instruction (segregated of course) and Morgan complied with their requests. Soon she was teaching more Bible classes than art classes, and though she continued to teach African American women, her primary pupils were white. Women from every congregation in town came to her for instruction and at the height of her activity she was teaching every day of the week in churches within a fifteen-mile radius of her home. Out of these efforts a number of Sunday schools were created.

Yet she continued to take photographs, and at one point she paused in her whirlwind of activity to mount her pictures in three albums, which she gave to close friends in her carpetbagger circle—the Hendersons, the Logues, and the Liddells. It was the owner of the Henderson album who gave Marian Furman permission to copy and publish the images you see here. Edith Morgan's health began to fail, but she kept working, even to the point of holding Bible classes from her hospital bed. When she died on April 2, 1939, the local newspaper summed up her life this way: "Camden and vicinity and Wilcox County will miss her untiring service, her kindly deeds, deeds inspired, deeds of sacrifice, deeds of mercy, deeds of love and friendship, accommodating deeds and deeds of every admirable and gracious character."

What the obituary did not mention was her art, but now, with this volume, that omission has been corrected. Edith Morgan lived a full life. A life of teaching and a life of creating. Here you have a sample of what she accomplished.

Preface

MARIAN PERDUE FURMAN

The family home where I spent much of my childhood and reside today is just a mile down the road from the old family home where Edith Morgan lived her entire life a hundred years ago. My childhood in the late 1930s and '40s was spent in Wilcox County, Alabama. Time then, as now, moved slowly, as the world beyond accelerated with changes coming at lightning speed. Progress and change, however, have slowly seeped into this place, and there are fewer and fewer people who experienced the life that prevailed here three or four generations ago. I am one who remembers.

In 1948, my father presented me with a twin lens Rolleiflex camera, the kind used by serious photographers at the time, and he built a tiny darkroom for me in our garage. Thus began my lifelong passion for photography. I operated a portrait studio for a time, but my special interest was darkroom techniques and fine-art, black-and-white images.

In the fall of 1986, on a visit to a home formerly owned by Edith Morgan, I noticed an old photograph album with black pages lying on a side table. Casually glancing inside, I was captivated and awash with nostalgia as I slowly turned the pages. I knew that I had stumbled on an artistic and historic treasure. My background in photography gave me an instant appreciation of the images in this album created by Edith Morgan. Edith, born and raised in Wilcox County, attended the School of the Art Institute of Chicago where she studied painting. This training is evidenced by her use of lighting and composition, which enhanced her art—and certainly enhanced her photography as well. I was especially impressed by her ability to show the strength and dignity in the faces of her subjects. Portraits are expected to capture the physical likenesses of the subjects, but great portraits capture the subjects' very essence. Edith Morgan has done this with many of her black subjects, especially the older ones; she not only captures their strength and dignity, but she also captures their nobility. Her photographs of blacks contrast dramatically with those of whites—presumedly her personal and family friends, primarily carpetbaggers and children of carpetbaggers. There are no photographs of poor whites, which is subject to speculation.

Even though my childhood in Wilcox County was thirty or forty years after the images presented in this book were created, some things were very much the same. As a child, I picked worms off the collards, put them in a soft drink bottle, and then fed them to the chickens. There is an image in this book of a boy doing exactly that (Plates 80 and 81). I have spent so many hours alone in the darkroom printing and working with these images that I feel I know each in a special way.

I felt compelled to preserve these images for future generations. I learned that there were three copies of the album; Edith had apparently given them to her special friends in the Henderson, Liddell, and Logue families. I gained permission from the Henderson family to copy the collection professionally. I am honored to be a steward of Edith Morgan's photographic legacy.

As a photographer myself, I always want photographs to stand on their own. If the visual arts are a form of communication and if art is to delight us and broaden our own perspectives, it should be able to do so without the commentary of experts. So, I try to approach art without preconceptions formed by others; I first try to experience a work of art itself as the only link between the artist and me. Only then do I turn to others. I must admit that their contributions, although secondary, do enhance my understanding and appreciation. For these reasons, I recommend that you first look at the photographs themselves. In the album, the photographs were arranged at random; they are presented here, however, in an order that seems to be more logical for appreciating them, an order that corresponds to Matt Mason's essay. Edith had trimmed and cut out some of the photographs with scissors before pasting them into the albums; these are presented in this volume against a black background to mimic their appearance in the albums. Experience the photographs yourself, experience them as something fresh, as images to broaden your perspective and your world. Only then, read the essays—and enjoy the photographs in a different light.

ACKNOWLEDGMENTS

This book has been in my heart and mind for many years. It would never have come to be published without the help and support of many people along the way. First, I want to thank the Hendersons who so graciously gave permission for me to copy their copy of the photograph album, and to George Alford at the Alabama-Tombigbee Regional Commission for supporting the project. Many thanks to my family who have been so supportive and patient with my efforts to preserve and promote the photographs. Special thanks to granddaughter Jade Miller Furman for her skilled and untiring technical assistance. Oida Woodson provided invaluable local history information. Thanks to Black Belt Treasures and especially Kristin Law for her help. I am grateful to Harvey Jackson who so willingly shared his experience and encouragement in my often faltering efforts. Matt Mason has provided an essay that broadens what was known locally about the Morgan family, and he has put Miss Edith's photographs in their contemporary context. Jeff Benton at NewSouth Books has earned my lasting gratitude for his patient and untiring assistance. Last and most importantly, thanks to NewSouth for agreeing to bring new life to these photographs and the remarkable woman who created them.

SOURCES OF ILLUSTRATIONS

Page ii, Edith Morgan, "Self-portrait." Courtesy of Marian Furman.

Pages 8–9, Unidentified photographers, "Wilcox County Courthouse," "Wilcox Female Institute," "First Presbyterian Church." Historic American Buildings Survey.

Page 11, Unidentified photographer, "Edith Morgan (1875–1939)." Published in Aleathea Thompson Cobbs, "An Unofficial Leader: Edith Morgan," in *Presbyterian Women of the Synod of Alabama, U.S.* (Mobile, Alabama: Woman's Auxiliary of the Synod of Alabama, U.S., 1935), 268.

Page 13, Map 1. NewSouth Books and Matthew Daniel Mason, "The Alabama Black Belt."

Page 14, Maps 2 and 3. NewSouth Books and Matthew Daniel Mason. "Wilcox County, Alabama," and "Locations in Camden, Alabama."

Page 27, Frances Stebbins Allen and Mary Electa Allen, "How D'y Do" (LC-USZ62-67233). Courtesy of the Library of Congress, Prints & Photographs Division.

Page 28, (top) Emma Justine Farnsworth, "La Cigal," from *Camera Notes,* Volume 3, No. 3, 1900; (bottom) Mathilde Weil, "The Embroidery Frame." Courtesy of the Frances Benjamin Johnston Collection, Library of Congress, Prints & Photographs Division, LC-USZC4-9066.

Page 29, Elizabeth B. Brownell, "A-Listnin' to the Witch-Tales 'at Annie Tells About" (LC-USZC2-5939); and Gertrude Käsebier, "Miss N" (LC-DIG-ppmsca-12056). Courtesy of the Library of Congress, Prints & Photographs Division.

Page 30, Zaida Ben-Yusuf, "The Odor of Pomegranates" (LC-DIG-ppmsca-15875). Courtesy of the Frances Benjamin Johnston Collection, Library of Congress, Prints & Photographs Division.

Page 31, Frances Benjamin Johnston, "Elderly African American couple posed outside of a building, near Hampton Institute, Hampton, Va." (LC-USZ62-118921); "Old African American couple eating at the table by fireplace, rural Virginia" (LC-USZ62-61017); and "Negro man, woman and three children at an old-time well" (LC-USZ62-51059). Courtesy of the Frances Benjamin Johnston Collection, Library of Congress, Prints & Photographs Division.

Page 32, Mary Morgan Keipp, "A Nurse of Eighty Winters." From *Mary Morgan Keipp, Negro Life,* courtesy of the New York Public Library, Miriam and Ira D. Wallach Division of Art, Prints and Photographs.

Page 33, Russell Bros., "Cotton Picking in Alexandria Valley, Alabama." Courtesy of the Randolph Linsly Simpson African-American Collection, Yale Collection of American Literature, Beinecke Rare Book and Manuscript Library, Yale University.

Page 34, Arthur Rothstein, "Gee's Bend Negro, Alabama" (LC-USF33-T01-002404-M5). Courtesy of the Farm Security Administration, Office of War Information Photograph Collection, Library of Congress, Prints & Photographs Division.

Page 35, Marion Post, "Angelina Parker and Children Working in Garden, Gees Bend, Alabama" (LC-USF33-030351-M3). Courtesy of the Farm Security Administration, Office of War Information Photograph Collection, Library of Congress, Prints & Photographs Division.

Page 36, Eva Lawrence Watson-Schütze, "Storm." From *Camera Work,* Number 9, January 1905.

Pages 39–136, Edith Morgan Photographs, courtesy of Marian Furman.

PART I

ESSAYS

Edith Morgan and Her World

MARIAN PERDUE FURMAN

I am a photographer and a lifelong resident of Camden, Wilcox County in Alabama's Black Belt. So too was Edith Morgan. My family has lived in Wilcox County since 1820, but I have traveled all over the world. It has given me perspective; it has enabled me to see my own home in a different way than had I never left Wilcox County. Edith Morgan had the perspective of Chicago and of growing up in a family of outsider carpetbaggers. What I have absorbed in eight decades of living in Camden—as well as some research—may help you understand and appreciate Edith Morgan's photographs. Her world was not so unusual at the beginning of the twentieth century, especially in the rural South. It was, however, a world away from the urban, internationally-oriented, fast-paced, impersonal world experienced by many Americans at the beginning of the twenty-first century.

THE MORGANS

Edith Morgan (1875–1939) was born into a world struggling to be reborn. With the defeat of the Confederacy, the politico-economic realities of the Old South had completely collapsed. During her lifetime, she would experience radical changes; yet, so much remained unchanged.

In 1866, Edith's parents and her older sister came to Camden from their native Chautauqua County, New York. Albion LaBat Morgan (1834–1917) had been a successful merchant in western New York State. He was ten years older than his wife,

Lydia Jones Morgan (1844–1896). Their older child, Minna "Minnie" Augusta, who was born in New York in 1864, married Charles C. Washburn. Edith was born in Camden on July 28, 1875, and with the exception of several years in Chicago, she made her life in her native Camden.

Albion Morgan was one of the thousands of carpetbaggers who came south after the Civil War to make their fortunes. The carpetbaggers were widely viewed by Southern whites as Northern opportunists who bought up land for rock-bottom prices, took control of the railroads, controlled local and state government to loot the public coffers and exploit patronage—in general, to profit personally from the destitute South. Carpetbaggers differed from Northerners who came into the South as early as 1862 in the wake of occupying Union troops. Those Northerners were likely to be abolitionists, schoolteachers, and missionaries, and, after 1865, agents of the federal Freedmen's Bureau. The motives of this other group of Northerners were most likely to have been to remake the South in their own image. Both groups were widely despised by Southern whites.

In 1866, Albion Morgan was one of the first carpetbaggers in Wilcox County. He had had two years of college in Ohio before marrying and coming south. Reconstruction federal authorities appointed him a county commissioner and clerk of the Wilcox County court. He represented Wilcox County in the Alabama Constitutional Convention of 1867. That convention produced the Constitution of 1868—which essentially enfranchised male freedmen and tried to disenfranchise many white men who had served the Confederacy. This Radical Reconstruction Constitution of 1868 was a reaction against the Presidential Reconstruction Constitution of 1866, which had been written by white delegates and which basically had tried to reinstate the old regime.

Federal military rule ended in 1867, and the following year Alabama was readmitted to the Union with its new Constitution of 1868. A civilian Republican governor and legislature were elected, with freedmen voting for the first time in Alabama history. The Radical legislature of carpetbaggers, freedmen, and cooperationists (scalawags and pre-war Southern Unionists) had no means to raise revenue for the state, since most wealth had been lost during the war. The price of cotton, an international commodity, had not risen to prewar levels, because during the war and Union embargo of the

4

Confederacy, Great Britain had encouraged cotton production in its empire, chiefly in India and Egypt. Even though the Black Belt cotton crops failed in 1865 and 1866, there was an international cotton glut and resulting low prices. To raise revenue, Alabama's Radical legislature responded by raising the property tax by 350 percent. This move actually united traditional antagonists: the planters of the Black Belt and the small farmers of the hill country of north Alabama. It also ignited widespread violence that resulted in up to a thousand deaths. Almost a quarter of Alabama's 90,000 Confederate troops had been killed in the war, and another quarter had been wounded or disabled. Those who had survived had lost heavily also; many of their farms had reverted to wilderness, but that land was all they had to begin anew. They were not going to lose their land. Even more federal troops were rushed in to maintain Republican control, but by 1874 Southern white Democrats had regained control of the governor's office and the legislature. Black men and poor whites were not disenfranchised en masse until the turn of the century; however, because the secret ballot was not introduced in Alabama until 1893, it was easy to intimidate poor voters who depended on the elite for their livelihoods.

Although Albion Morgan's political base was shrinking, he was reelected after Reconstruction ended and served in his Wilcox County positions until 1881 when President Hayes nominated him U.S. internal revenue collector for the First Collection District, Mobile. He held that position for three years. Morgan's political outlook changed in time, and eventually he affiliated with the Democratic Party, the party of the Southern white Redeemers. In the U.S. Census of 1880—and in all subsequent censuses through 1910, Morgan was listed as a farmer. He had first acquired property in 1867 with the purchase of 950 acres near Boiling Springs, about twenty-five miles northwest of Camden. Soon afterwards, he bought some adjoining tracts. Still later, he acquired ten small properties nearer Camden.

The U.S. Census of 1880 notes that in addition to his wife and two daughters, the Morgan household included a relative of Lydia Jones Morgan, John C. Jones, a miller, and his wife, Jinnie Jones, both in their early thirties and both Northern-born. The Morgan household also included Emma Chapin, single and forty years old, an art teacher; she too was born in the North.

Camden and Wilcox County

When Edith was born on July 28, 1875, Camden was a small town and the county seat of Wilcox County (Maps 2 and 3) whose population was about 30,000. In the flush times of the 1850s, the county's population had grown 42 percent. This was the result of the 1837 invention of the steel plow by John Deere of Illinois. The ancient wooden plow, even with iron augmentation, was incapable of breaking the rich soil of the Midwest—and the rich, dark soil of the Alabama prairies, the Black Belt (Map 1). But it would take imported British steel before Deere was able to produce a thousand plows a year in the late 1840s. Subsequently, Alabama's Black Belt became one of the richest areas in the United States, its wealth based on cotton produced by slave labor on the prairies and in the river bottomlands. In the decade before the Civil War, Wilcox County wealth was evident by its having many steamboat landings on the Alabama River. In 1860, well over half of the white families in Wilcox County were slave owners, and slaves comprised 72 percent of the population. In addition, in 1860 there were seventy free blacks in the county. However, by 1875 when Edith was born, all that had changed. Although Wilcox County's population had grown slightly in the 1870s, it then began to decline and did so throughout Edith's life. During the Great Migration between 1915 and 1930, some 174,000 Alabama blacks left the state for the North. In 1930, Wilcox County's population was down to 25,000.

In the immediate post-war period, the region that had depended almost entirely on cotton was trying to work out a new economy for a radically changed reality. At the heart of the problem was labor and, to a lesser degree, land ownership. Freedmen did not have land, and landowners did not control labor. Three solutions came to the fore. Landowners signed contracts with freedmen who worked for wages. This solution was preferred by the landowners who could work the field hands in gangs, thereby continuing the antebellum economy of scale; freedmen found this solution the most onerous. A second solution was to divide large landholdings into small farms that were leased to tenants. Landowners disliked this inefficient method; freedmen preferred it, but could seldom get credit for equipment and seed, and even when they could, were generally unable to produce enough to make a decent living for themselves. The third solution, which came to dominate, was the crop-lien system. Sharecroppers signed one-year agreements with landowners. Depending on how much of the seed and equipment was supplied by the landowner and how much by the sharecropper, the harvested crop was divided, usually with the cropper getting a third or a half. Inevitably, these three solutions were not solutions at all, and yield and income proved inadequate to support either the laborers or the landowners.

Cotton dominated the economy of Wilcox County from the pioneer days of Alabama Fever that began in 1817 until the early twentieth century. However, it took almost to the turn of the century to return to the 1860 cotton production level. For almost fifty years, Wilcox County was one of Alabama's main cotton-producing counties. However, what amounted to a one-crop economy was not a stable economy. The vagaries of weather and the price of cotton on the world market resulted in unpredictability. One thing that was predictable was that after high prices for cotton, more acres would be planted, and that usually resulted in more cotton produced and, consequently, lower prices. Farmers, of course, understood the cycle of supply and demand, but there was nothing they could do about it short of government quotas. Depending on one crop exacerbated the inherent reality of agriculture. In Morgan's day, there was no machinery to aid in cotton production; it was a labor-intensive enterprise, and the cost of labor was the only economic variable that could be controlled, to a degree, by the cotton farmer. In the 1910s, cotton production dropped precipitously. In the Black Belt especially, the destructive boll weevil was an impetus for a degree of agricultural diversification that included corn, sweet potatoes, and livestock. To make the situation even more difficult, there were no improved roads in Alabama before 1895, no paved roads before 1915, and even no paving company until 1925. Steamboat traffic on the Alabama River was still important for rural Wilcox County until the 1920s when it was eclipsed by the railroads. In the 1930s, the final decade of Edith Morgan's life, Wilcox County's economy was boosted by the completion of the J. Lee Long Bridge over the Alabama River.

Camden (Map 3) had been the county seat since 1819, when the county was formed. Union troops entered the town in 1865 and ransacked the 1857 Greek Revival-style courthouse, but the records had been removed for safekeeping. The troops, headquartered in the Wilcox Hotel, did not destroy the town. However, much of it was

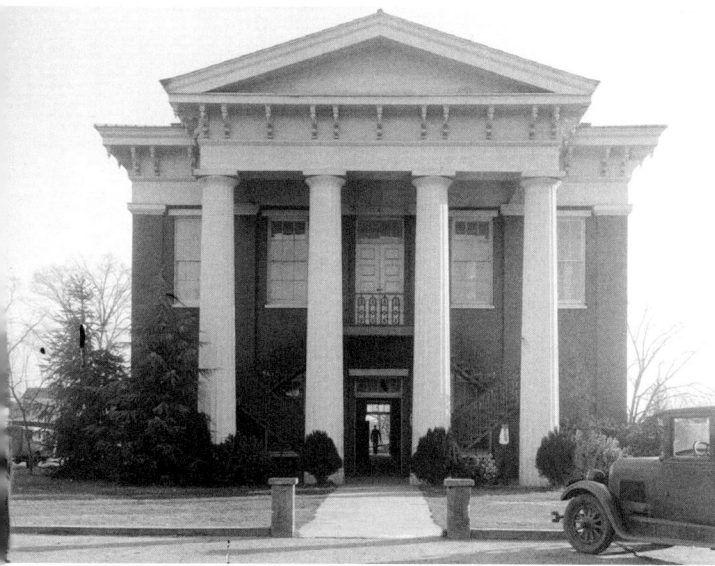

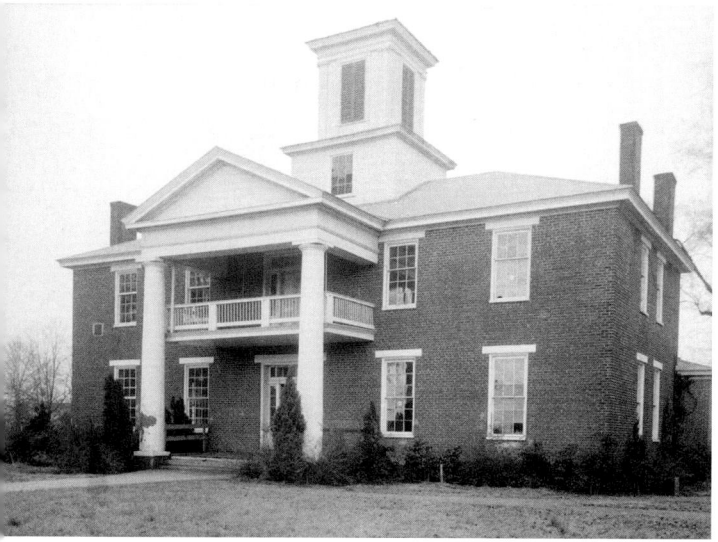

Wilcox County Courthouse (top) and Wilcox Female Institute, Camden, Alabama. (Photos from Historic American Buildings Survey, circa 1930s)

destroyed in 1869 and 1870 by two devastating fires; the former consumed about two-thirds of the town. Yet, the Camden that Edith Morgan knew was much like Camden before the two fires. The business district centered on the courthouse square, an almost ubiquitous feature of Southern county seats. Roads radiated out from the courthouse towards half a dozen ferries across the Alabama River. The main public buildings (the churches, Masonic Hall, and Wilcox Female Institute) were along Broad Street, which led to the Gee's Bend ferry landing a mile and a half out of town. The other streets radiating out from the courthouse square were residential, with frame houses set on large lots that also included numerous outbuildings, vegetable gardens, chicken yards, etc.

EDITH MORGAN

With her family, Edith attended the First Presbyterian Church—established in 1845, constructed initially in 1856, burnt in the fire of 1869, and rebuilt in 1885. She also most likely attended the Wilcox Female Institute, the only choice for education other than being taught at home. One of the most successful of Alabama's many academies, the Institute was founded in 1850 so the local elite would not have to send their daughters to Virginia or the Carolinas for schooling. (By 1850, the reception of Southerners in the North had started to become so unpleasant that many of the Southern elite avoided summering in the North or sending their children there to school.) In its antebellum years, the Institute offered "primary classes, more advanced classes, higher English, languages—ancient and modern, music with use of instrument, painting and embroidery." The enrollment was consistently between 175 and 200 students. After the Civil War, of course, the local elite's financial wherewithal was strained; consequently, the education level declined.

Although there is no hard evidence that Edith led a semi-isolated childhood because of her carpetbagger family status, there is oral history evidence that some children were forbidden to play with the children of the carpetbaggers. Eventually, in the second generation, Edith's generation, the children of carpetbaggers were accepted into the community and became valued members. Nevertheless, Edith did maintain lifelong friendships with the Hendersons, Logues, and especially Liddells, other carpetbagger families. The Liddells feature prominently in the photograph album.

In the U.S. Census of 1900, Edith's occupation is listed as "artist," but later censuses give "none" as her occupation. Between 1900 and 1908, Edith attended the School of the Art Institute of Chicago (SAIC) for five school

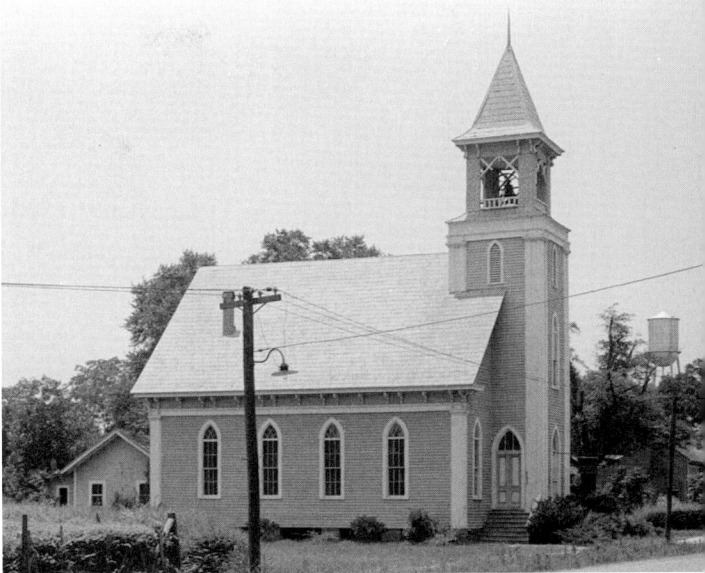

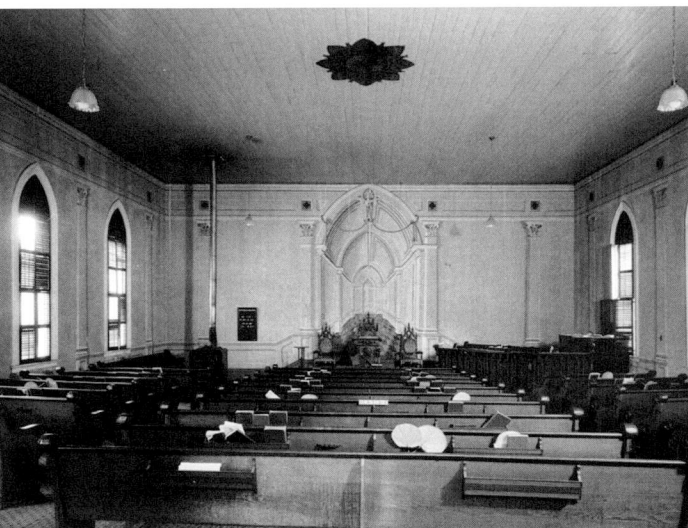

Exterior and interior of Camden's First Presbyterian Church. (Photos from Historic American Buildings Survey, circa 1930s)

9

years (1900–01, 1901–02, 1903–04, 1905–06, 1907–08). She did not take a degree. As a student in the school of drawing and painting, she would have taken courses in the elementary, intermediate, antique, and life divisions. SAIC's 1901–02 catalogue describes the divisions as follows:

I. Elementary: Chiefly early charcoal practice from antique fragments in outline and general light-and-shade, together with practice from blocks and familiar objects. The sketch classes give all students the opportunity to draw from life from the beginning.

II. Intermediate: More advanced. More important outlines and shadows carried farther. Perspective. Pen-and-ink from objects. Still life in monochrome.

III. Antique: Heads and figures from cast in full light and shade. Still life in colors. Artistic anatomy. Modelling recommended.

IV. Life: Costumed and Nude Life. Composition. Separate life classes are maintained for very advanced students.

The study of the human figure, including artistic anatomy and working from the nude, was regarded as the basis for the practice of art. For example, the course in artistic anatomy included forty lectures, as well as much practice. Construction of the human head and figure included thirty lectures, as well as large drawings.

Just where Edith learned photography is unknown; however the principles learned in her art classes are beautifully apparent in her photographs. Since Camden had no professional photographer during her early adult years and Selma was about forty miles by rail or unpaved road, she presumably learned in Chicago, although photography was not taught at SAIC until 1935. Her father did have a darkroom built for her behind the family home. He probably had the necessary equipment shipped by steamboat up the Alabama River from Mobile or possibly by railway express, although Camden itself was only served by freight trains.

In 1878, just three years after Edith's birth, her father bought property from J. Paul Jones that became the Morgan homeplace on the old Clifton Ferry Road (Map 3). The nineteen-acre property is one mile from Camden's courthouse square. Edith lived out her life in her family's home. Her father deeded the homeplace to Edith and her sister

Minnie in 1904. The two-story, frame house, constructed about 1840, has a porch across the front first floor supported by six simple box columns. The second story has a small porch in the center with a door leading out directly over the front door. There were numerous outbuildings. Minnie, who outlived Edith and died in 1946, left the house in her will to Glen David Liddell and thus the Morgan homeplace became the property of the Liddell family and eventually the residence of Janet Liddell Phillippi (1925–2010) and her husband, William Robertson Phillippi (1922–2000). In Camden, it is known as the House on the Hill or the Liddell-Phillippi House (Plates 1 and 2).

In August 1905, before returning to Chicago for her 1905–06 year at SAIC, Edith hosted an art reception at her art studio, which was near her home. The reception was to display to the public the work of her students. After her father's death in 1917, Edith supported herself with income from the land her father had purchased and by giving lessons. She never married; rather she devoted herself to enriching the lives of her neighbors. As is to be expected, Miss Edith was devoted to sharing her love of art. She offered pastel and water-color painting lessons to Camden's young ladies and gentlemen. She also taught photography, which at the time included not only the use of the camera, but also developing and printing the photographs. Appreciation of other arts enriched her art classes. Edith offered classes in drama, some of which are depicted in her photographs. In fact, an appreciation of music and other cultural endeavors were part of the curriculum of her classes. Today, a number of Edith's own paintings hang in Camden homes.

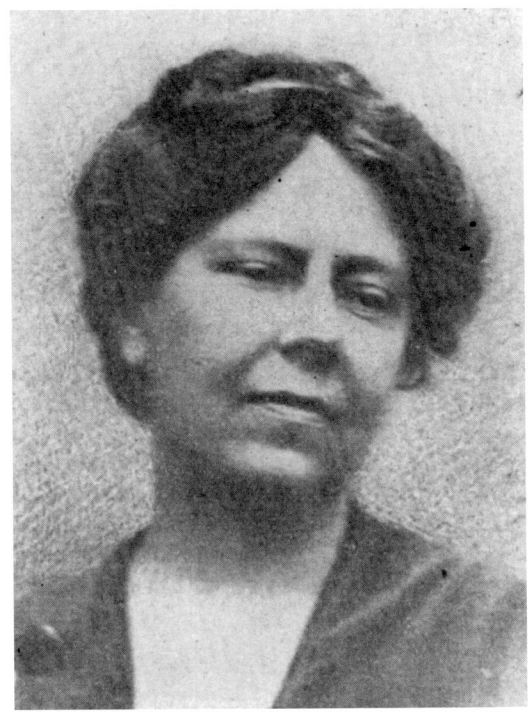

Edith Morgan, circa 1935. (Presbyterian Women of the Synod of Alabama)

11

In addition to her efforts to enrich the cultural life of her hometown, Miss Edith taught numerous women, black and white, to read. This work, perhaps surprisingly, is what endeared her to her neighbors. Illiteracy had always been high in Edith Morgan's world. Of course, almost all slaves had been illiterate, but as late as 1900, 44 percent of American blacks were illiterate. Even in 1930, a quarter to a third of Wilcox County's total population was illiterate. Miss Edith first taught reading by chance. It began in her kitchen; her first student was her middle-aged cook who wanted to read the Bible. Soon other blacks sought Miss Edith's help, and she set aside an area in her kitchen to teach black children to read. The Sunday School Movement had begun in the latter half of the eighteenth century in England and had spread to the mill towns of Rhode Island by 1790; Sunday was the only day of the week that the urban working class had off, so they were given religious instruction on Sunday afternoons. Of course, they first had to be taught to read. The motivation of the middle-class women who sustained the Sunday School Movement was religious, so the Bible was central in literacy training. So it was with Miss Edith. In the local agricultural economy, however, the poor were not as constrained as urban factory workers; they had slightly more flexible schedules. Almost until her death in 1939, every day of the week Miss Edith taught reading classes for blacks and whites within a fifteen-mile radius of Camden. She even navigated the treacherous logging roads to teach men in the logging camps. Miss Edith's living her faith and displaying her love, regardless of station in this life, assured her place in the hearts of her neighbors.

Two of Edith Morgan's obituaries have survived. Both are remarkable testimonies, especially considering that Miss Morgan was the daughter of a carpetbagger and that she was teaching blacks and poor whites to read—which flew in the face of the prominent Social Darwinism beliefs of the day. One obituary reads: "The great heart of Camden was wrung with pain and anguish, when tidings of the departure of Miss Edith Morgan, were received early Monday morning. She left at 9 o'clock Sunday night, April 2nd, 1939, for home in heaven." This obituary continues: "Camden and vicinity and Wilcox County will miss her untiring service, her kindly deeds, deeds inspired, deeds of sacrifice, deeds of mercy, deeds of love and friendship, accommodating deeds, and deeds of every admirable and gracious character."

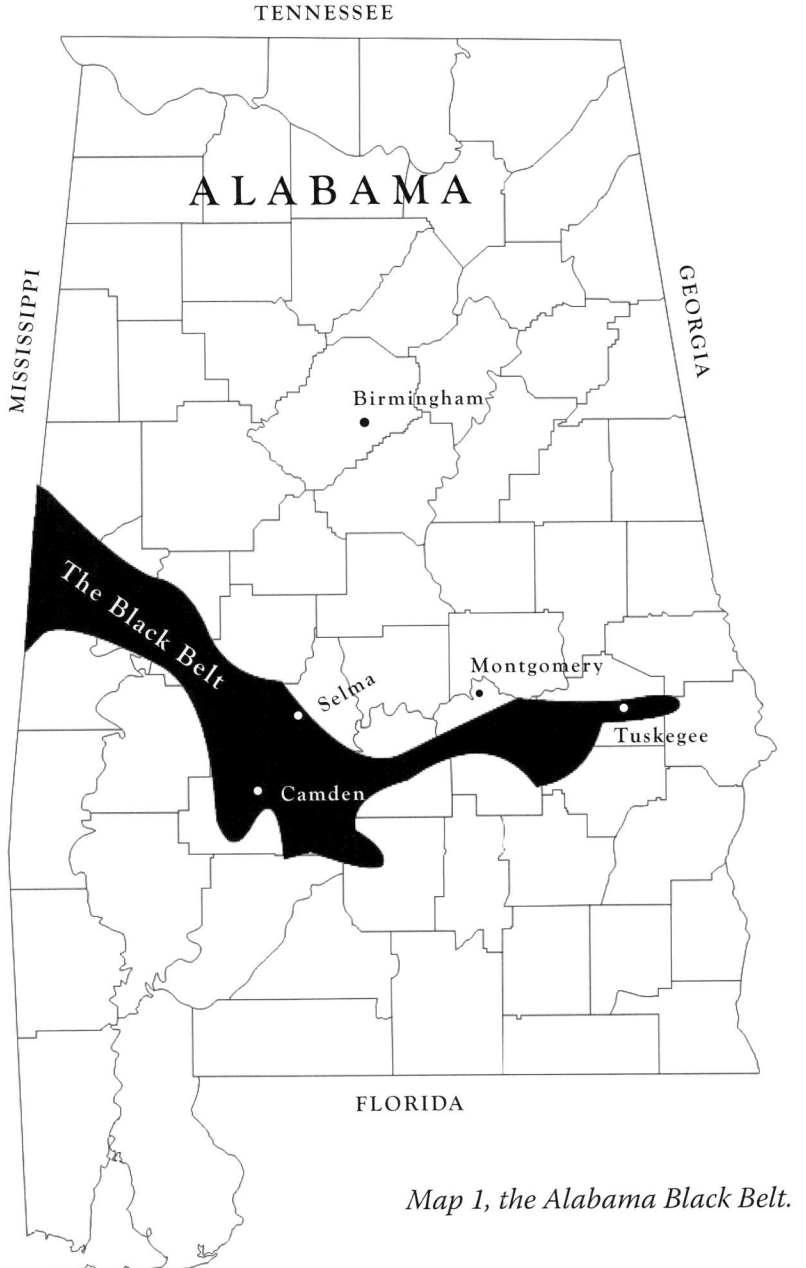

Map 1, the Alabama Black Belt.

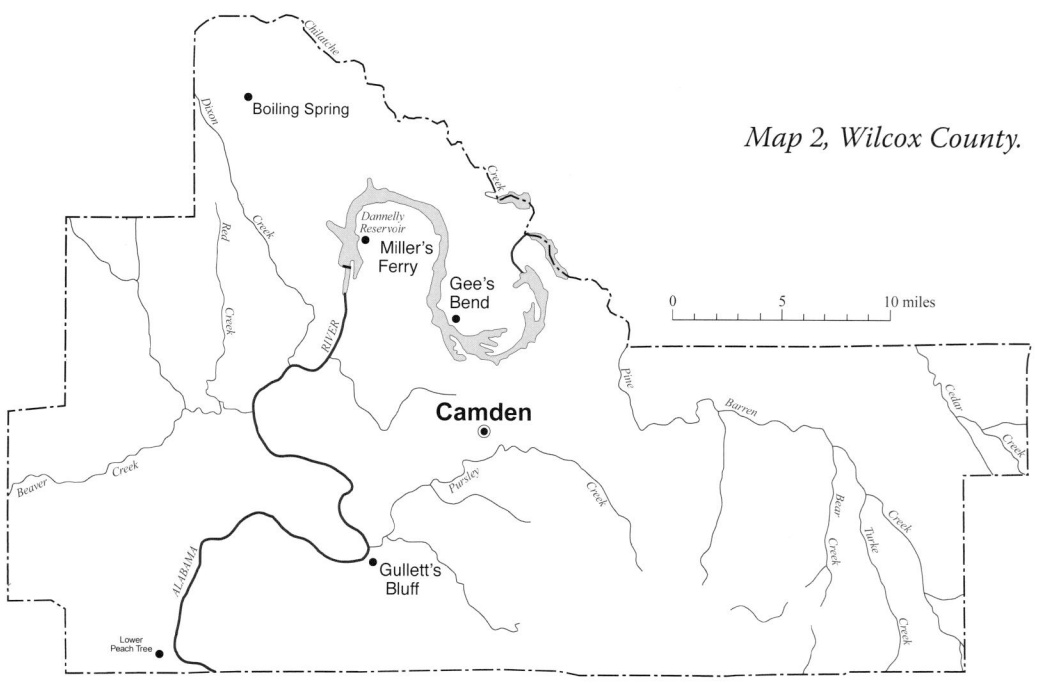

Map 2, Wilcox County.

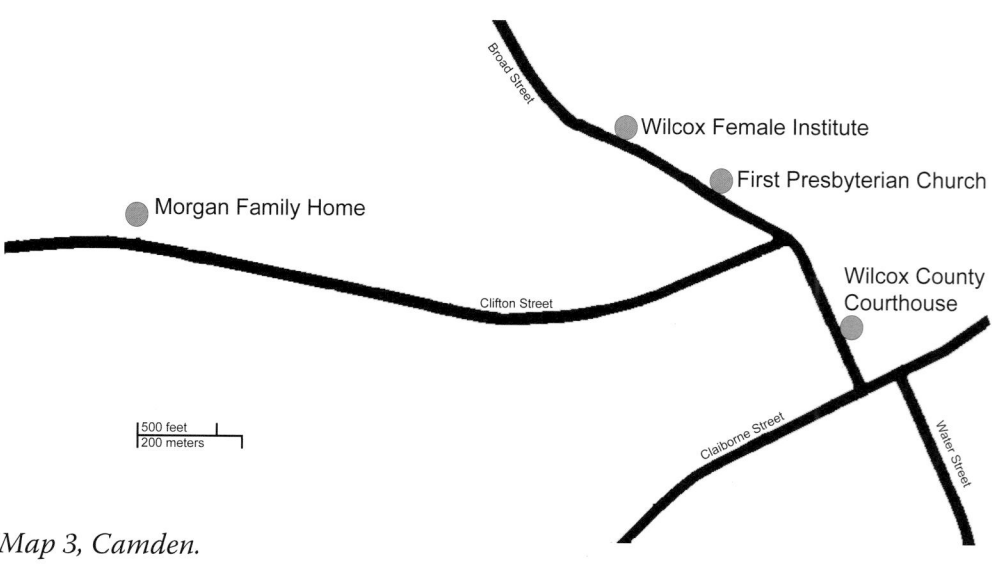

Map 3, Camden.

More than Black and White

Edith Morgan's Family, Life, and Photography

MATTHEW DANIEL MASON

The photographs Edith Morgan created and compiled in albums for her friends in the early twentieth century provide unique perspectives on her time and place.

To provide context for her photographs, the first part of this essay provides Morgan's family background, including short biographies of her extended and immediate kinfolk, as well as describing her life in Camden, Alabama. The Morgan family did not leave any publicly available papers, diaries, or letters, so this exploration of her ancestry and activities relies primarily on contemporary records, the reminiscences of others, and Morgan's photographic images.

A sense of place provides an understanding Morgan's photographs. She lived most of her life in Camden, the county seat of Wilcox County in south-central Alabama in the middle of the Black Belt, an agrarian region that extends from southwestern Tennessee into east-central Mississippi and east through Alabama's midsection towards Georgia (Map 1). The productivity of this agricultural region relies on a physical geography that combines a thin layer of rich black topsoil with a mild climate and deep artesian water wells. Before the American Civil War, thousands of African American slaves worked on cotton plantations in the area, and their descendants continued to work chiefly as sharecroppers and laborers during much of the century after the war. Consequently, scholars use "Black Belt" to designate the territory physically and demographically. The photographs and albums crafted by Morgan document people and locations in the heart of the Alabama Black Belt from around 1900 to 1910.

After investigating the environment surrounding Edith Morgan, the second part of this essay assesses her photography alongside the work of other image-makers, including the work of the leading women photographers in the United States at that time, as well as amateur and professional photographers in Alabama. In her leisurely pursuit of photography, Morgan captured different facets of Camden and Wilcox County. She made empathetic portraits of its people, and documented their lives in the natural and built landscapes. The photographic images she created and compiled in albums employed different photographic genres, including vernacular photography, documentary photography, and art photography. Often a single image combined multiple genres. This work expresses her eye for composition and detail that reflects her training and work as an artist and art teacher. The visual narratives that Morgan compiled in photographic albums demonstrate the mosaic of her place and time, especially the physical and cultural separation and commonalties of its black and white populations.

LOVE SOWED IN THE PAST AND PRESENT: BACKGROUND AND PUBLIC LIFE OF EDITH MORGAN

Morgan came from solid old American roots. Her genealogy reaches back to the founding of the United States and geographically to New England and the western region of New York State. Her great-grandfather, William Hall (circa 1753–1828), lived in south-central Massachusetts, fought at the Battle of Lexington, and served with several militia companies during the Revolutionary War. Her paternal grandmother, Abigail Pease Hall Morgan (died 1849), was a daughter of William Hall; in 1832, she married Edith Morgan's paternal grandfather Benjamin Townsend Morgan [Sr.] (1806–55), and they ultimately settled in western New York. Their family included Edith Morgan's father, Albion LaBat Morgan (1834–1917), as well as his older brother, Delavan G. Morgan (1832–66), and younger siblings, including two brothers, James Morgan (1837–58) and Benjamin Townsend Morgan [Jr.] (1845–91), and two sisters, Polly Morgan (1839–86) and Mary Morgan (1840–86). After the death of Albion's mother in 1849, his father married Eunice Odell Carey (1809–89), and Benjamin and Abigail Morgan's children gained two half-brothers, Frank Carey Morgan (1852–66) and Frederick William Morgan (1854–1921).

In western New York, the elder Benjamin Townsend Morgan participated in the founding of Kiantone, a small town in Chautauqua County, immediately south of Jamestown and near the state boundary with Pennsylvania. He served as a town clerk in November 1853 and as a justice of the peace shortly before his death in 1855. His eldest son, Delavan, also served as a town supervisor of Kiantone in 1858.

For two years during his young adulthood, Albion Morgan attended Richmond College in Richmond, Ohio. By June 1860, he lived in Kiantone with his brothers Delavan and Benjamin, and worked as a merchant. On March 6, 1861, Albion married Lydia Elizabeth Jones (1844–96), the daughter of Austin Jones and Rosa B. Stewart Jones (born circa 1815). Born and raised in western New York, Lydia was a middle child with two brothers, Jesse Jones (born circa 1840) and John C. Jones (born 1850). Immediately before her marriage, Lydia also lived in Kiantone with her older brother and worked as a schoolteacher.

In June 1863, Albion and Lydia lived in Ellicott in Chautauqua County. During the Civil War, Albion registered for the military draft, but he did not serve in the conflict. His brother Delevan did serve as a colonel in the New York Militia and an aide-de-camp to New York Governor Reuben Eaton Fenton (1819–85). In March 1865, Fenton appointed Delavan as the general superintendent of the New York State Military Agency, which provided relief to sick and wounded soldiers. Delavan died suddenly at his home in Kiantone on August 8, 1866.

On June 23, 1864, Albion and Lydia welcomed the birth of their daughter Minna "Minnie" Augusta (1864–1946), probably in Ellicott. About two years later, in 1866, the young Morgan family relocated to Camden, Alabama. According to family lore, Albion blazed a path to the American South for his younger brothers. Benjamin Jr. reportedly lived briefly in Camden, but returned north and became a partner in the B. F. Goodrich Company in Akron, Ohio. Frederick also worked in rubber manufacturing, but in Chicago as a partner in Morgan & Wright and a founding director of the Rubber Goods Manufacturing Company.

In 1867, Albion purchased 950 acres of farmland near Boiling Springs, Alabama. Over the years, he obtained adjoining tracts to this property, as well as smaller properties closer to Camden. It remains uncertain why the Morgan family moved to Camden. Likely, they followed economic and ethical impulses that attracted many Northern whites to the postbellum South, a group that many native Southerners pejoratively called "carpetbaggers." One historian asserts that for many Northerners migrating south, "joined with the quest for profit, however, was a reforming spirit, a vision of themselves as agents of sectional reconciliation and the South's 'economic regeneration.'" He continues that as many Northerners were "accustomed to viewing Southerners—black and white—as devoid of economic initiative and self-discipline, they believed that only 'Northern capital and energy' could bring 'the blessings of a free labor system to the region.'" These men actively participated in the Reconstruction of the South, which intended to transform the South and its socioeconomic and political landscape.

Following the examples of his father and elder brother, Albion involved himself in local politics. At the Alabama Constitutional Convention in Montgomery (November 5–December 6, 1867), Albion represented the 10th Election District which encompassed Wilcox County. In December 1867, the outgoing governor of the Reconstruction Third Military District, Major General John Pope, appointed Morgan clerk of the circuit court for Wilcox County to replace Confederate sympathizer Thomas Bell McMillan.

Many expatriate Northerners entered government services during Reconstruction. Albion Morgan later recalled that only seven Northern whites settled in Wilcox County immediately after the war, and six of them held political office. Of these, he became friends with another recent Northern arrival, Scotsman William Henderson (1839–1924), a former captain of Ohio cavalry. Both Morgan and Henderson were active in the Republican Party and jointly purchased property throughout Wilcox County. Henderson served in the state legislature from 1868–70, and as a probate judge in Wilcox County, 1870–76. Another Northerner, John Russell Liddell (1848–1930), moved to Camden in 1870 at Henderson's suggestion. For more than a decade, a coalition of the newly free blacks, carpetbaggers, and white Southerners who supported Reconstruction, derisively called "scalawags," reelected Morgan, Henderson, and others to public office. Many white Democrats felt that Morgan in particular mobilized the black vote in Wilcox County.

Over the next decade, Morgan remained intimately involved with Reconstruction. For example, on March 23, 1875, Morgan provided a deposition for his role as an election supervisor related to the congressional case of *Frederick George Bromberg v. Jeremiah Haralson*. In the election of 1874, Bromberg unsuccessfully ran against African American Haralson to represent the Alabama First District in the House of Representatives in the Forty-fourth U.S. Congress. In this race, Bromberg received 46 percent of the vote compared to Haralson's 54 percent plurality. Bromberg contested the election, but Congress accepted the results as valid. In his deposition, Morgan provided testimony about the nominating convention of the county Republicans, as well as his role as court clerk and as a speaker for the Republican Party in the county. Vindicated by the verdict, Representative Haralson sought a general amnesty for former Confederates—to help create harmony between blacks and whites. In his role as circuit court clerk, Morgan also certified the result of the next election in 1876, when Haralson lost to Charles Miller Shelley in a three-way race with another African American candidate, James Thomas Rapier. This election also marked the end of Reconstruction with the Compromise of 1877 settling the contested presidential election.

Morgan continued to serve as clerk of the circuit court until 1881. In December 1880, departing Republican President Rutherford B. Hayes nominated Morgan as internal revenue collector for the First Collection District, Mobile; the United States Senate confirmed the nomination. Morgan held this position for three years. He and other Republicans gradually lost their political influence in Wilcox County during this period. They attempted to regain power by joining the ill-fated Greenback Party, which advocated the use of fiat money in the United States and opposed any reduction of paper currency. Local sources recall that Morgan consequently changed his political affiliation to the Democratic Party, especially his support of President Woodrow Wilson, but a posthumous biographical entry maintains that he remained a Republican.

Despite his political offices, most census records describe Albion Morgan as a farmer. However, the definition of agricultural employment ranged widely in these decadal tabulations. For example, the census enumerator instructions for censuses from 1870 and 1880 directed, in part, "Be very particular to distinguish between farmers and farm laborers." In general, a census designation of a farmer was a person who managed his own farm, whether he owned or rented the land. Farm laborers were employees, and this included sharecroppers whose remuneration came after harvest in the form of a portion of the crop. For the 1900 census, the enumerator instructions stated that "farmer" represented an individual who earned more than half of his income from farming.

EDITH MORGAN WAS BORN in Camden on July 28, 1875, and her childhood and adult life were led in post-Reconstruction Alabama. Although technically a native Southerner, the Northern background of the Morgan family and the political activities of her father probably excluded Morgan from established white Southern society. The Morgan family probably did not initially socialize with long-established Southern families of Camden and Wilcox County. Rather, the Morgans had deep relationships with other families that relocated from the North, including the Henderson and Liddell families. Well into the first half of the twentieth century, families with their roots in different regions of the country did not generally socialize. Viola Goode Liddell (1901–98), a neighbor in Camden and a prolific author, wrote that the children of the carpetbaggers gradually broke down some of the social barriers between families. She stated, "the new generation born here to these people were still called Yankees and would be for many years, [but] they were less and less called damn-Yankees."

In 1878, the Morgan family purchased a simple house constructed in the Greek Revival style about forty years earlier and formerly owned by Dr. John Paul and Camilla Boykin Jones. Apart from her years studying art in Chicago, Morgan lived in this large two-story frame house at 428 Clifton Road in Camden (Map 3). Set back from the road with a dirt wagon path leading to it, the house had a first-floor porch that ran the width of the house with wide front steps and six columns, as well as a smaller second-floor porch. Morgan created several photographs of her home (Plates 1 and 2). The first-floor porch would prove an ideal outdoor studio for Morgan, and she posed many of her exterior portraits on it (Plates 3, 4, and 14).

During her childhood, the Morgan household included Edith, her parents, and her older sister, as well as black servants, extended family, and lodgers. For instance, in 1880, her home included her maternal uncle John C. Jones and his wife Jinnie (born circa 1850). The Morgan household also included Emma Chapin (born circa 1840), an unmarried art teacher from New York, who may have inspired Morgan to pursue a teaching career. The Morgan home also served as a gathering place for Northern expatriates. For instance, in 1890 Fred Henderson was born in the Morgan home, although his family lived on a farm in Miller's Ferry about nine miles northwest of Camden.

As a white girl and woman, Morgan did not interact on an equal footing with her family's black servants or neighbors (Plate 5). Throughout her life, the African American population outnumbered the other inhabitants in Wilcox County four to one. In 1900, almost all of the Morgans' neighbors were black. This racial ratio in the county contrasted with the demographic changes in Alabama during her life. Despite being the minority in Wilcox County, Viola Liddell recalls that until the 1960s, "most Black Belt whites still boasted that 'their' Negroes were as contented and as faithful as they had always been." During the period between Reconstruction and the civil rights era of the mid-twentieth century, whites expected deference from blacks. Nevertheless, Morgan's photographs and her activities demonstrate that she had empathy toward her black neighbors, even if she often expressed it in stereotypical ways.

Morgan probably attended Camden's Wilcox Female Institute (established 1850). The Reverend John Miller (1825–78) of the Associate Reformed Presbyterian Church purchased the school in 1867 and initially administered it. The Miller family continued to own the school until 1908, although different principals would run it during the intervening years. In the late nineteenth century, the school maintained an enrollment of around 170 students, drawn chiefly from the wealthy families of the region. Parents often sent daughters to female academies or seminaries like the Wilcox Female Institute to fulfill parental aspirations for their offspring. These schools allowed the young women to exchange daily domestic responsibilities for education and prepared many of their students for careers as schoolteachers. Morgan may have learned drawing and painting in school or from local artisans during her childhood and adolescence. The deep bonds cultivated between students at these schools persisted into adulthood as friends and confidants, and many of Morgan's former classmates probably appear in her photographs.

The bonds forged in female academies continued in women's organizations that typified the "New Woman" at the turn of the twentieth century. The New Woman, popularized by the literary heroines created by author Henry James (1843–1916), represented an educated and independent woman with a career. According to one historian, "The term New Woman always referred to women who exercised control over their own lives be it personal, social, or economic." In adulthood, Morgan epitomized the New Woman in Alabama.

The Morgan family attended the First Presbyterian Church in Camden. The church aligned with the Mobile Presbytery of the Presbyterian Church in the United States (PCUS). Throughout most of its history, the PCUS represented a conservative branch of Presbyterianism based chiefly in Southern and Border states. It stressed adherence to the Westminster Confession of Faith and the Scottish School of Common Sense as it evolved into the Princeton theology. Morgan was active in the church throughout her life, and she taught Bible classes and Sunday School widely in Wilcox County. In 1935, the Presbyterian Women of the Synod of Alabama featured her in a volume about women's work for the church. It states, "Seeking nothing for herself, she has followed the Inner Light and spoken as the Spirit gave her utterance and in so doing she has found an ever-widening circle of influence."

In her early adulthood, Morgan remained active in her church and participated in women's clubs and organizations, including the Roundtable Chautauqua Circle. On September 6, 1896, her mother, Lydia, died in Camden. Soon after their mother's death, Morgan and her sister, Minnie, joined the recently established local chapter of the Daughters of the American Revolution. The Morgan girls may have sought emotional support from other women in these groups. Viola Liddell recollected that Northern and Southern women eventually "found rapport through their mutual efforts in music, art, writing, teaching, and handiwork." These activities especially served Edith Morgan to rehabilitate her family name in the hearts and minds of many white families in Wilcox County.

In 1900, Minnie married Charles Campbell Washburn (1868–1954); the newlyweds initially lived in Birmingham. From 1913 to 1918, he worked as a music instructor at several schools in Nashville, including the Harpeth Hall and Ward-Belmont schools. In 1918, Washburn served as a social and musical director of the Medical Officers' Training Camp in Fort Oglethorpe, Georgia, and later in the same position for the Young Men's Christian Association, which included providing entertainment and support for American servicemen in Great Britain and France during World War I. The Washburns eventually moved to Nashville, where he served as a music instructor for several schools in the city, including the Scarritt College for Christian Workers and the George Peabody College for Teachers. Washburn also edited several hymnals for the United Methodist Church.

By June 1900, Edith Morgan was working as an artist in Camden. She lived with her father and their black servants, including a cook, Marcila James (born 1860), and her brother Wash James (1875–1958). In the kitchen of the Morgan family home, Morgan taught Marcila to read using a Bible as a primer. Similar to many New Women of the period, Morgan valued education, and in this vein sought to support the instruction of African Americans. Initially, she taught only Marcila, but soon she included other black adults and children in the community. For example, her black neighbor Mary Riley Boykin (1901–78) benefited from this tutoring as a child, and later her own children received books from Morgan. Some of Morgan's education outreach may have connected to the Camden Academy, a school for African Americans established by William Henderson in 1885. Morgan also documented the importance of this educational outreach in her photography, especially a portrait of a young African American writing beside a fireplace (Plate 6).

In the fall of 1900, Morgan traveled North and probably lived in the family home of her uncle, Frederick Morgan, to attend the School of the Art Institute of Chicago (SAIC). She would attend the art school for five school years between 1900 and 1908. Founded in 1866, the school bore several names before it became the SAIC and formed a separate entity from its associated museum, the Art Institute of Chicago. The school thrived under its director, William Marchant Richardson French, from 1879 until his death in 1914. Under French, the school had a European bias in its instruction, which mirrored the Kunstakademie Düsseldorf, a leading German art school of the time. This included a distribution of class levels: the elementary form, the intermediate form, antique form, and life form. During her second year in 1901–02, Morgan achieved an intermediate level in the school. Morgan probably attended the Normal Art School of the SAIC as well, which accounts for the five years of her attendance. Beginning in 1901, the first year she attended, the SAIC began formal Normal School training for art teachers. The course included three years of academic work, with the last two years focused on pedagogy.

Morgan may have learned photography in Wilcox County before attending school in Chicago. Local photographer Samuel Ross Thompson (1853–1937) began dabbling in photography in the mid-1880s in Gullett's Bluff, about ten miles southwest of Camden. If she learned photography from Thompson or another local photographer earlier in life, then she may have used glass plate negatives. Many photographers continued to use glass negatives into the twentieth century despite the later availability of roll film. Self-portraits of Morgan with an African American laundress (Plates 7 and 8) depict what might be a paint box or a camera case, which could have held either a roll camera or a glass plate camera. Still, considering the evolution of photographic technology, the images she created and compiled in her albums probably derive from a roll-film camera. Widely available after 1890, film negatives weighed considerably less than glass-plate negatives and occupied less physical space.

Morgan probably purchased her camera in Chicago; a couple of images in the album depict snow-covered landscapes of sites in the city, possibly in Lincoln Park, a large lakefront park established in 1843 (Plates 9 and 10). She may have learned photography as a tool to support her own artwork. Many artists used the camera to capture scenes that they planned to place on canvas. Conversely, Morgan may have purchased a camera simply to document her activities, family, and friends. Nevertheless, Morgan probably created the other images in Camden and Wilcox County during the summers of her attendance at SAIC or shortly thereafter. In 1902, her Chicago cousin Agnes Josephine Morgan (1883–1967) accompanied her to Camden, and she may appear in the photographs as well. Morgan's portrait subjects wear clothing styles popular between 1900 and 1910, and the white and light-colored dresses that white women wear in many of Morgan's photographs represent the fashion dictate to wear these colors only between Easter and Labor Day.

After completing her schooling in Chicago, Morgan returned home and lived with her father, as well as their married African American servants, Mary McWilliams (born 1872) and Taylor McWilliams (born 1863). Morgan probably made the portrait of her father in the album more than a decade before his death on March 17, 1917 (Plate 11). After Albion's death, Morgan oversaw the family home, which she owned with her sister, and the other properties their father acquired during his life in Camden. Later the sisters rented most of their family home to Glen David Liddell (1892–1965) and his growing family, while the sisters kept the second floor.

During the remainder of her life, Morgan supported herself financially as an art teacher, augmented by revenue from the real estate and investments inherited from her father. She offered art and music classes to students in Camden and the greater Wilcox County area, which included drawing and painting, as well as photography. Her students include children and adults at a small art studio near her home. One of her music students was Narcissa Logue (1887–1981), who lived in the home of her aunt and uncle, local artisans Narcissa Mayo Cooper (1848–1925), a textile artist, and Frederick Cooper (1837–1923), a woodworker. The elder Narcissa also taught school in Camden, while Frederick constructed the wooden easels that Morgan used in her instruction. To highlight the work of her students, Morgan hosted exhibitions of their work, such as a reception at her art studio in August 1905, which displayed the work of Narcissa Logue, Martha "Mattie" Mobley Hollinger (1888–1978), and Nettie Floyd Harris (born 1887). Morgan also sold and presented her paintings to families in Camden and Wilcox County.

Morgan died at her home in Camden on April 2, 1939, and her body was interred beside her mother and father in the Morgan family plot in the Camden Cemetery. Her gravestone bears the inscription, "Edith Morgan / 1875–1939 / It soweth here with toil and care, but the harvest time of love is there." The sentiments of these lines underscore the love she felt for her family, and friends, and neighbors—which she captured in her photographs and compiled in the pages of albums, as well as the generations of adults and children she influenced with her instruction. For Edith Morgan, the harvest time for love lay in heaven after the toil and care she took during her life in Camden.

Reminiscent and Prescient: Photography of Edith Morgan

The photographs created by Edith Morgan in Camden and compiled by her in albums for her friends depict a multifaceted view of her hometown and time. Overall, her photographs exemplify vernacular photography by a talented amateur photographer. Her work runs the gamut of photographic practice in the early twentieth century. It includes portraits, genre works, landscapes, still life, and documentary studies. To our knowledge, Morgan did not pursue photography professionally. Instead, she created photographs, trimmed individual prints, and arranged them in the albums to please herself and her friends. At the turn of the twentieth century, many middle-class women acquired cameras and began to photograph their friends and families. By photographing within their families and social circles, they consequently had noninvasive relationships with their subjects. She may have also had personal relationships with many of her African American subjects; they may have worked as servants or laborers for the Morgan family, or attended her Sunday School or reading classes.

Overall, many of Morgan's photographs, especially her portraits, are reminiscent of the work of the leading women photographers of her time, as well as amateur and professional photographers in Alabama during the early twentieth century. Conversely, many of her photographs, especially her images of African Americans in Wilcox County, are prescient of the documentary photography of the Farm Security Administration photographers during the Great Depression. Morgan additionally created stereotypical imagery of African Americans, but with a decidedly empathetic eye. The following explores both the reminiscent and prescient aspects of her work.

Morgan may have found inspiration for her photography from a series of single-page picture spreads, "The Foremost Women Photographers of America," compiled by leading female photographer Frances Benjamin Johnston (1864–1952) and published in the *Ladies' Home Journal* from May 1901 to January 1902. The target audience for this "monthly Bible of the American home" was native-born, middle-class white women. By January 1904, the magazine had a monthly circulation of more than one million copies. Like Morgan, many of the women featured in Johnston's series also cultivated individuals from their social circles to serve as some of their subjects. The photographers highlighted in the articles included sisters Frances Stebbins Allen and Mary Electa Allen, as well as individual photographers including Gertrude Käsebier, Mathilde Weil, Emma Justine Farnsworth, Eva Lawrence Watson, Zaida Ben-Yusuf, and Elizabeth Brownell.

Frances Johnston and the women photographers she highlighted in the pages of the *Ladies' Home Journal* chiefly identified with the prevailing Pictorialist movement in photography in the early twentieth century, a style that stressed aesthetic beauty over reality. For many photographers, optical sharpness and exact replication of subjects inhibited individual artistic expression. Instead, they sought a "pictorial effect" that frequently mirrored the imagery of the painters from the earlier Barbizon School, circa 1830–70, such as Jean-Francois Millet (1814–75), whose softened brushwork in paintings created atmospheric effects. The Pictorialists believed that their artistic photographs paralleled other artwork. To this end, some photographers manipulated the surface of the prints for artistic effect similar to painters. Although Morgan did not physically manipulate the surface of her prints, she did trim several of them to remove presumably

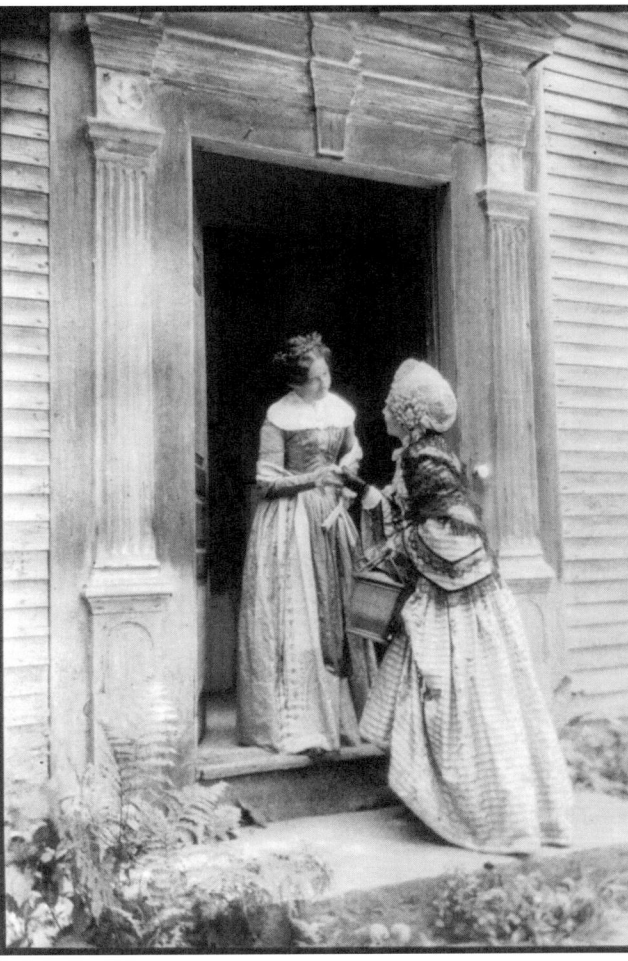

Frances Stebbins Allen (1854–1941) and Mary Electa Allen (1858–1941), "How D'y Do?," circa 1900. (Library of Congress)

extraneous or distracting information (Plate 12). In general, the portraits and other images created by Morgan echo the work by these leading women photographers.

Genre works and tableaux were a popular pursuit of many professional and amateur

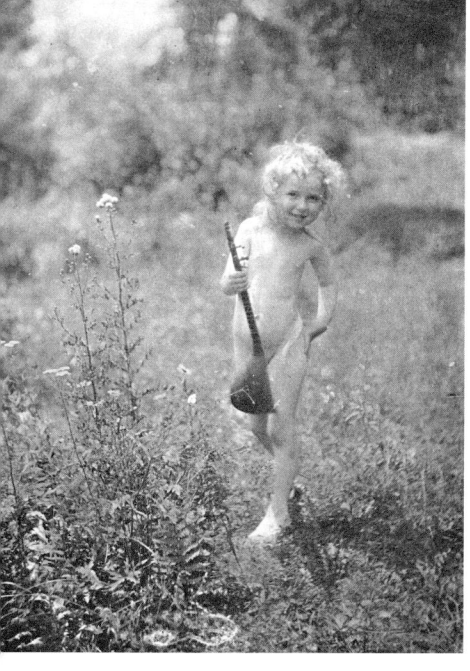

Above, Emma Justine Farnsworth (1860–1952), "La Cigal," Camera Notes, *Volume 3, No. 3, 1900.*
Below, Mathilde Weil (1872–1918), "The Embroidery Frame," circa 1900. (Library of Congress)

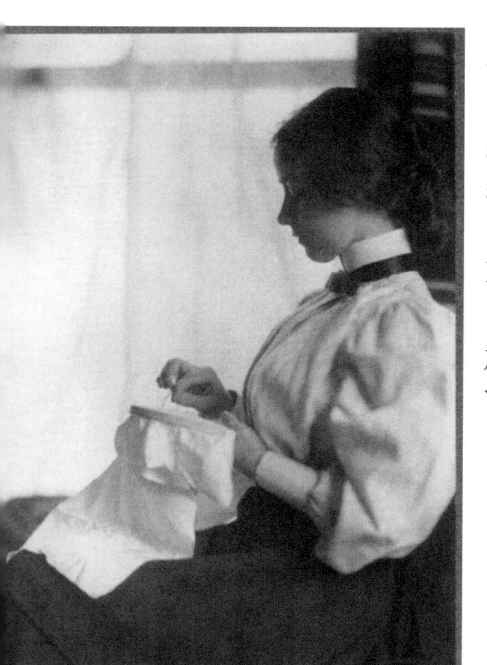

photographers around the turn of the twentieth century. Frances Stebbins Allen (1854–1941) and her younger sister Mary Electa Allen (1858–1941), teachers in Deerfield, Massachusetts, created genre works that recreated images of American colonial life by positing their friends and family members in local eighteenth-century homes (Page 17 and Plate 13). Morgan may have viewed the Allen sisters' work at an exhibition that included their photographs at the Art Institute of Chicago in 1908. In the *Ladies Home Journal,* Johnston also highlighted the portraits of Emma Justine Farnsworth (1860–1952), an art photographer in Albany, New York. Similar to the Allen sisters' practice, Farnsworth used genre works portraying figures in open landscapes that allude to historical Greek classicism.

As mentioned, Morgan created many of her portraits of friends and family, in front of a makeshift backdrop on a front porch of her home. Portions of the house's clapboard siding and columns are visible in several of the images (Plates 3, 4, 14). This south-facing location probably provided ample sunlight to illuminate her subjects. In much of her genre work, Morgan provides visual narratives related to courtship. One narrative includes two women approaching a man, who coincidentally holds a photograph album. This narrative also includes another young man choosing between the two women, the dejected woman, and the happy resolution (Plates 14–20). In other genre work, likely illustrative of her work as a teacher, Morgan depicts William Lithgow Liddell (1895–1988) as a traveling student with a bag of books and carrying a lunch pail (Plates 24 and 25), as well as a teacher with a student, again William Lithgow Liddell (Plate 26), or painters at easels (Plate 27 and 28).

Morgan also positioned many of her African American subjects in tableaux related to their lives and work, such as men and women talking (Plates 29, 30, 31) and women working with girls' hair (Plates 32 and 33). This work bears similarities to photographs by Mathilde Weil (1872–1918), a professional photographer in Philadelphia, highlighted by Johnston. Weil excelled at capturing portraits of women engaged in traditional tasks, such as a young woman with embroidery. Morgan captured similar portraits of her subjects, especially African American women at work. This includes women hand-carding cotton and spinning thread (Plates 34 and 35), as well as shelling peas and feeding the discarded pods to a hungry mule (Plate 36).

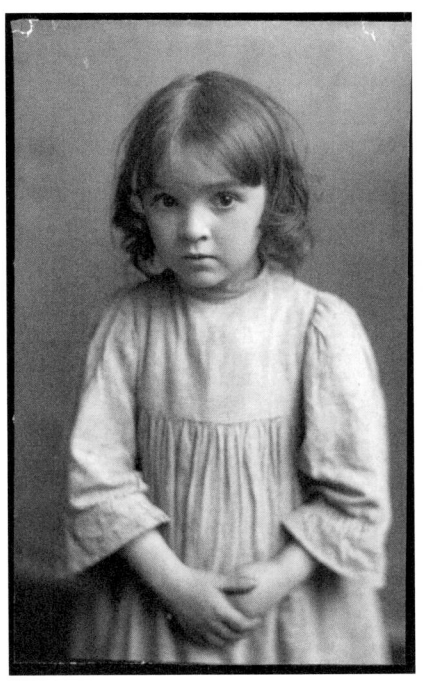
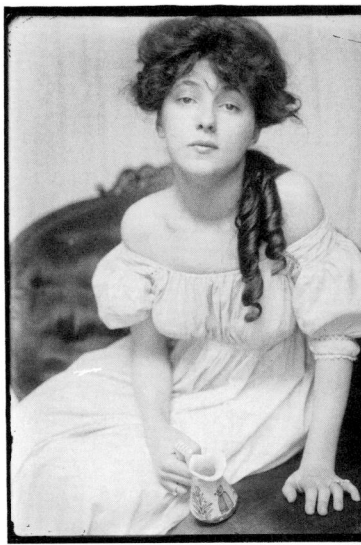

Left, Elizabeth B. Brownell (born circa 1867), "A-Listnin' to the Witch-Tales 'at Annie Tells About," circa 1900. Above, Gertrude Käsebier (1852–1934), "Miss N," circa 1900. (Both, Library of Congress)

Morgan also employed genre work in some of her portraits of African American children in a manner similar to Elizabeth B. Brownell (born circa 1867). In her volume, *Dream Children* (1901), Brownell created portraits of children based on literary characters, such as a portrait of a young girl to illustrate the poem, "Little Orphant Annie," by James Whitcomb Riley. Morgan evokes similar portraits in her portrayals of African American children, such as older children caring for younger siblings (Plates 37 and 38).

Many of Morgan's traditional portraits echo the work of other contemporary women photographers highlighted by Frances Johnston. Gertrude Käsebier (1852–1934) created evocative images of motherhood and powerful portraits of Native Americans that focused on the emotions and self-expression of her subjects. Her portrait, "Miss N," shows the sixteen-year-old chorus girl and artist's model Evelyn Nesbit (1884–1967). Usually a frontal view of a subject in a portrait instills a greater aura of authenticity. The eyes of the subject and the photographer—and by extension the viewer—meet and provide a forthright acknowledgment of the portrait process.

Averted glances and expressions, on the other hand, may create a sense of intimacy. For the example by Käsebier, the forthright portrait of Nesbit expresses the young woman's implicit sexuality and innocence. Several of Morgan's portraits similarly express the emotions of her subjects, including a self-portrait (Plate 39) where her eyes meet those of the viewer, as well as portrayals of young women whose averted expressions impart a sense of intimacy in their portraits (Plates 40–42). Interestingly, two of the portraits include the women holding flowers. Morgan created several self-portraits in the album that explicitly depict her as an artist (Plates 7, 8, and 27). Given the implicit goal of her albums to document her relationship with her friends, she likely included these images as self-definitions.

MORGAN ALSO CREATED ATYPICAL portraits similar to those of leading women photographers of her day. Zaida Ben-Yusuf (1869–1933) operated a fashionable portrait studio on Fifth Avenue in New York that catered to celebrities and rising young professionals. Her portraits departed from conventional methods of the time; Johnston writes that Ben-Yusuf "imbues all her studies with a touch of the picturesque, and at her best combines a rich effect of light with sweeping lines of drapery and distinction of pose." This is particularly evident in Ben-Yusuf's "The Odor of Pomegranates," circa 1900, which depicts a woman wearing a long flowing gown, standing in front of a curtain and holding a pomegranate. Morgan also departs from traditional portraiture in some of her photographs, such as the woman with her hair down (Plate 61).

Much of Morgan's other work, especially her photographs of African Americans, compares favorably to the photography of Frances Benjamin Johnston herself. In January 1888, Johnston received her first camera from family friend and photographic innovator George Eastman (1854–1932). By 1901, she had an established career as a professional photographer in Washington. In 1897, she had published an article in

Zaida Ben-Yusuf (1869–1933), "The Odor of Pomegranates," circa 1900. (Library of Congress)

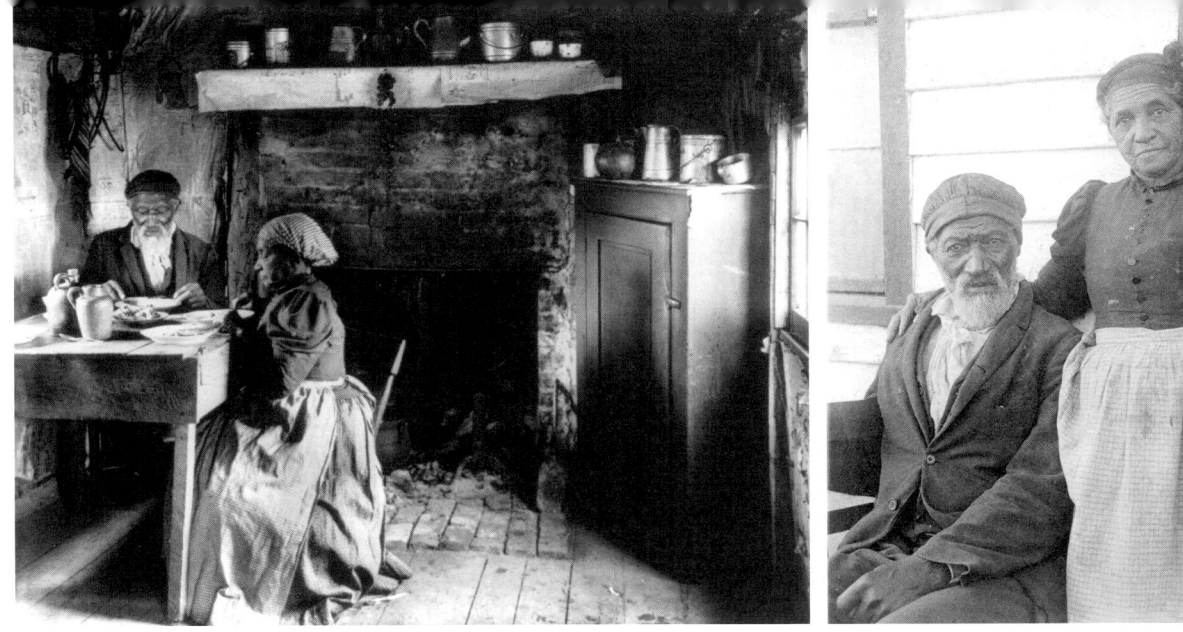

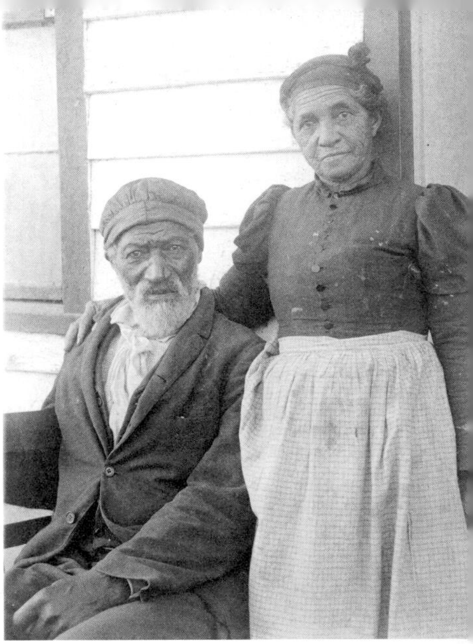

Frances Benjamin Johnston (1864–1952). Above left, "Old African American couple eating at the table by fireplace, rural Virginia," 1899 or 1900. Above right, "Elderly African American couple posed outside of a building, near Hampton Institute, Hampton, Va.," 1899 or 1900. Below, "Negro man, woman and three children at an old-time well," 1899 or 1900. (All, Library of Congress)

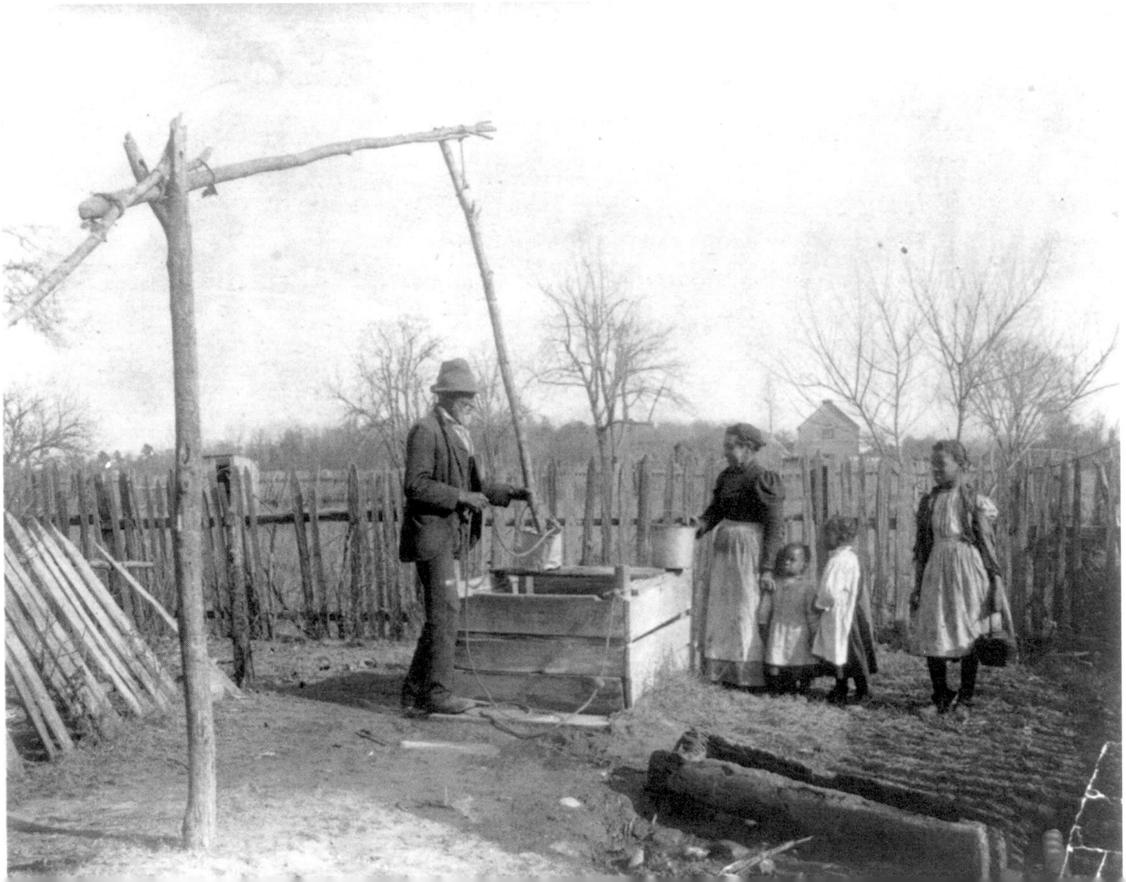

Ladies' Home Journal entitled, "What a Woman Can Do with a Camera," that advised women how to become professional photographers. She stated, "The woman who makes photography profitable must have, as to personal qualities, good common sense, unlimited patience to carry her through endless failures, equally unlimited tact, good taste, a quick eye, a talent for detail, and a genius for hard work." These qualities defined the image work of Johnston.

In 1899, Hollis Burke Frissell, the president of Hampton Normal and Agricultural Institute in Virginia, commissioned Johnston to photograph the school's buildings and the school's African American and Native American students. Based on this work, Booker T. Washington, an alumnus of Hampton Institute and president of Tuskegee Normal and Industrial Institute in Alabama, asked her to document his school and its African American students. Both institutes trained, in the bellicose words of Hampton founder Samuel Chapman Armstrong, "an army of black educators." These teachers emphasized self-improvement and job training to enable African American students to support themselves as artisans or industrial workers. Johnston's well-known photographs of Hampton and Tuskegee depict the environs of each and overviews of students in classes. She also created intimate and lesser-known portraits that bear striking similarities to Morgan's work, such as a series of images of an elderly African American couple posed outside and in their home near Hampton Institute.

Other Morgan images of African Americans bear similarities to the work of other photographers of Alabama's Black Belt region, especially her contemporary Mary Morgan Keipp (1875–1961) of Selma and the later work of Prentice Herman Polk (1898–1984). Keipp was the daughter of German immigrants and captured images of African Americans in rural Dallas County, immediately north of Wilcox County. Her portraits of African Americans during the early twentieth century are similar to Morgan's in content and composition. They depict children, agricultural workers, laundresses, and elders. Rather than an album, Keipp compiled a slim volume of six photographs, *Negro Life* (circa 1900), as well as exhibited images, that

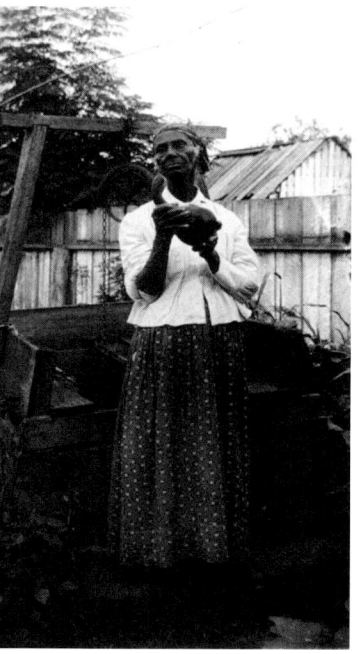

Mary Morgan Keipp (1875–1961), "A Nurse of Eighty Winters," circa 1895–1900, from Mary Morgan Keipp, Negro Life *(circa 1895–1900). (New York Public Library)*

document different aspects of African American life in the Black Belt.

Born in Bessemer, Alabama, African American photographer Prentice Herman Polk attended Tuskegee Institute, but left before he graduated. In 1927, he returned to Tuskegee as a photography instructor and later became the head of its photography department and official photographer for the school. For much of his working life, P. H. Polk was the only professional photographer—black or white—in Alabama's Black Belt region. Many of his earliest portraits, which intimately depict African American subjects, parallel those by Morgan, such as his portrait of an African American woman, "The Boss" (1932).

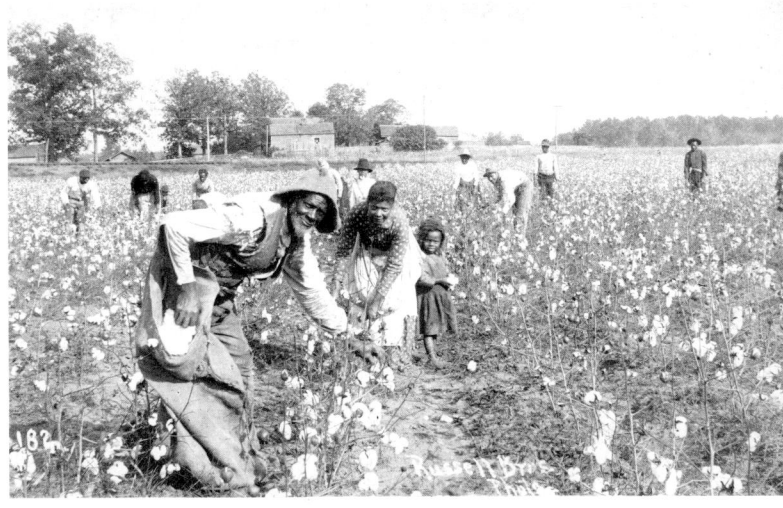

Russell Bros., "Cotton Picking in Alexandria Valley, Alabama," circa 1895–1900. (Beinecke Rare Book and Manuscript Library, Yale University)

Aside from portraits, Morgan created many images of African Americans and others engaged in cotton agriculture, including a black family picking and collecting bolls in split white oak baskets (Plates 72–76), as well as the production of cotton bales (Plates 77–79). This imagery mirrors contemporary photographs of the cotton industry, especially of African Americans working in the fields, such as a view by brothers Samuel and Robert Russell in Anniston, Alabama, circa 1895–1900.

WHILE MORGAN'S PHOTOGRAPHS ECHOED the work of contemporary photographers, she made images that foresaw the development of documentary photography in the 1930s, in which photographers endeavored to supply straightforward images of their subjects, usually people. In the middle of the Great Depression, President Franklin Delano Roosevelt created the Resettlement Administration, headed by Undersecretary of Agriculture Rexford Guy Tugwell, to aid poor rural Americans uprooted from their tenant farms and moving to urban areas to find industrial jobs. Tugwell appointed Roy E. Stryker as chief of the historical section; its mission was to use photography to publicize the work of the Resettlement Administration. Stryker hired a group of photographers, whose work became known as the Farm Security Administration (FSA) project. Following Stryker's directives and to support the government programs of the New Deal, these photographers used documentary photography to elaborate on the lives of rural people in the middle of the economic and social tumult of the time. Stryker's photographers generally employed camera angles and distances from a normal eye-level that imparted viewpoints of equity and cooperation between the viewer and subjects.

Several FSA photographers captured images of Black Belt Alabama, including locations in Wilcox County. Arthur Rothstein (1915–1985), a recent graduate of Columbia University, became the first photographer Stryker hired for the FSA. In February and April 1937, Rothstein documented a community of African American tenant farmers at Gee's Bend, a peninsula surrounded on three sides by the Alabama River. Rothstein visited the area to document the Gee's Bend inhabitants and the primitive character

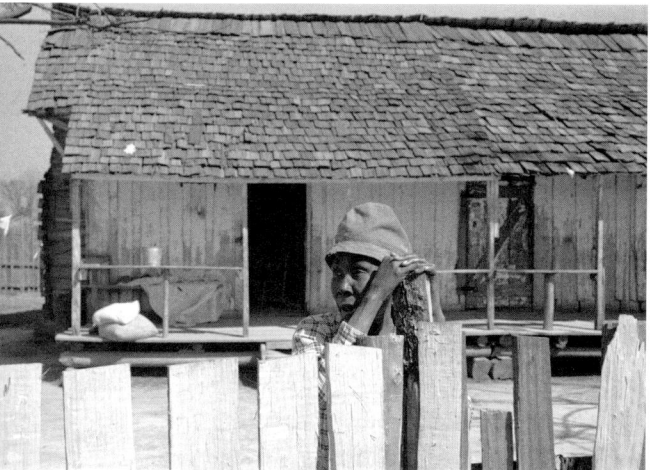

Arthur Rothstein (1915–85), "Gee's Bend Negro, Alabama," February 1937. (Farm Security Administration, Library of Congress)

of the community. These images illustrated a story in the *New York Times*. Later that year, the FSA purchased the land at Gee's Bend, divided it, and rented it to the tenants.

Another FSA photographer, Marion Post (1910–90), who became Marion Post Wolcott when she married in 1941, visited Wilcox County in late April 1939, a few weeks after Edith Morgan's death. A native of New Jersey, Post trained as a dancer and studied child psychology in Europe from 1932 to 1934, and then worked as a teacher in Massachusetts and a freelance photographer in New York City and Philadelphia before she joined the FSA in 1938. Her photographs for the agency often emphasized the role of people with nature.

Post made several images of the African American families living in Gee's Bend to document improvement since Rothstein had visited two years earlier. Post's images included Angelina Parker (born circa 1892), Mark Parker (circa 1867–1946), and their children working in the cooperative garden. The photographs created by Rothstein and Post for the FSA parallel depictions of African Americans made by Edith Morgan decades earlier.

While Morgan created photographs of African Americans that presaged the work of the FSA, she also produced images that reflected prevailing stereotypes of her time: the "pickaninny" and the watermelon. The word *pickaninny* is a vulgarized version of the Portuguese-based pidgin word *pequenino*, which

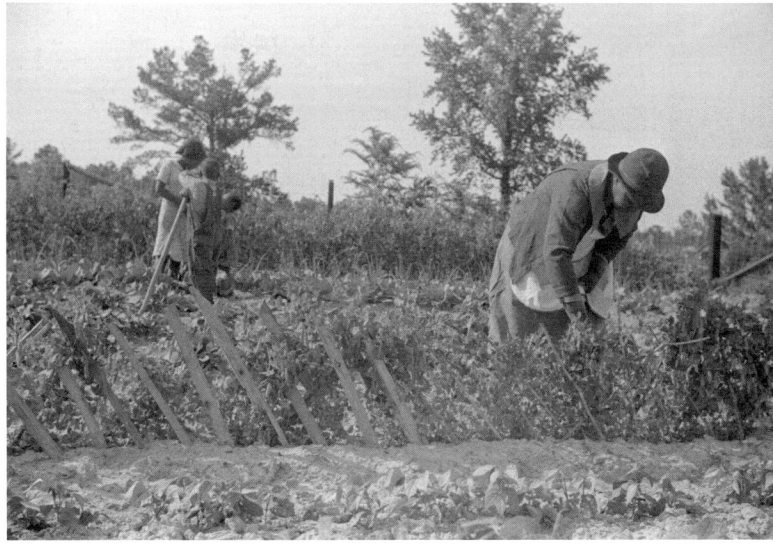

Marion Post (Wolcott) (1910–90), "Angelina Parker and Children Working in Garden, Gees Bend, Alabama," April 1939. (Farm Security Administration, Library of Congress)

means *little ones* and was used in the seventeenth-century Atlantic slave trade. The pervasiveness of African American children in imagery contributed and reinforced white perceptions of wanton breeding in Southern black communities. Often depicted in groups, and occasionally with maternal figures, pickaninnies served to support the myth of nonexistent nuclear families among African Americans. Morgan created several images of black children portrayed as stereotypical pickaninnies (Plates 37, 38, 87, 91, and 92).

These stereotypes are particularly clear when images of black children are combined with watermelons. Imagery and black collectibles from the period after Reconstruction through World War II depict African Americans eating watermelons. Additionally, in many antebellum stories, masters caught slaves stealing watermelons from gardens at night after the whites of their eyes revealed their location like scavenging animals, such as raccoons. Morgan created several images of black children with watermelons (Plates 94–97) as well as black adults (Plate 98). Nevertheless, her educational work with African Americans belies any sense that Morgan created these stereotypical images in a mean-spirited way. More telling is her inclusion of a group of white men and women also eating watermelon with wild abandon (Plate 99).

Morgan also created a few landscape photographs that compare favorably to the work of Eva Lawrence Watson (1867–1935), later Watson-Schütze after marrying Martin Schütze in 1901. Women photographers, unlike male practitioners, came relatively late to landscape photography, for the practical reasons of heavy equipment, in addition to the artistic tradition of women artists selecting themselves as subject throughout the history of art. Nevertheless, Watson-Schütze's landscape, "Storm," published in *Camera Work* in January 1905, is similar in composition to Morgan's examples of landscape (Plates 100–104).

In her life, Edith Morgan fulfilled many roles: daughter, friend, artist, and teacher. The photographs she created document these aspects and transmit her experience over the century from her time to ours. Her empathetic eye captured her home and its people for her friends. Their stewardship of these albums allows us to view a place in time.

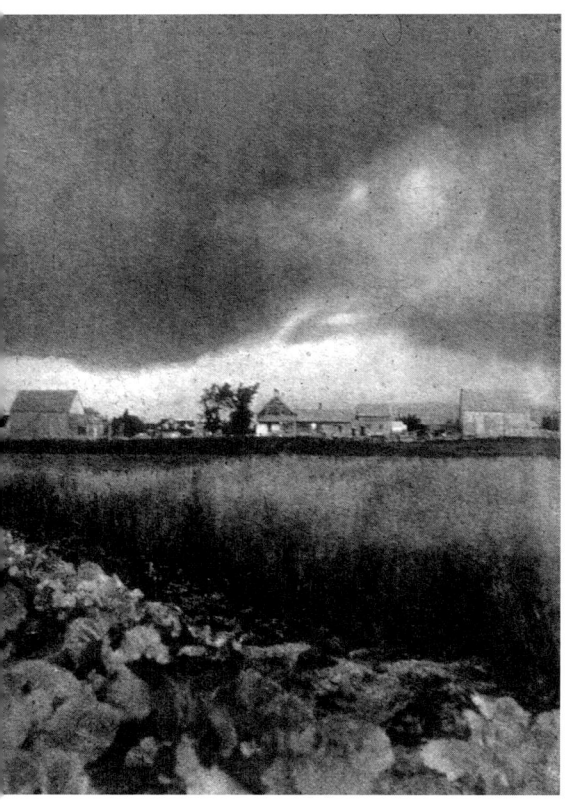

Eva Watson-Schütze, "Storm," Camera Work, *Number 9, January 1905.*

PART II

THE ALBUM

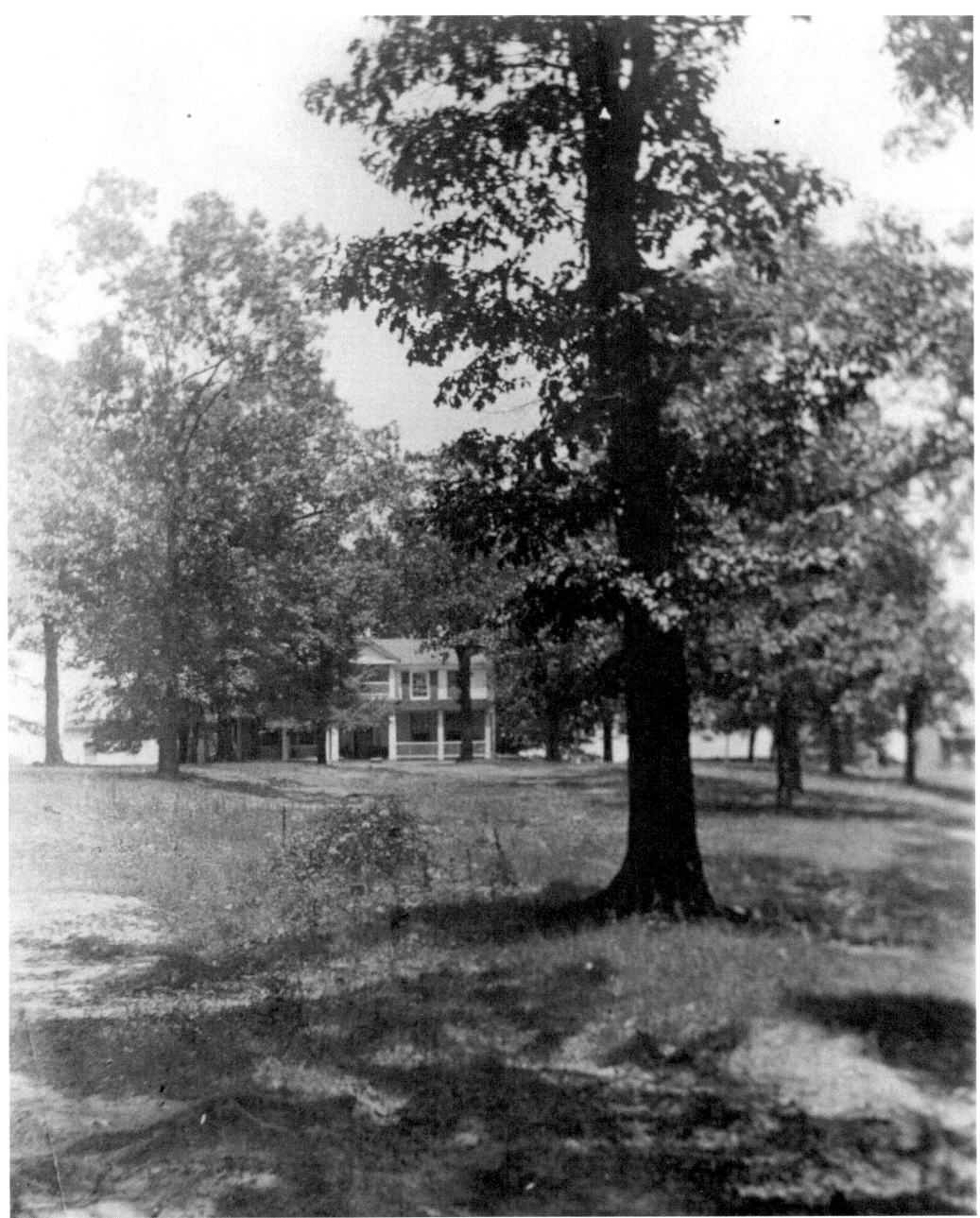

Plate 1.

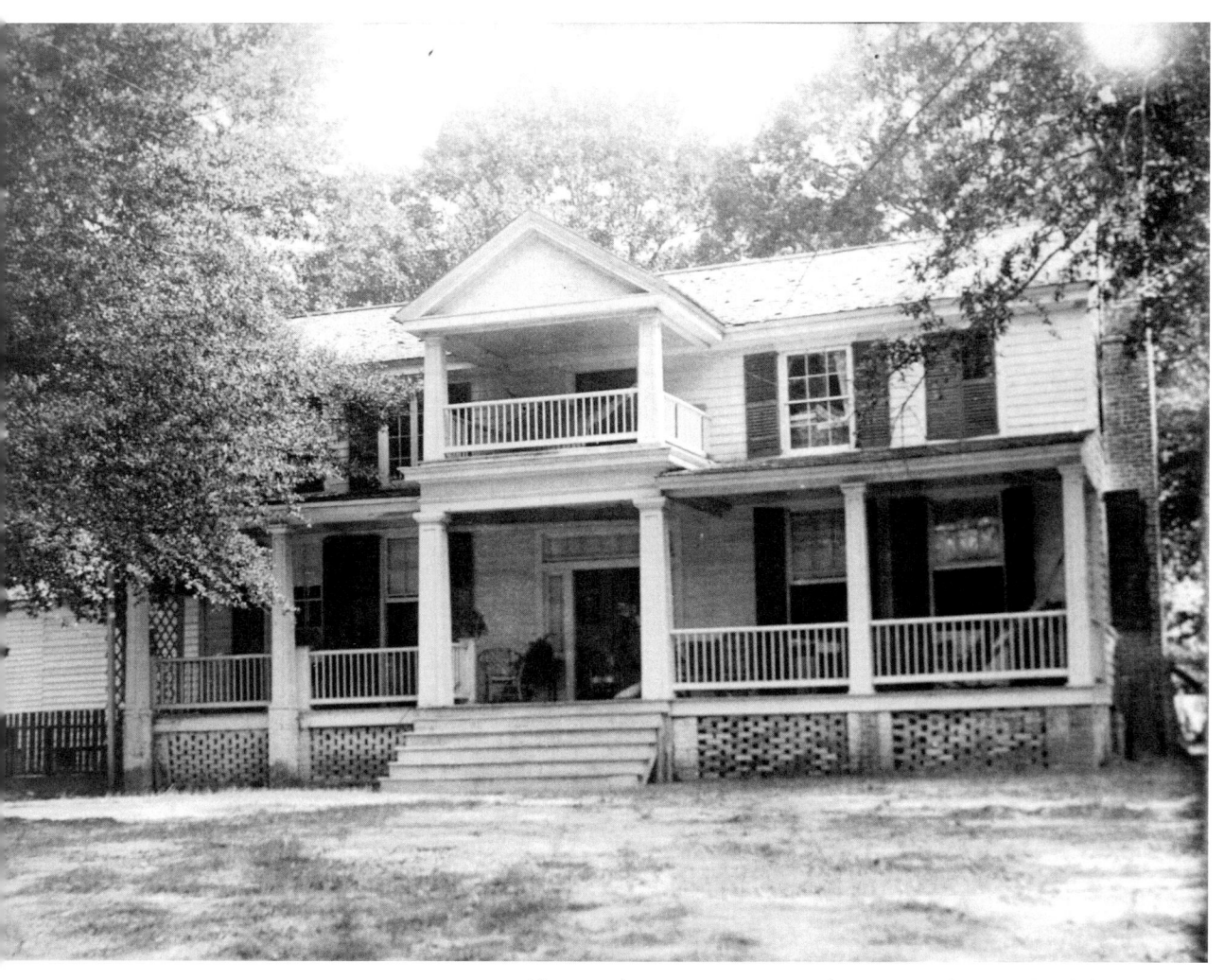

*Above, Plate 2. Opposite, Plate 3, on the porch of the Morgan
home; Minnie Miller (later Jones) at far left.*

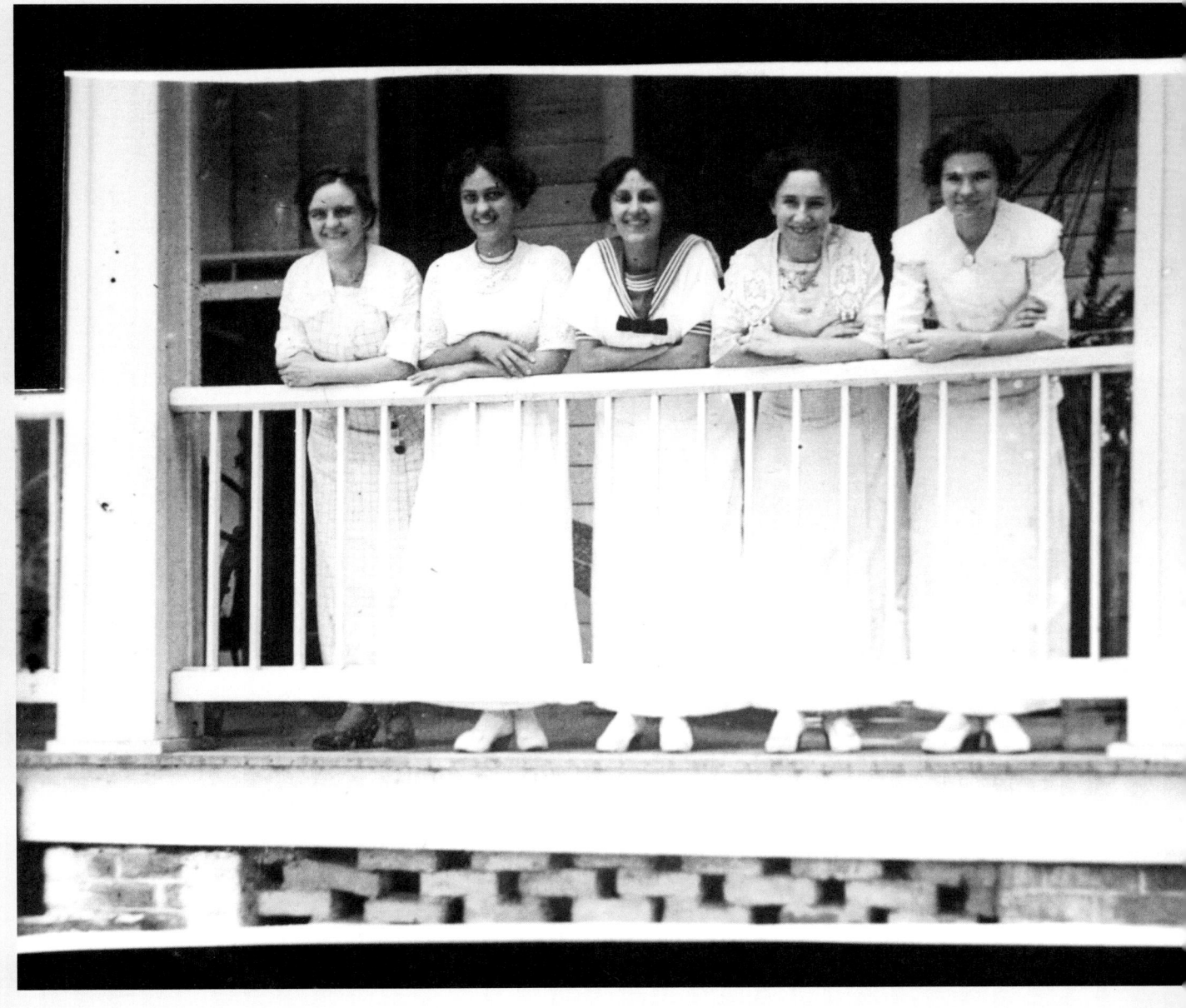

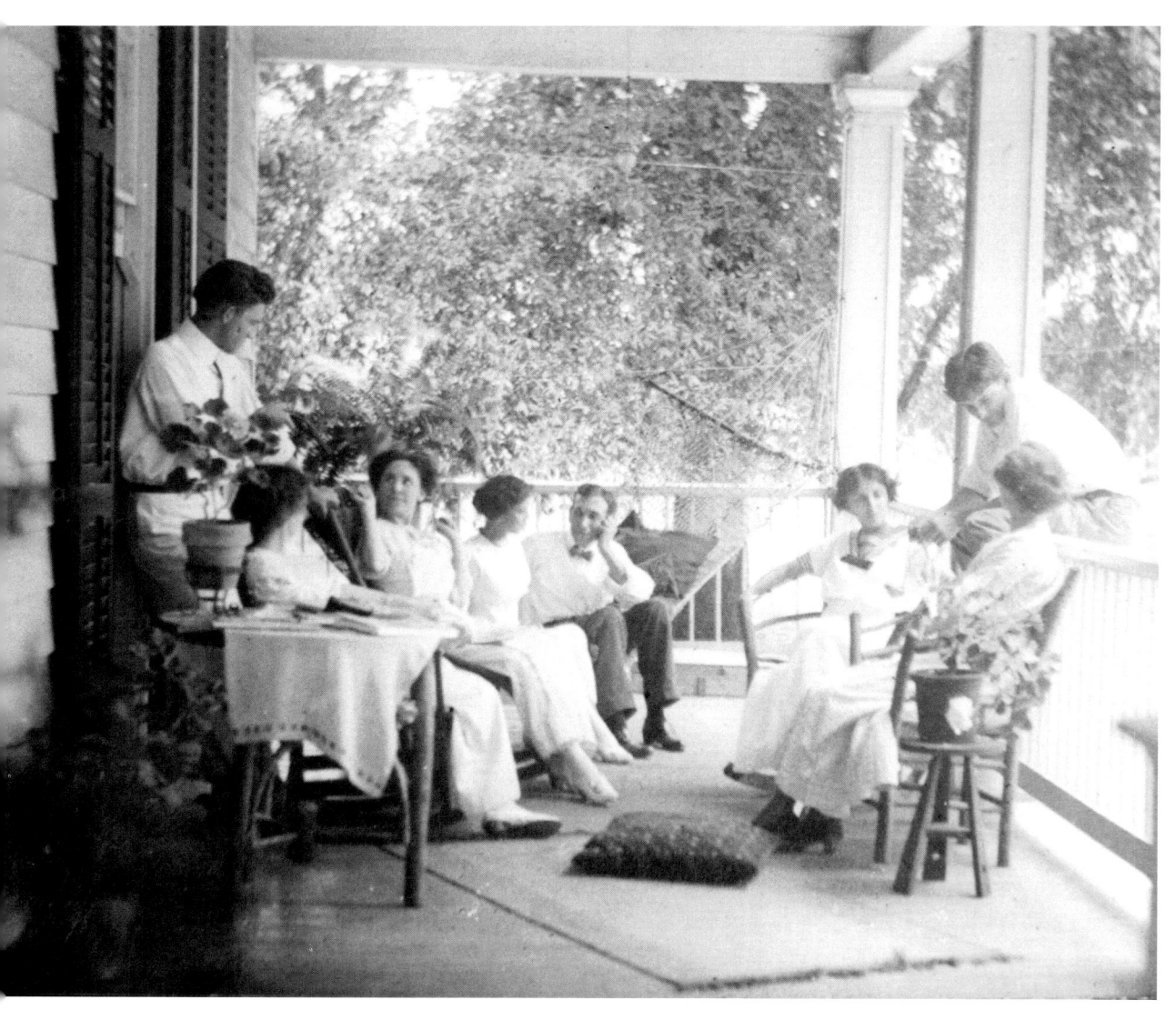

Above, Plate 4. Opposite, Plate 5.

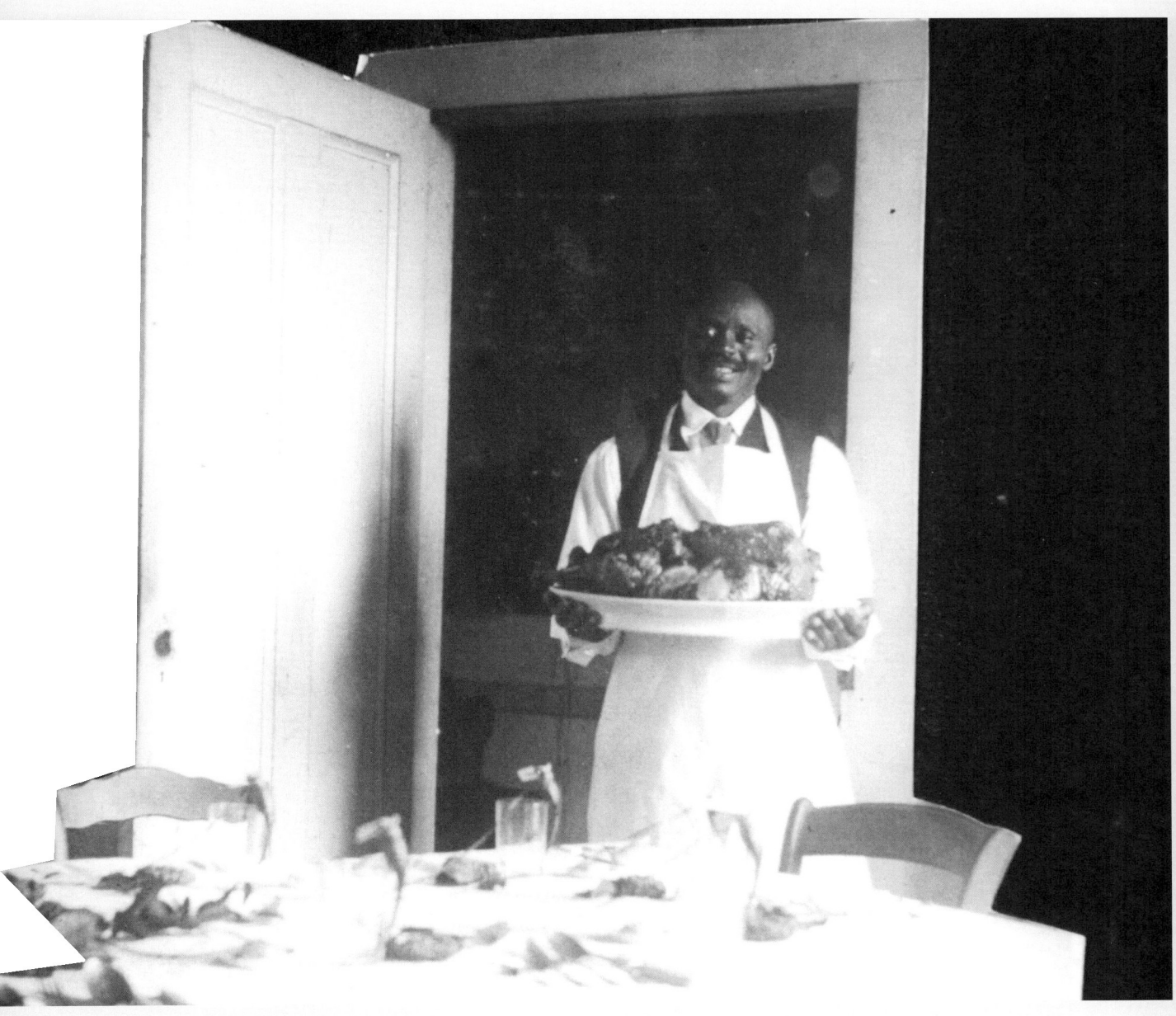

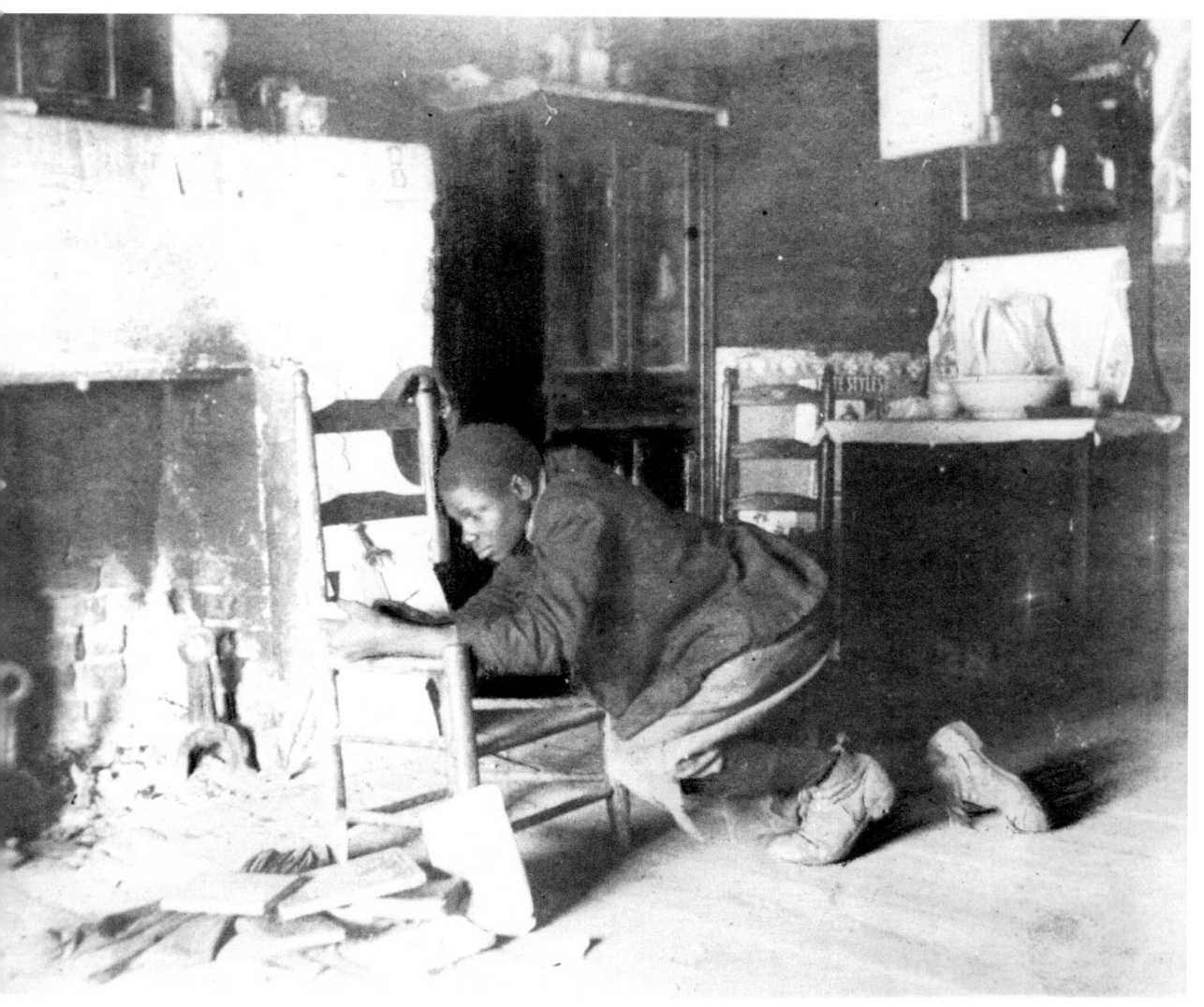

Above, Plate 6. Opposite, Plates 7 and 8, Edith Morgan with a washerwoman.

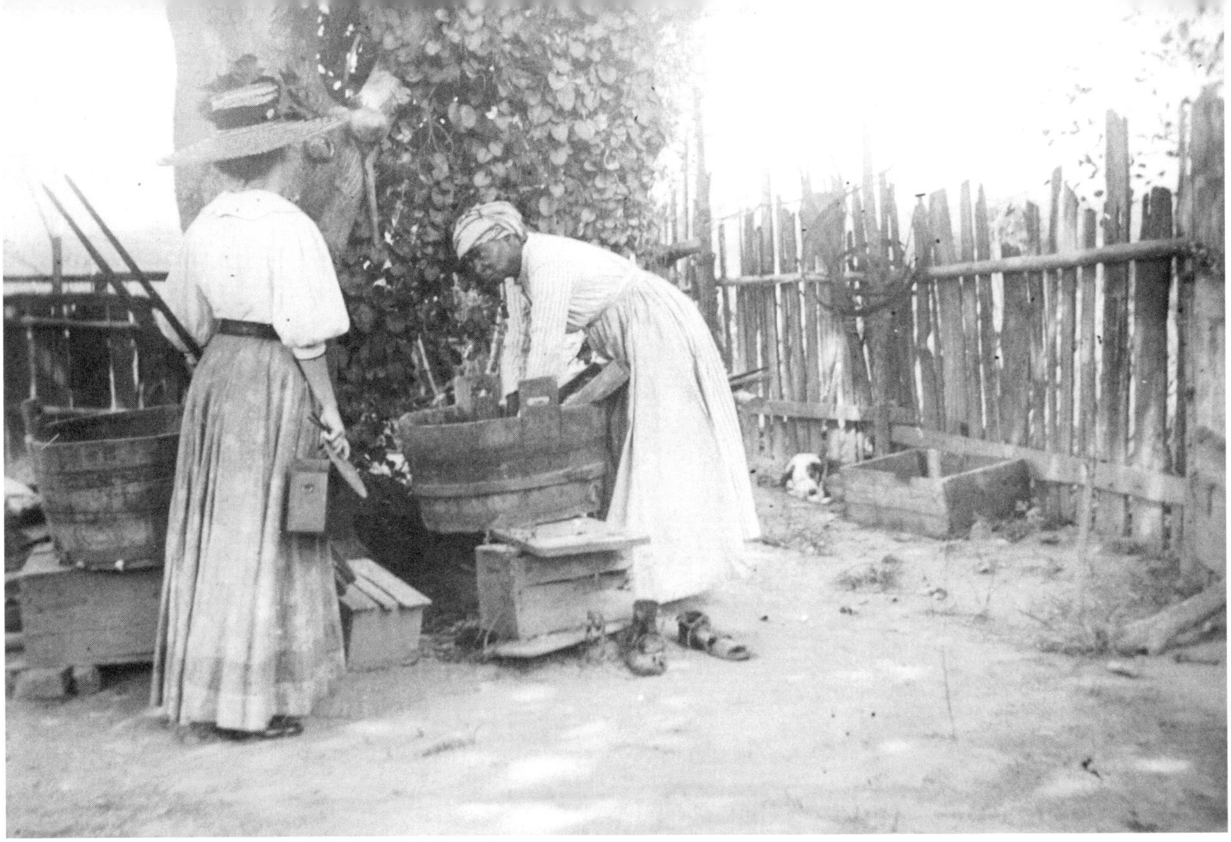

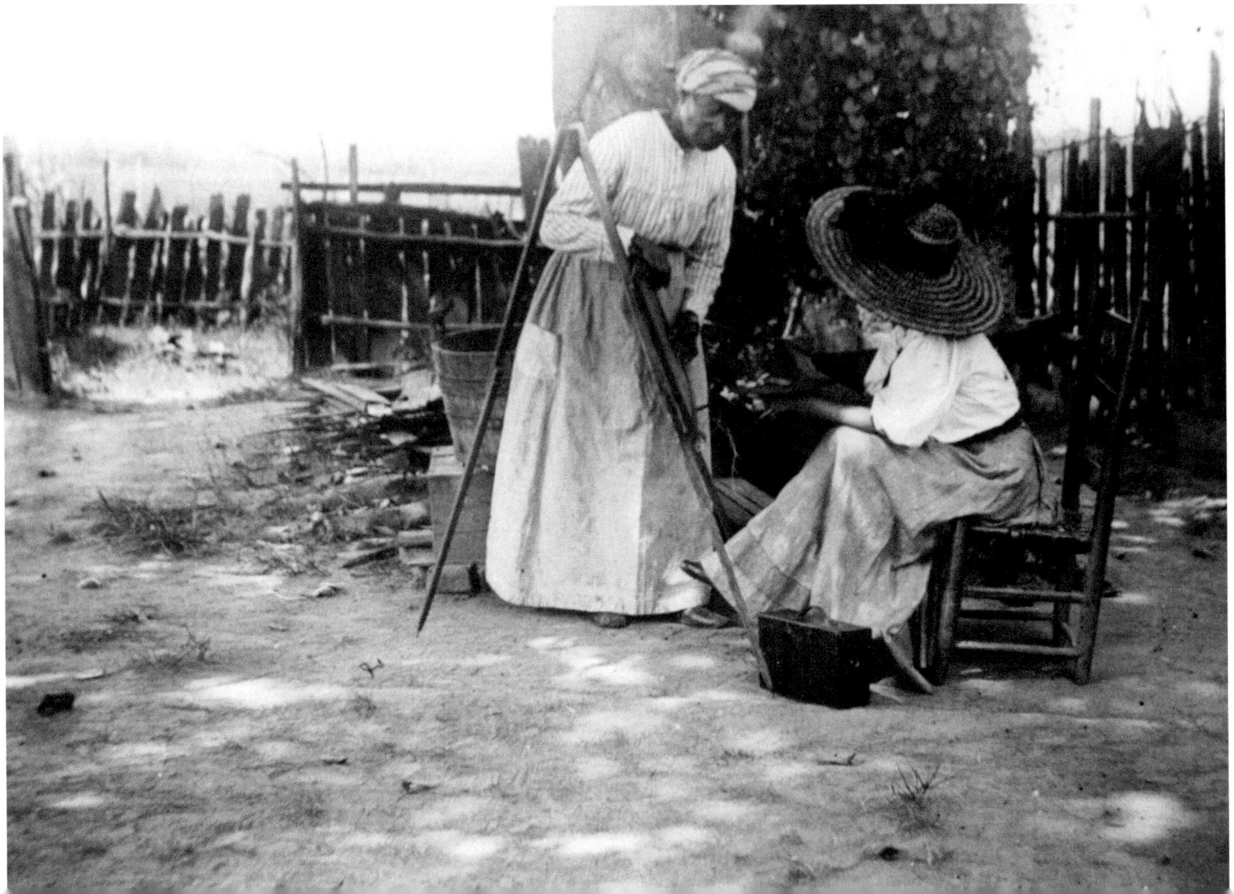

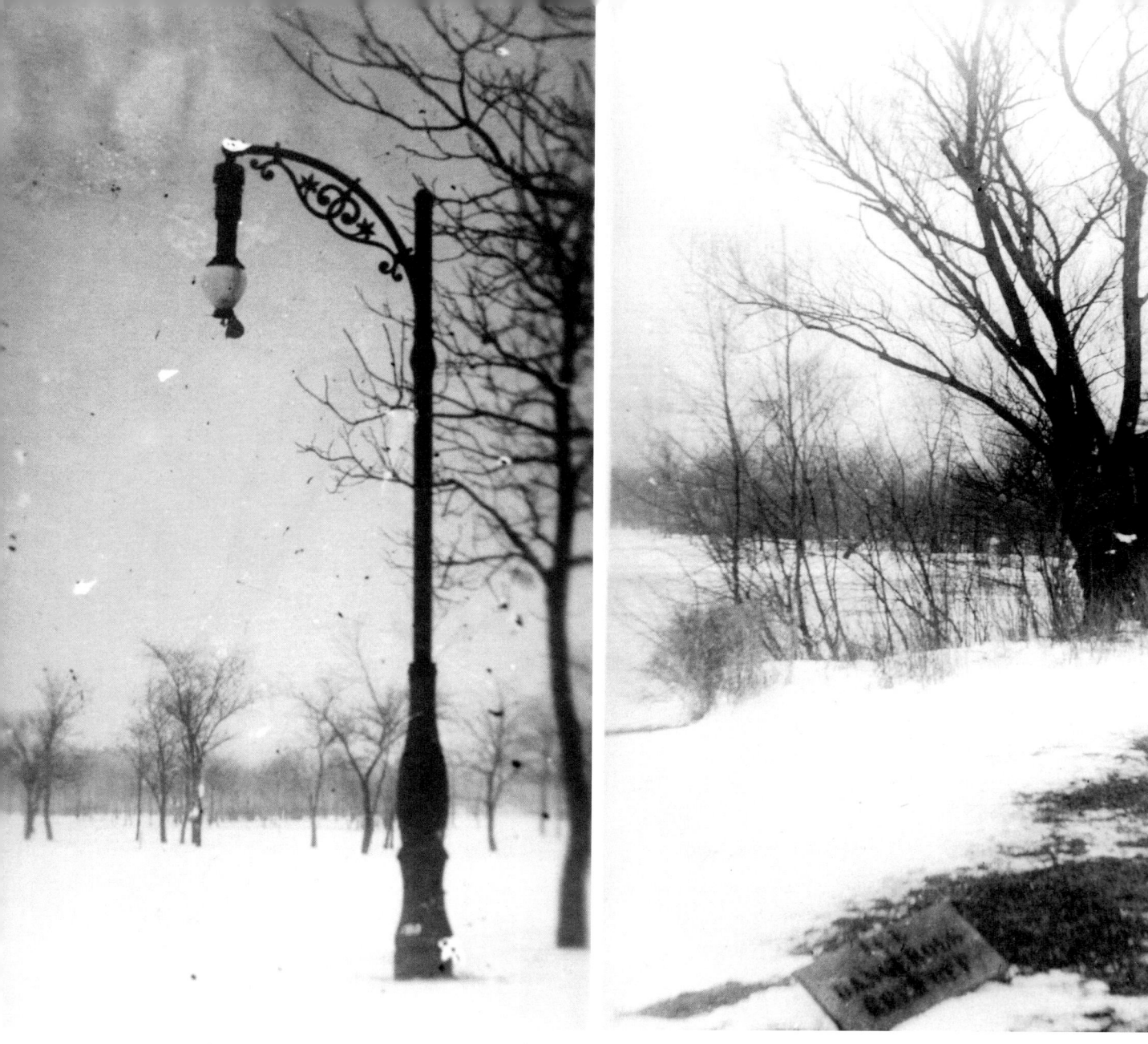

Plates 9 and 10, Chicago, Illinois.

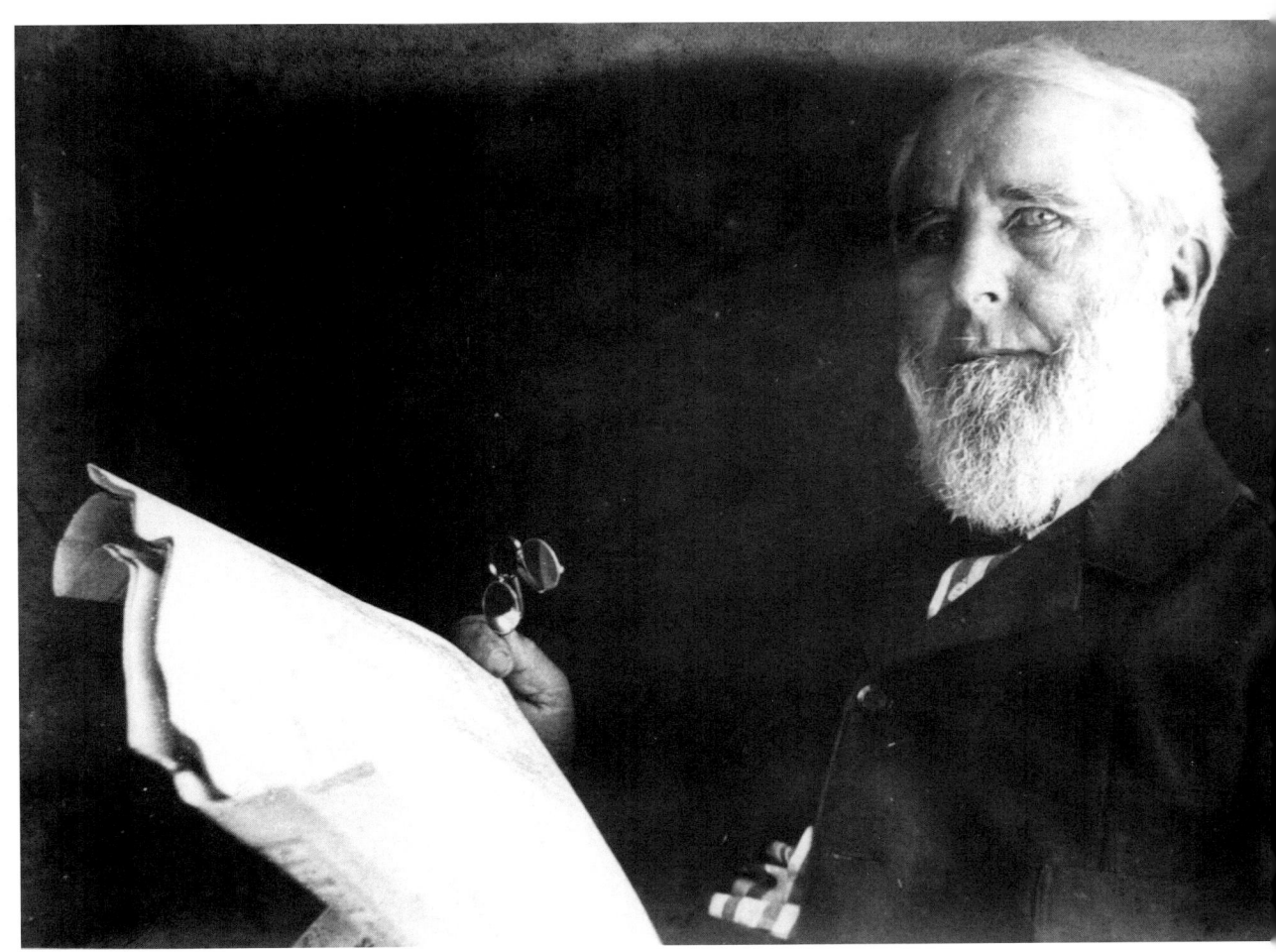

Plate 11, Albion Morgan.

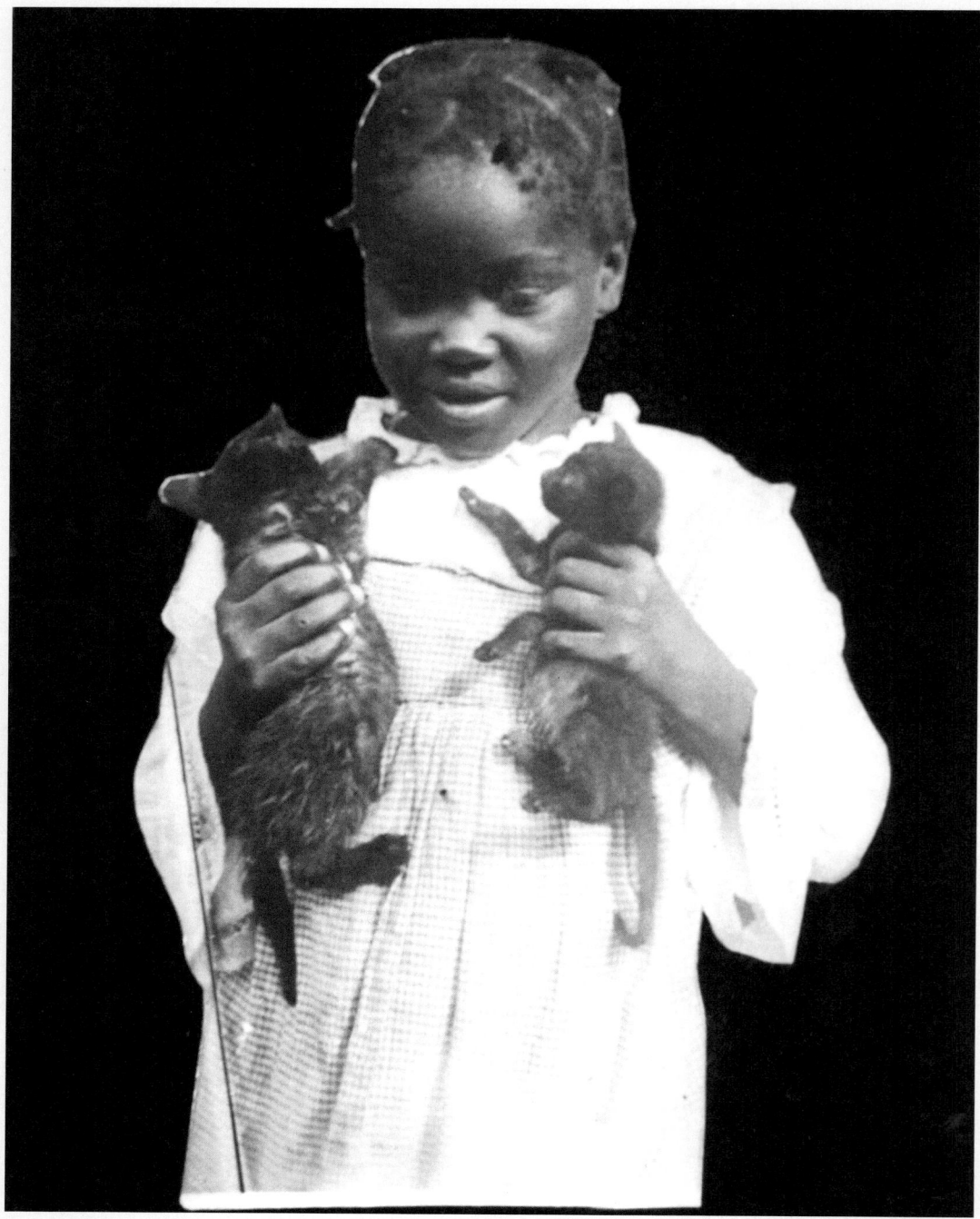

Plate 12. This image was labeled "Three Brunetts" in the album.

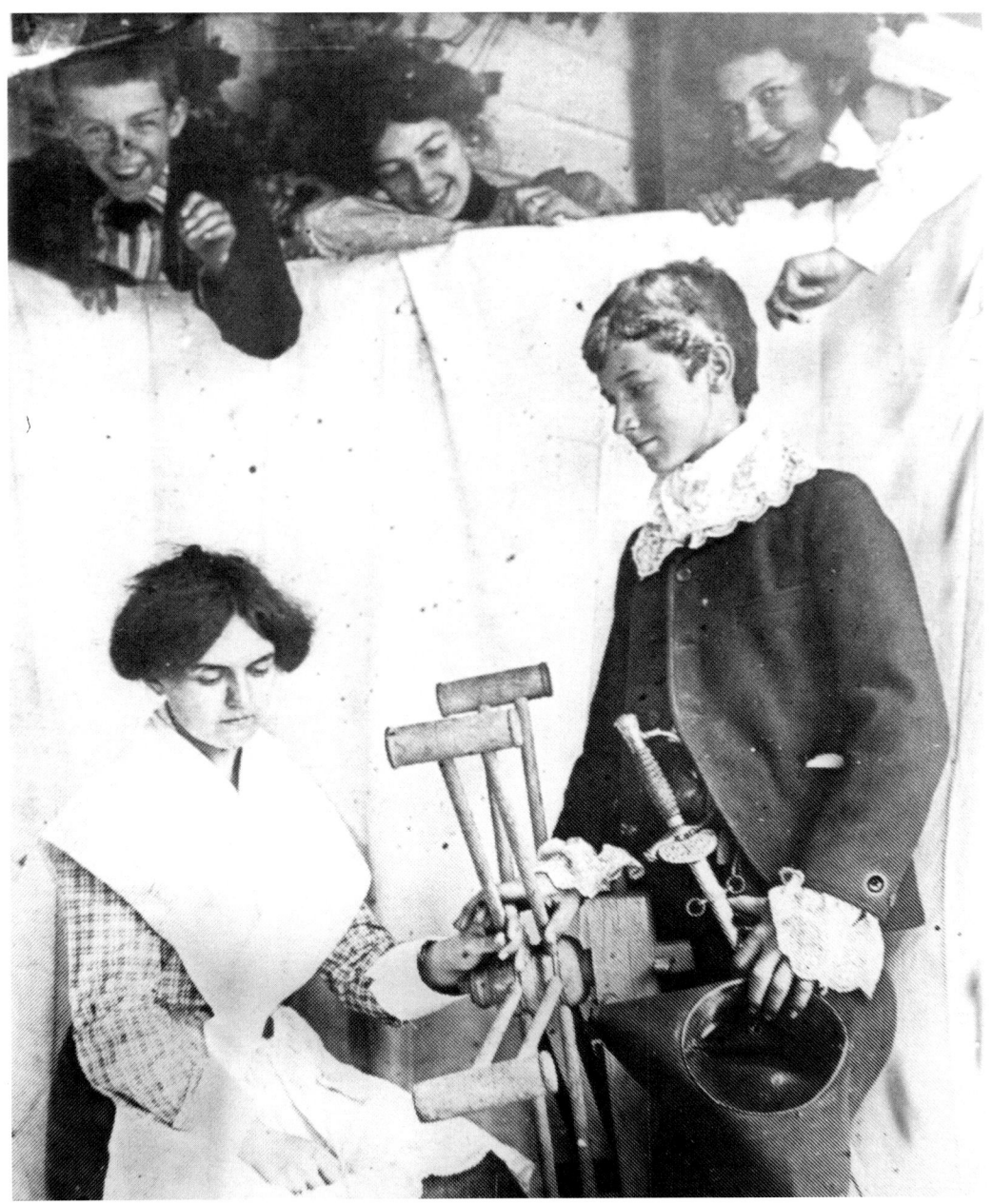

Plate 13. Foreground, Minnie Miller (Jones) and Roy Henderson Liddell. Rear, Glen David Liddell, Ellen Boykin (Jones), and Annie Brice Miller (Boykin).

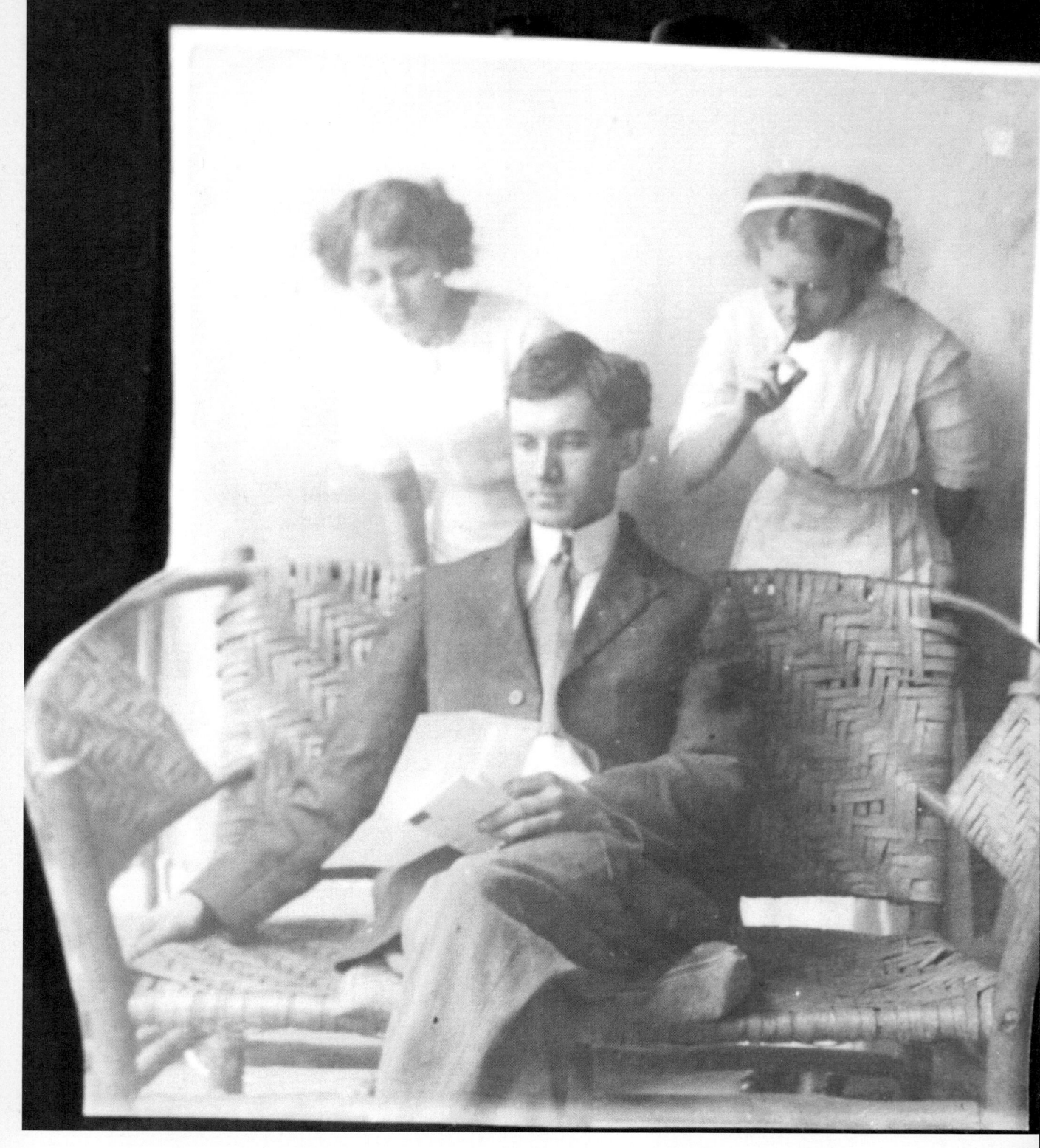

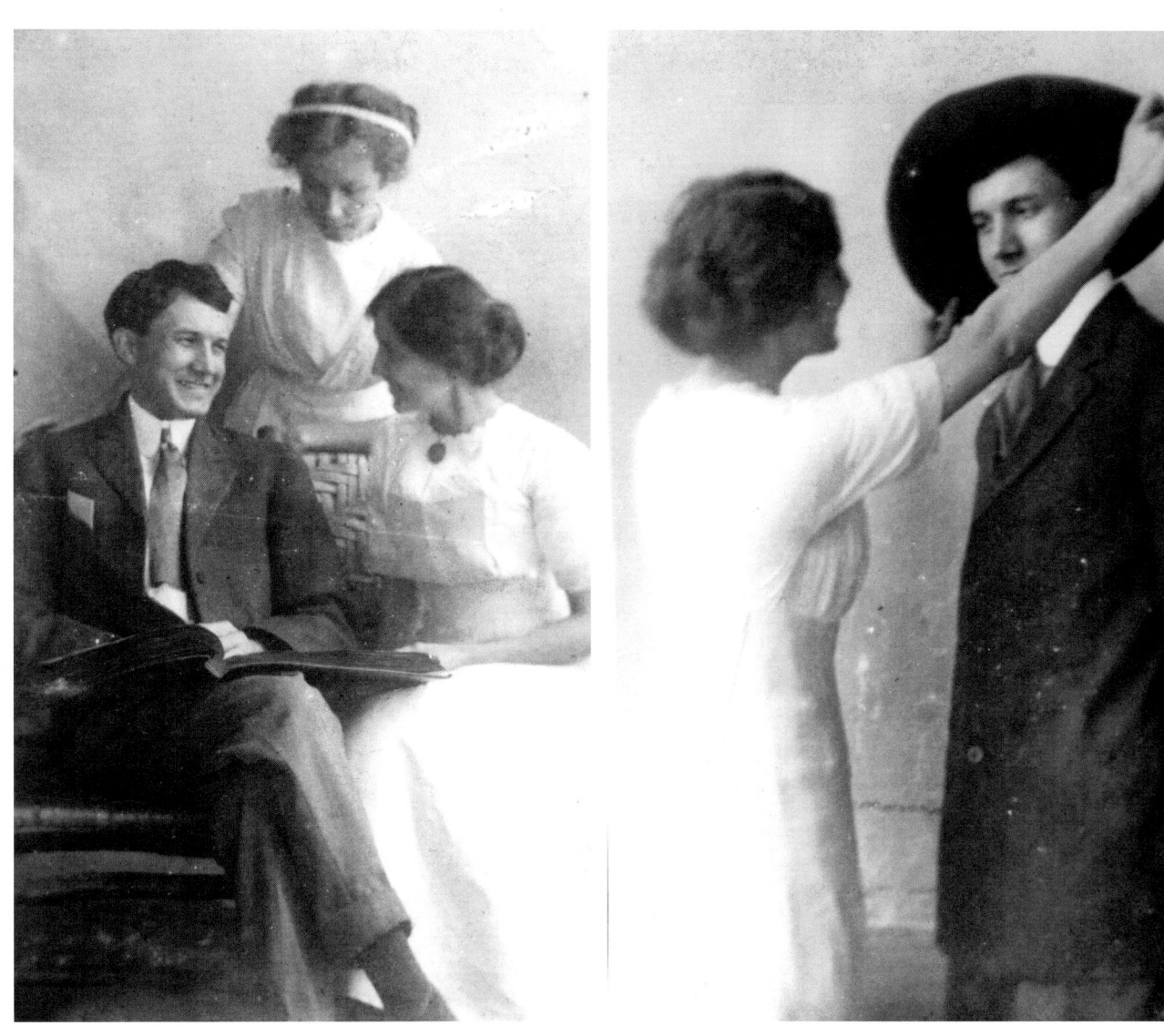

Opposite, Plate 14. Above, Plates 15 and 16.

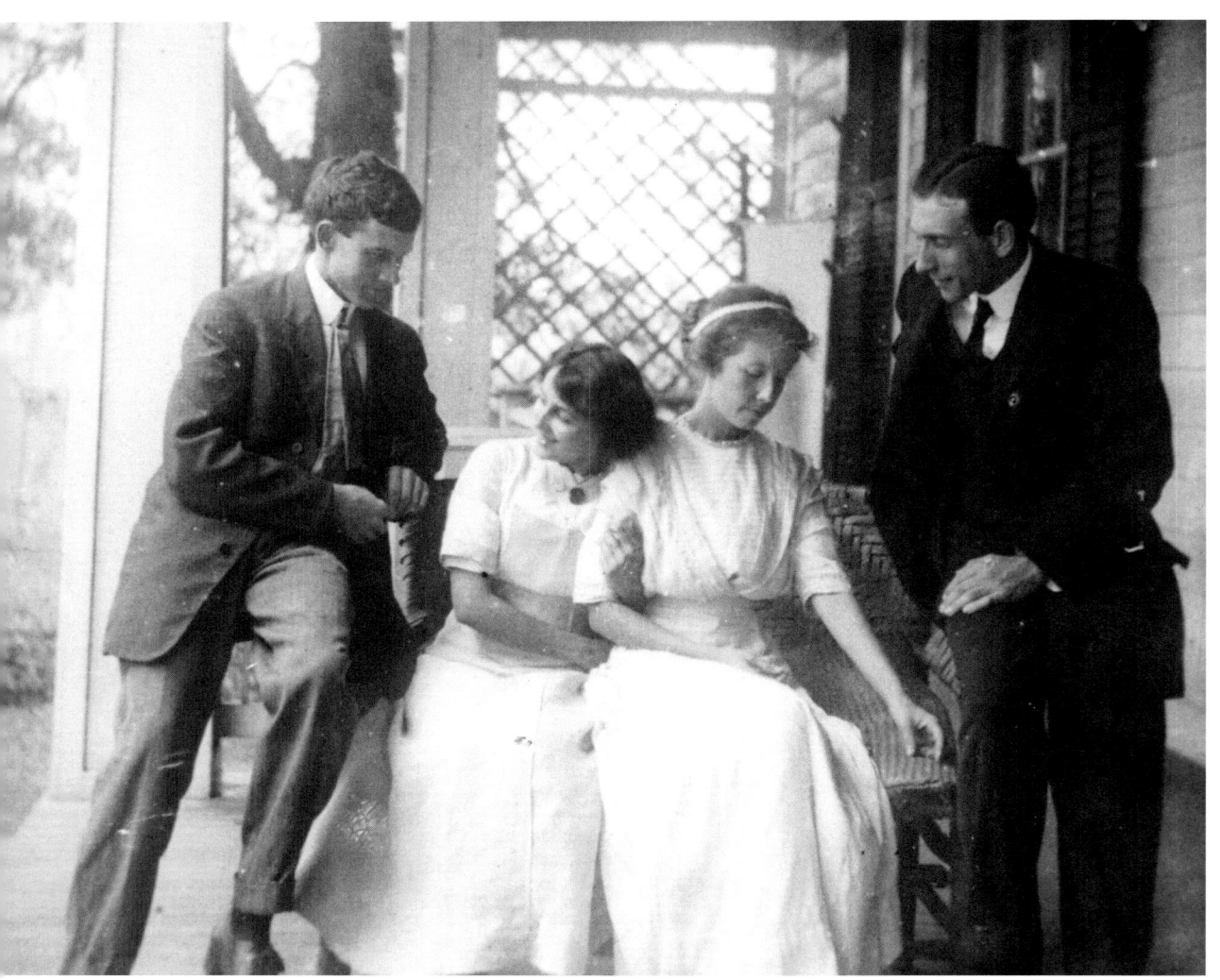

Above, Plate 17. Opposite, Plates 18 and 19.

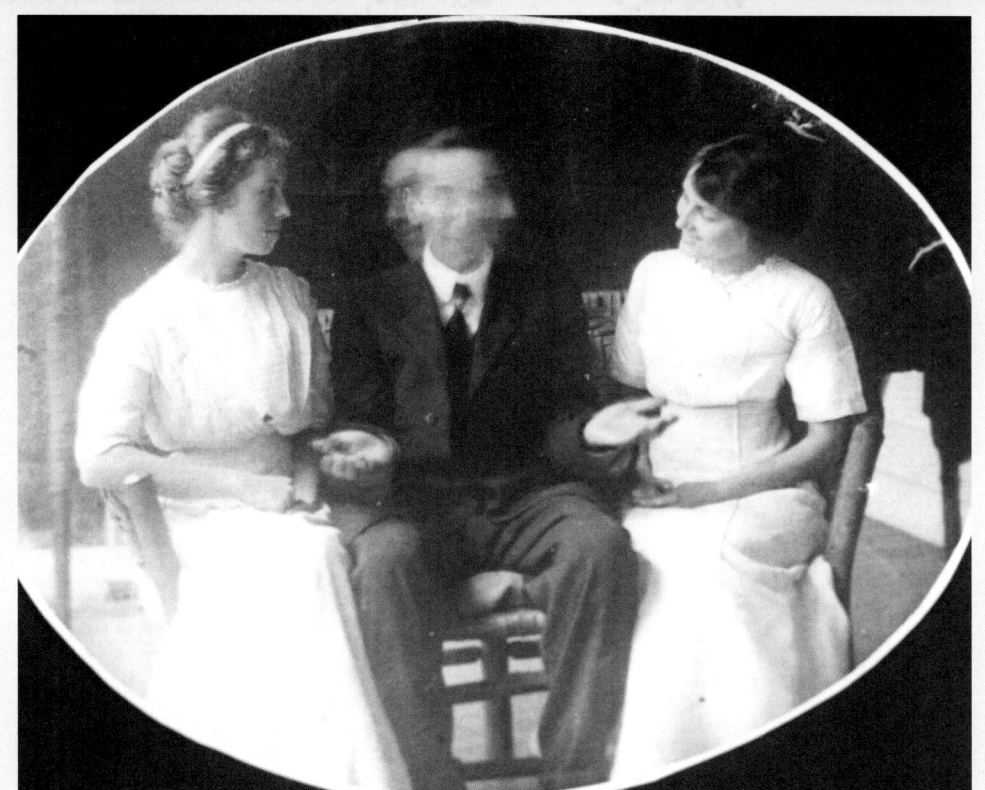

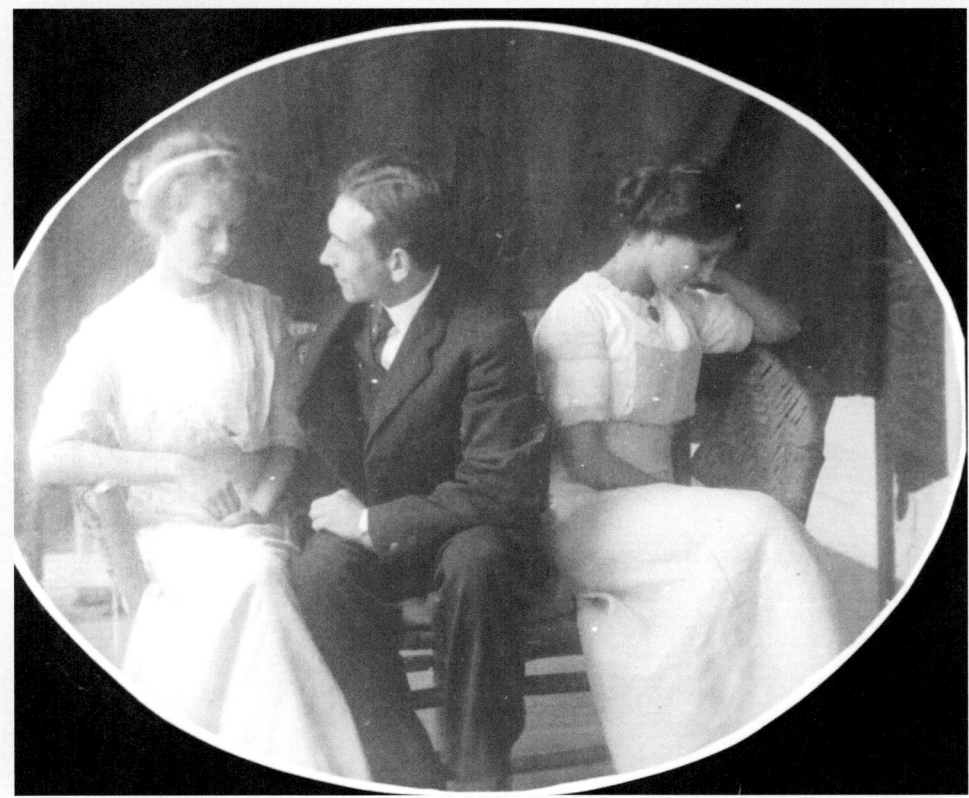

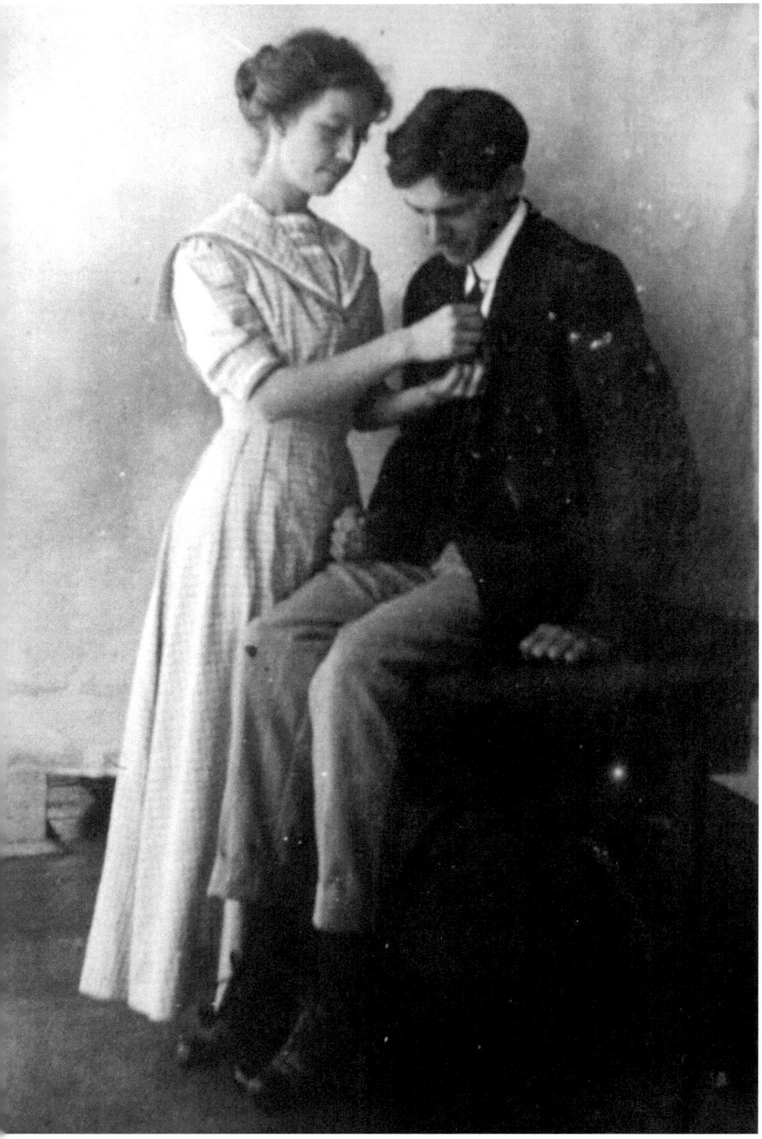

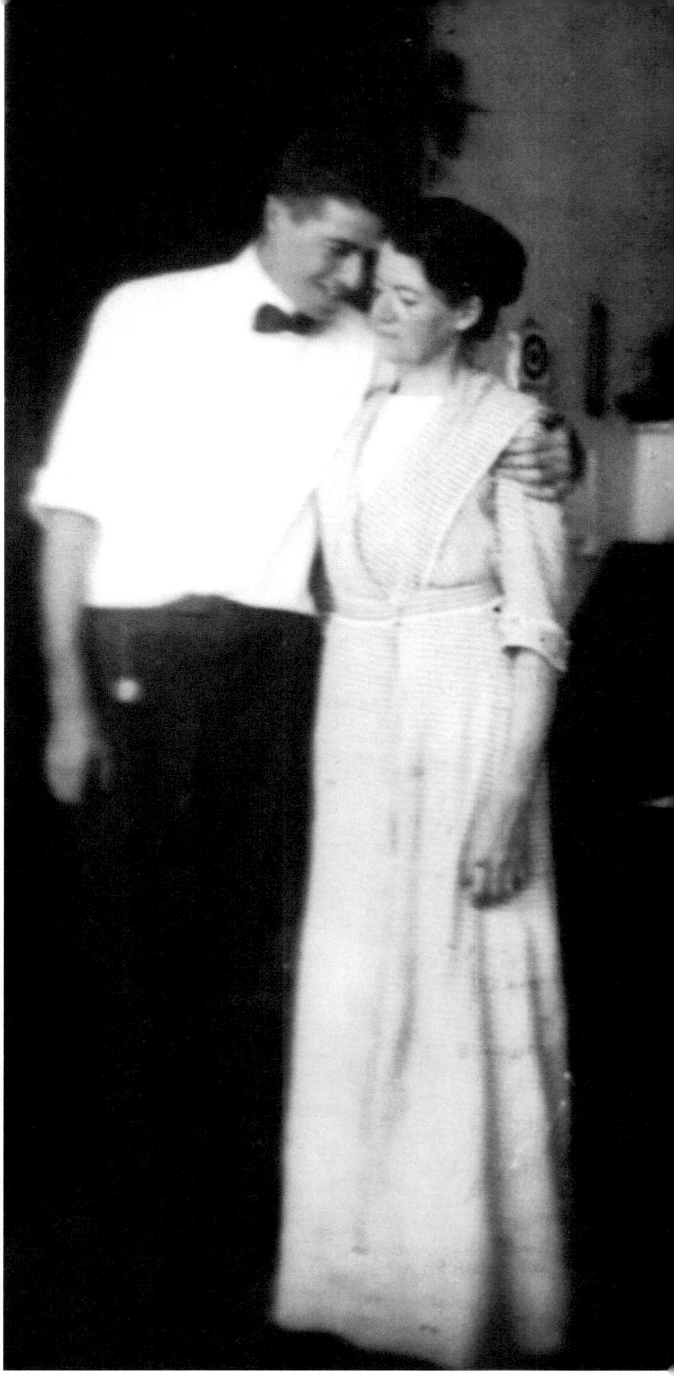

Plates 20 and 21.

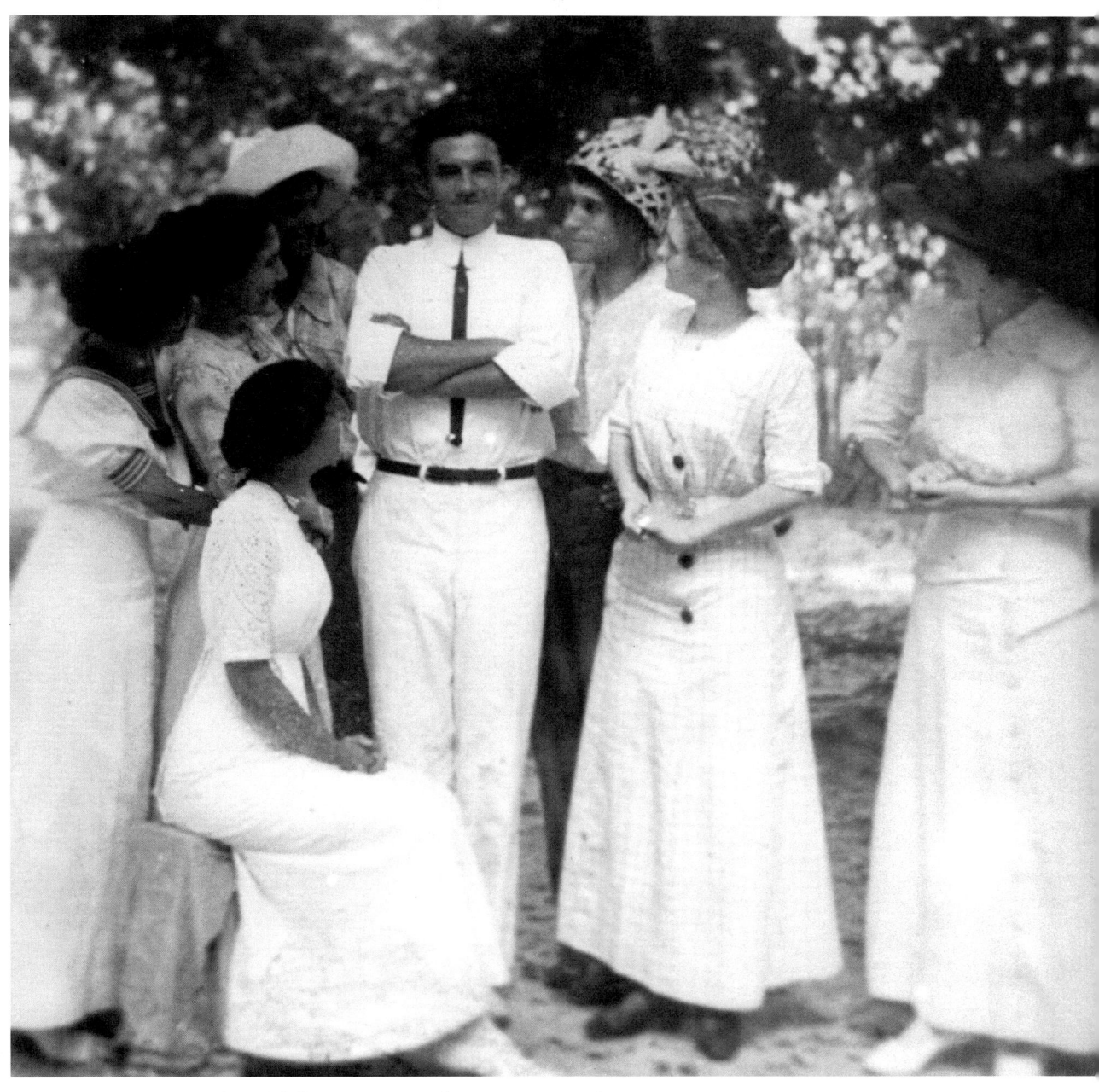

Plate 22, John Russell Liddell Jr. in center, between two other young men wearing women's hats.

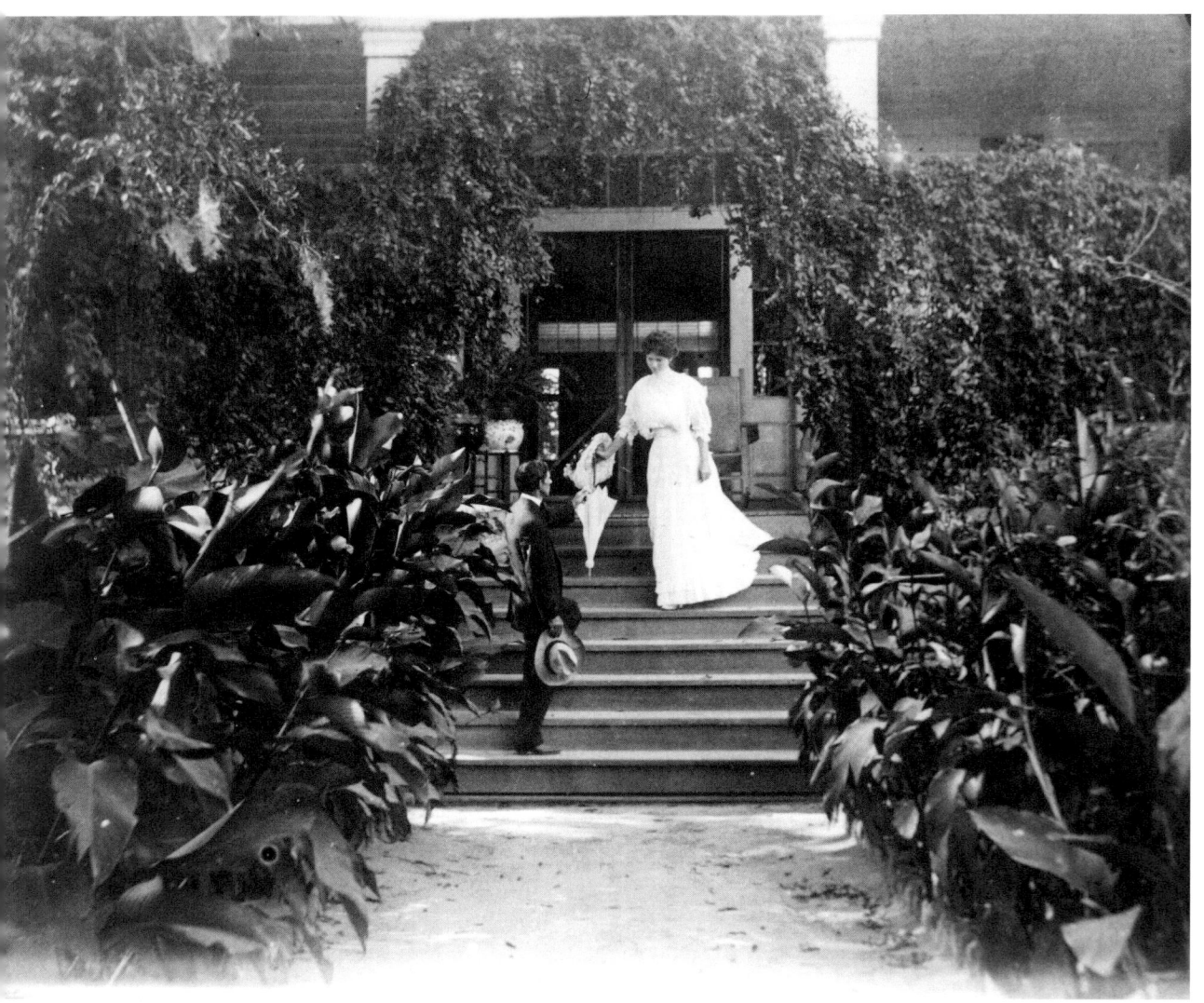

Plate 23.

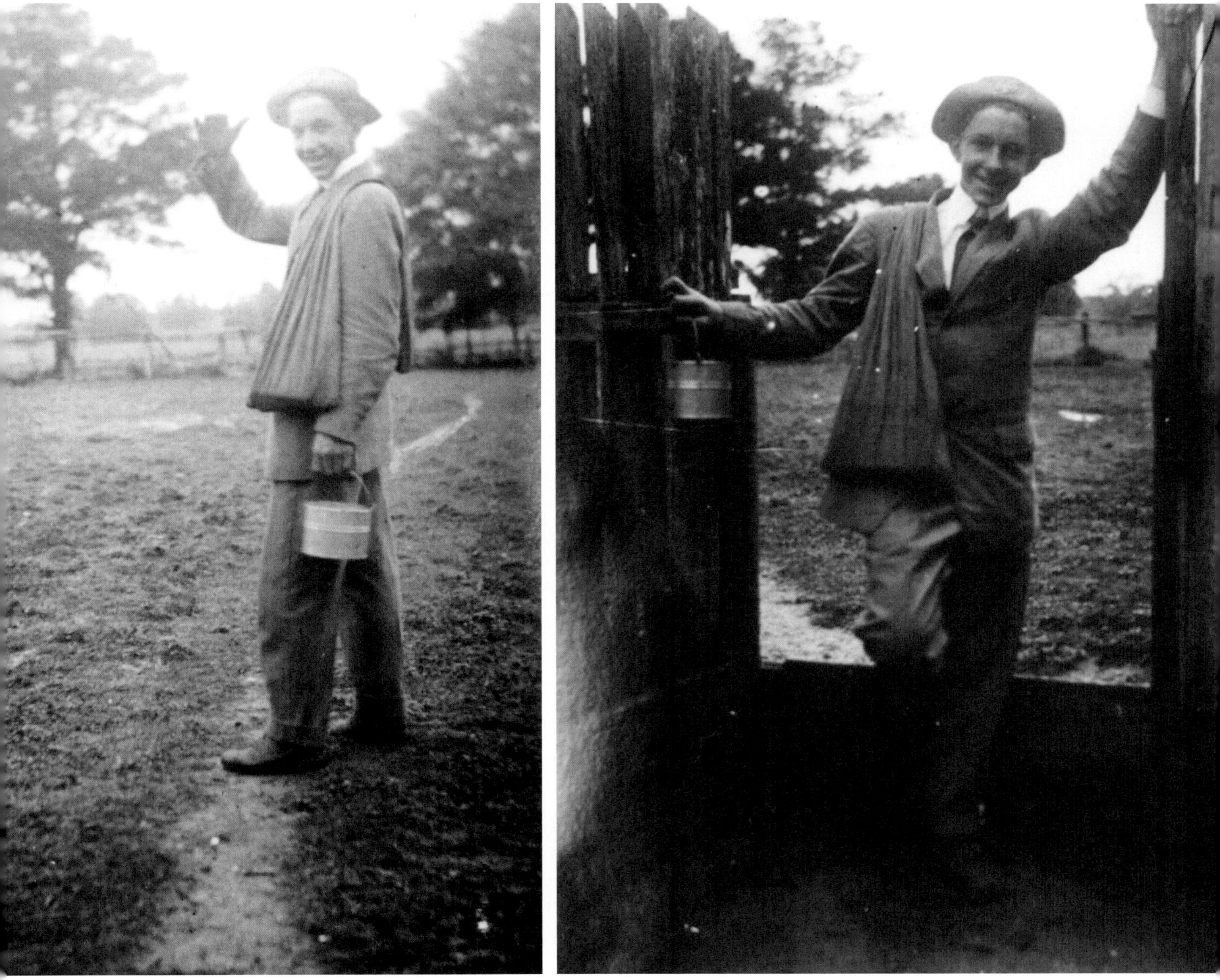

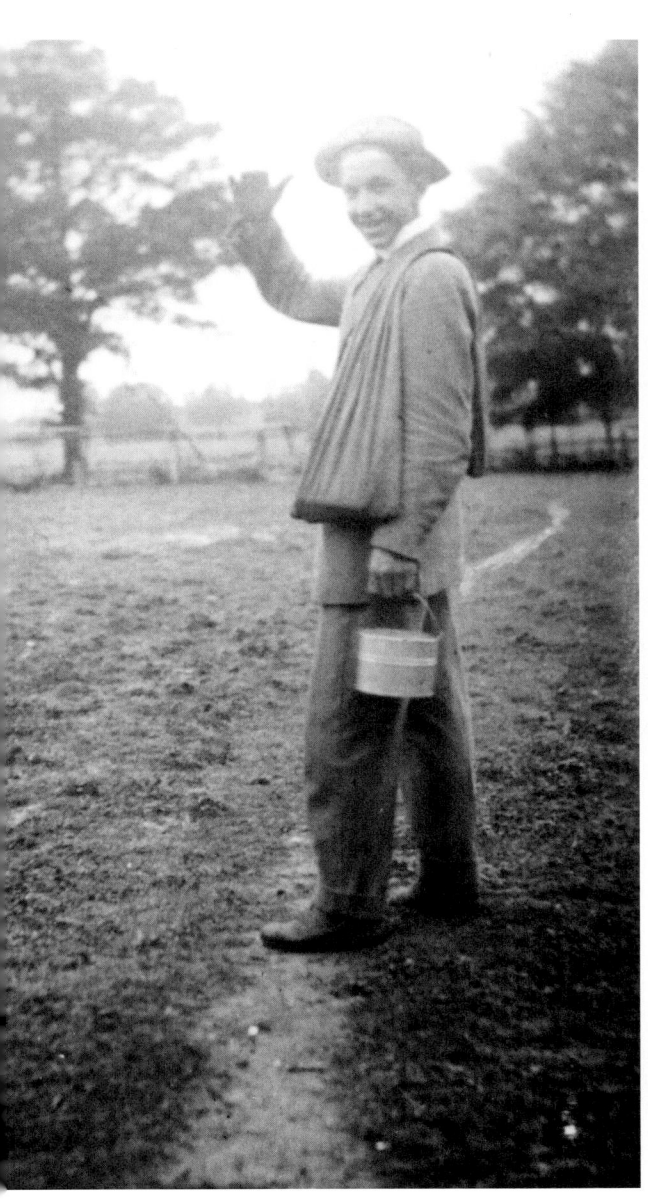

Plates 24 and 25, William Lithgow Liddell.

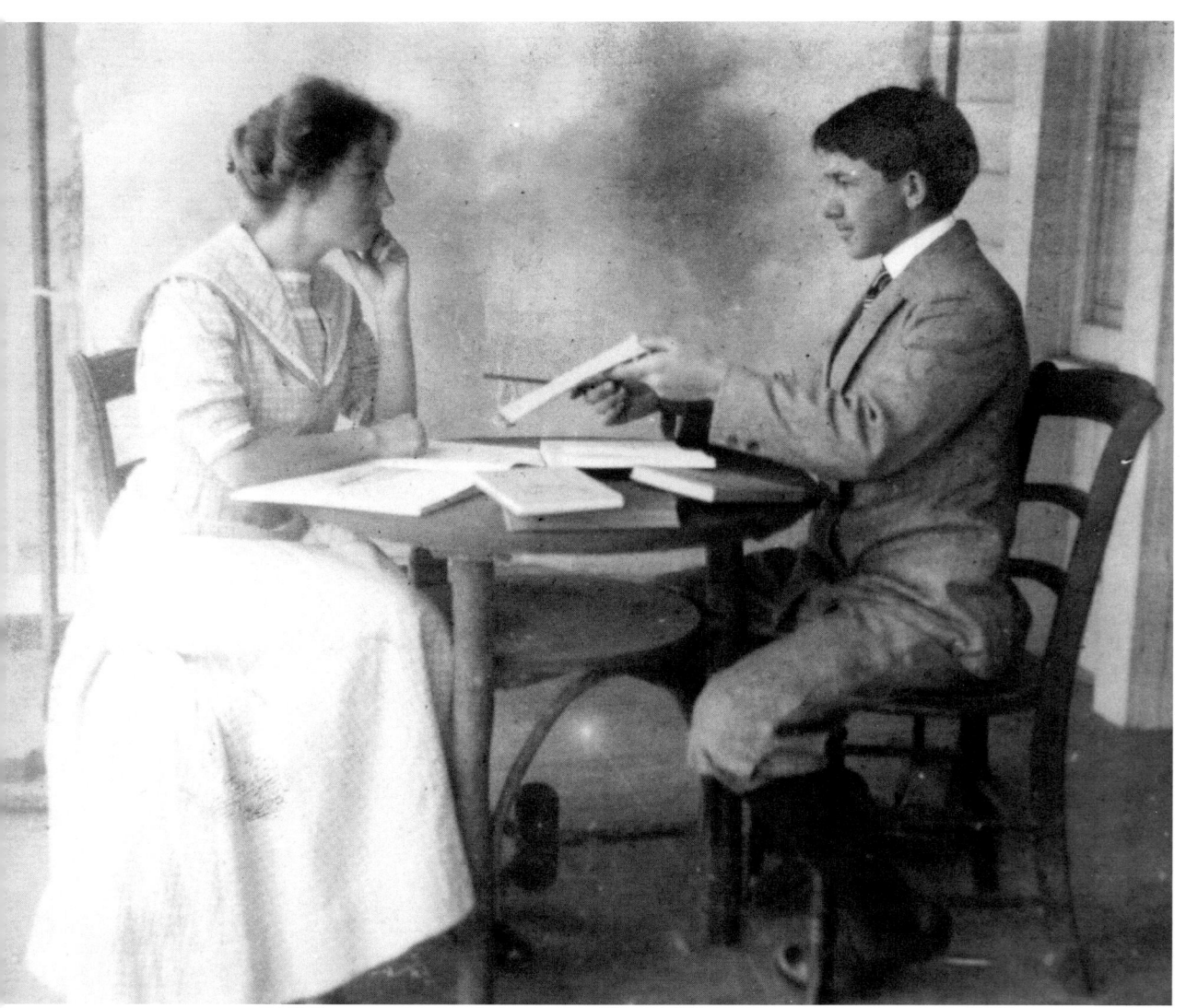

Plate 26, Edith Morgan and William Lithgow Liddell.

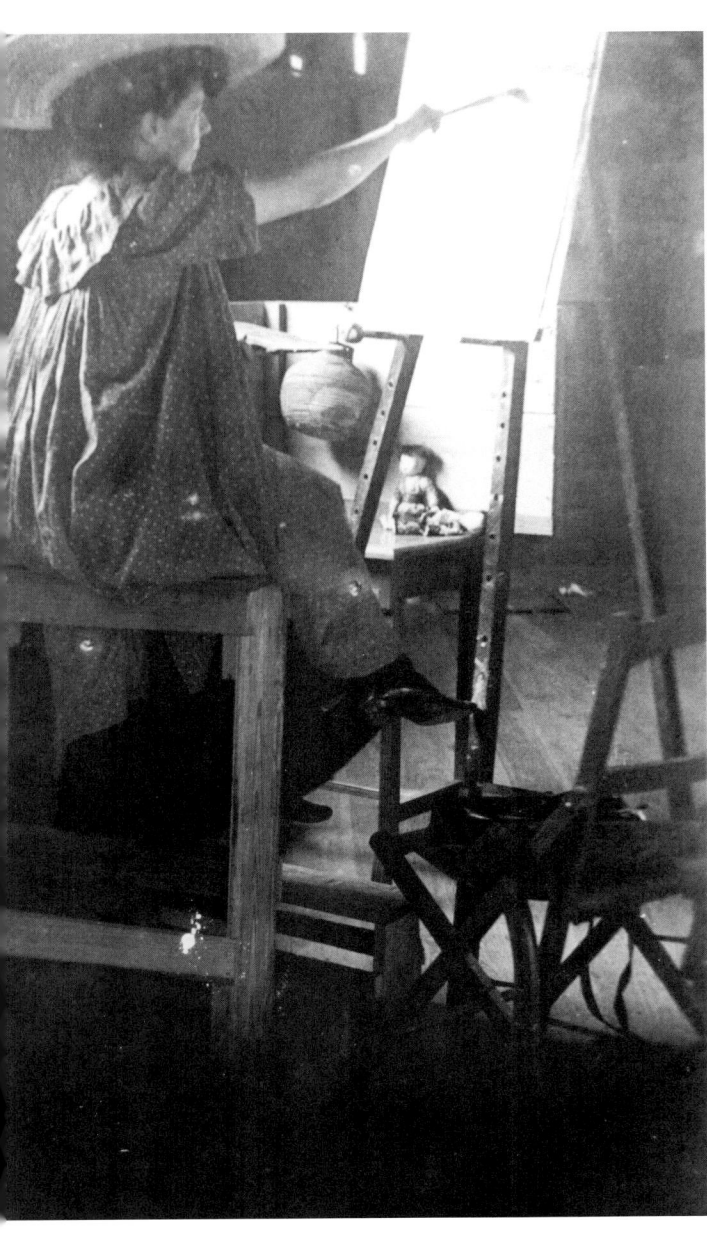
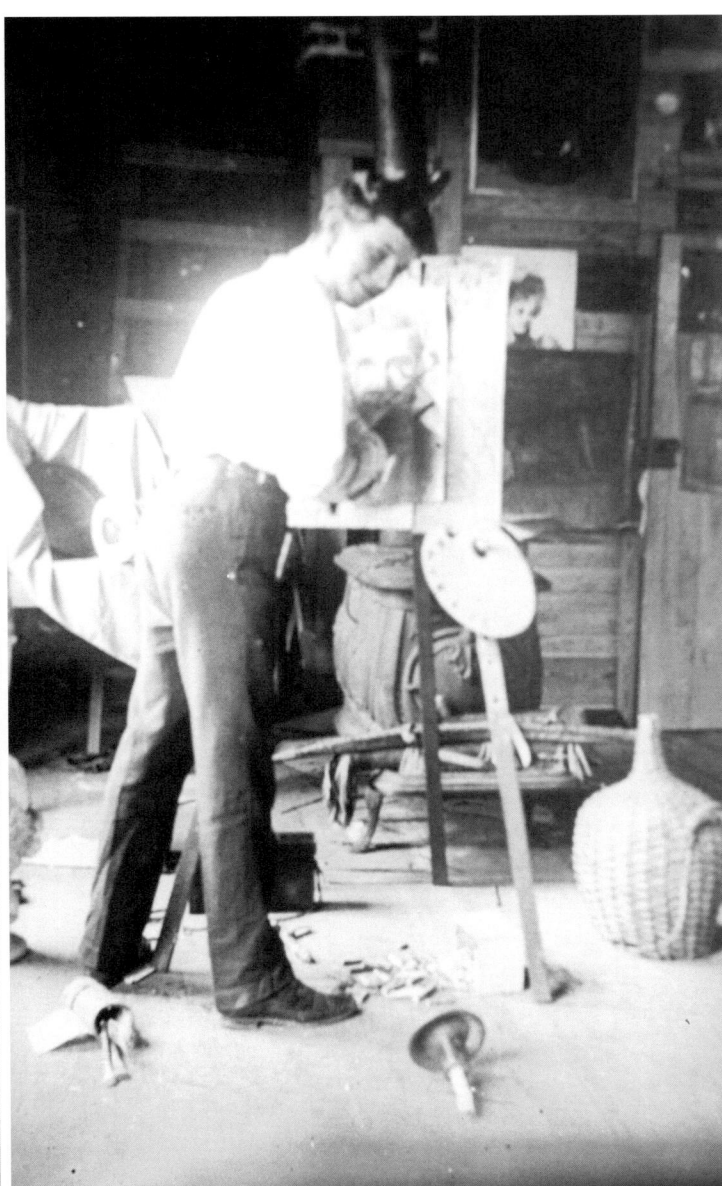

Plates 27 and 28.

59

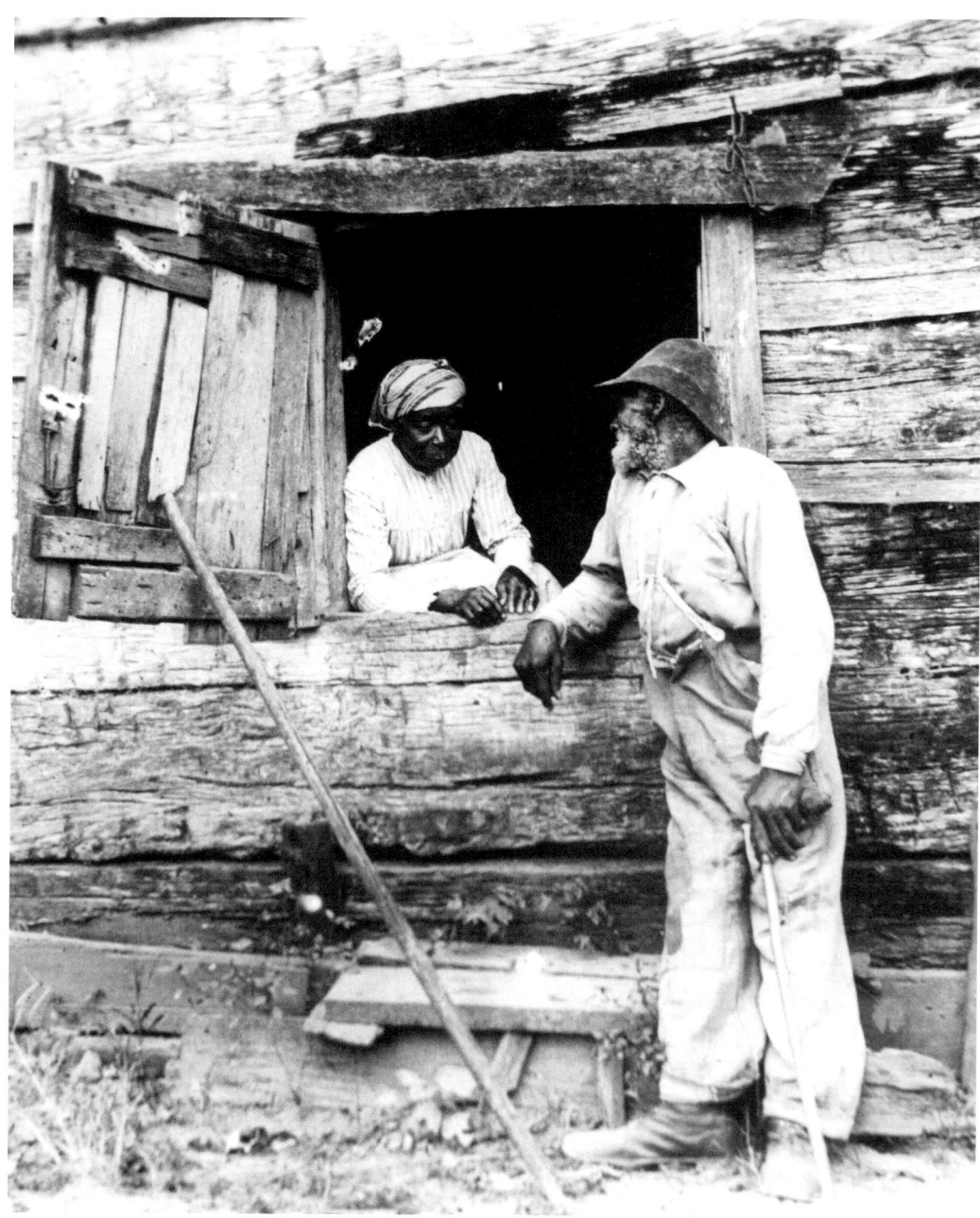

Plate 29.

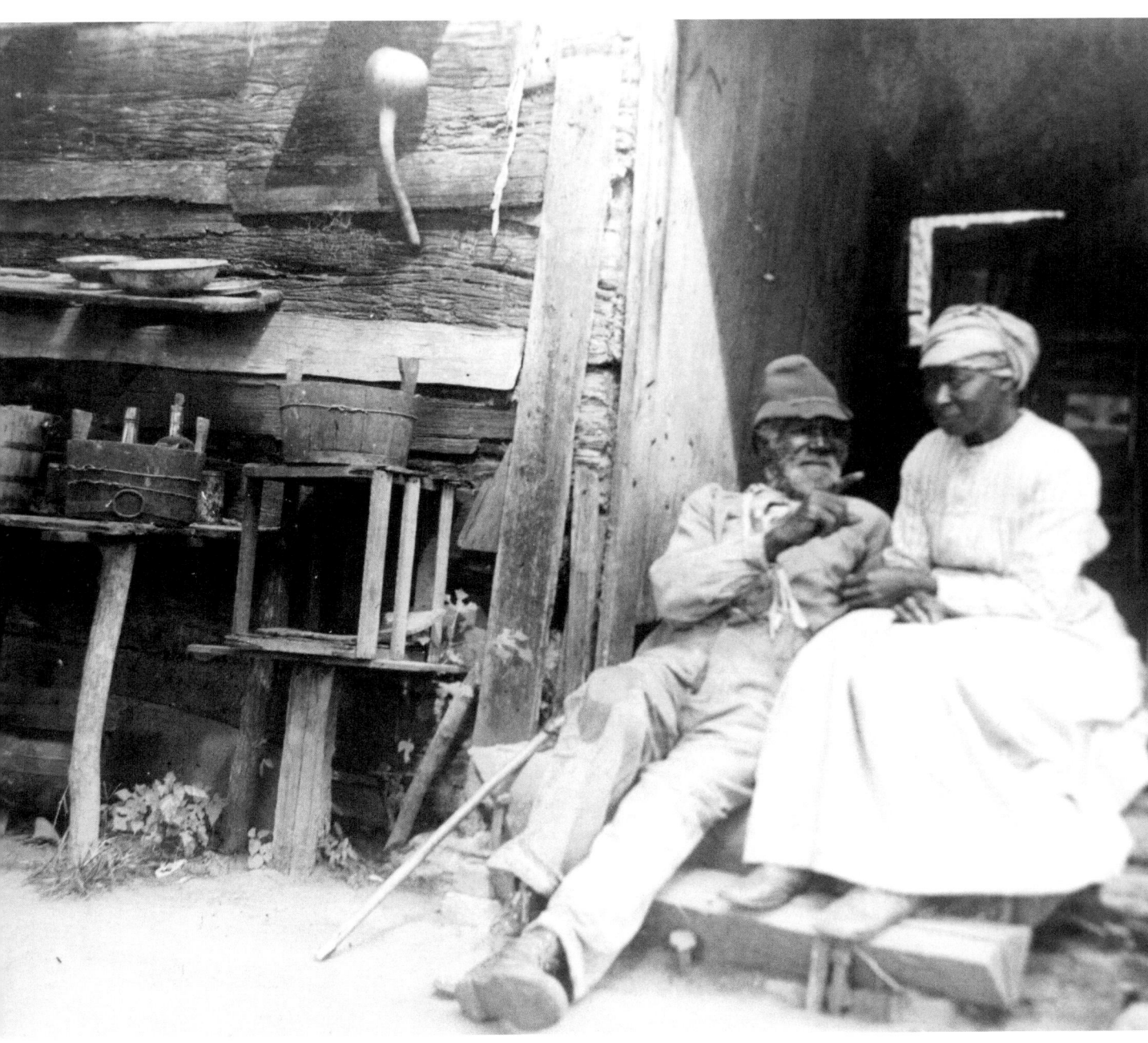

Plate 30.

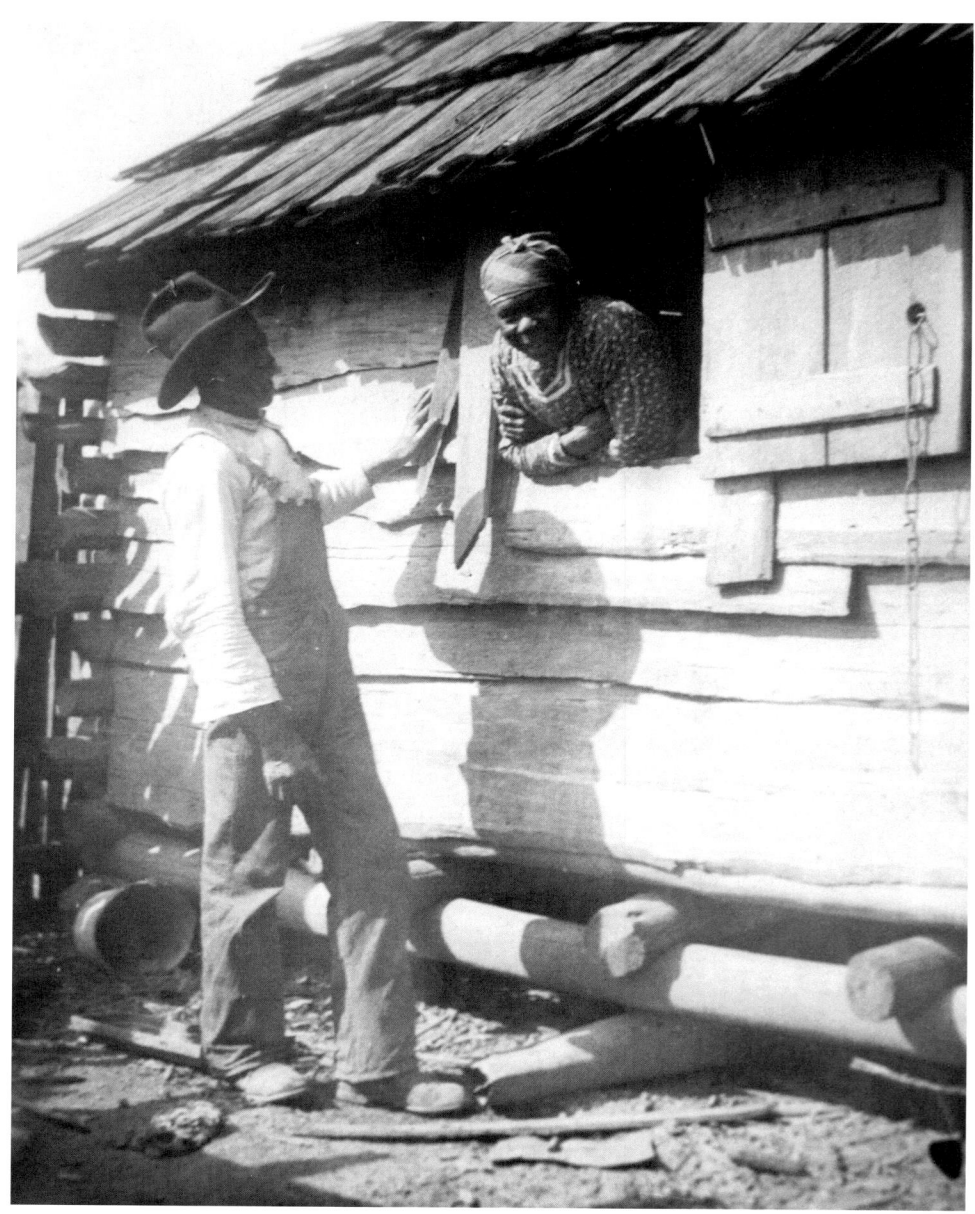

Plate 31.

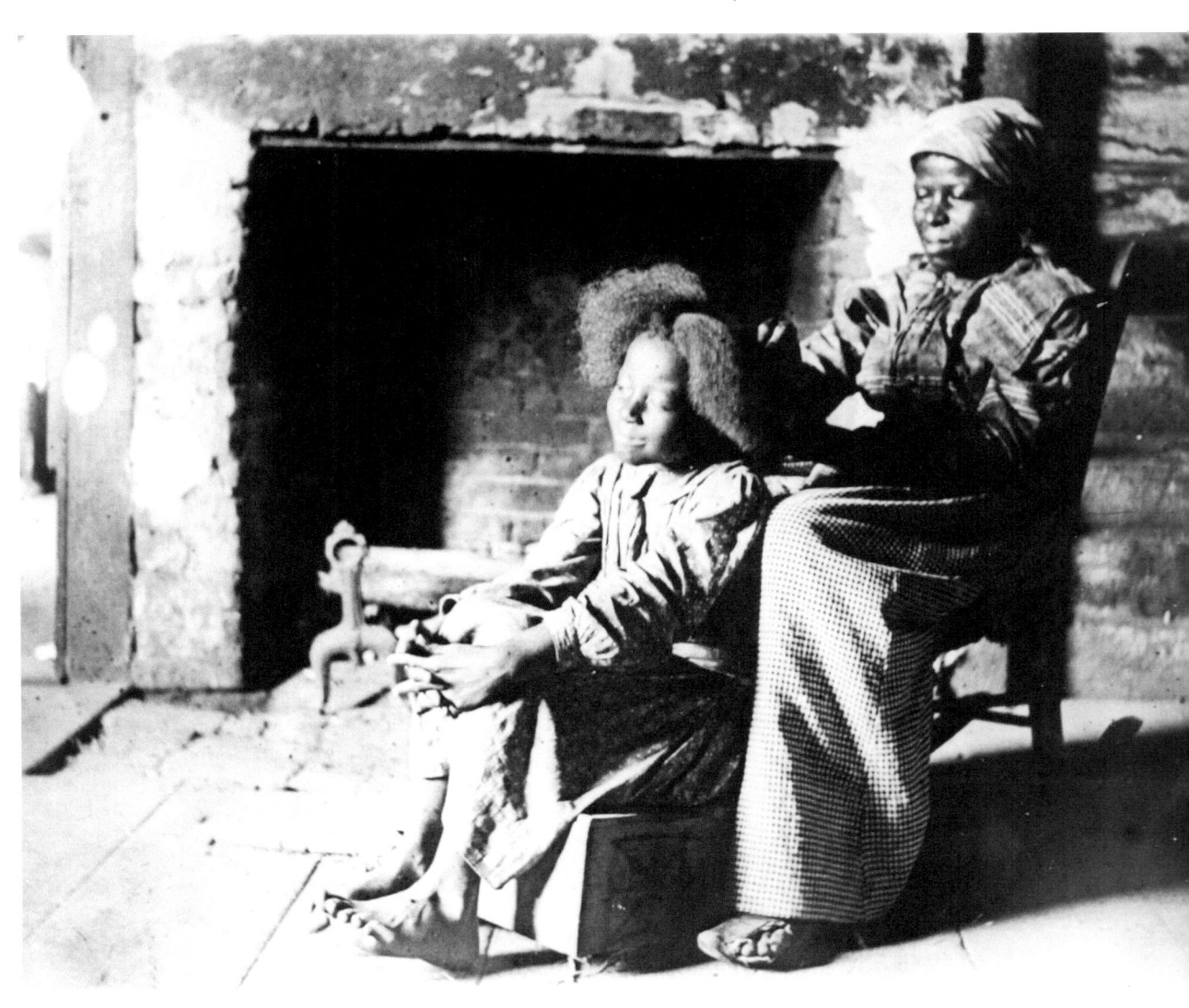

Plate 32.

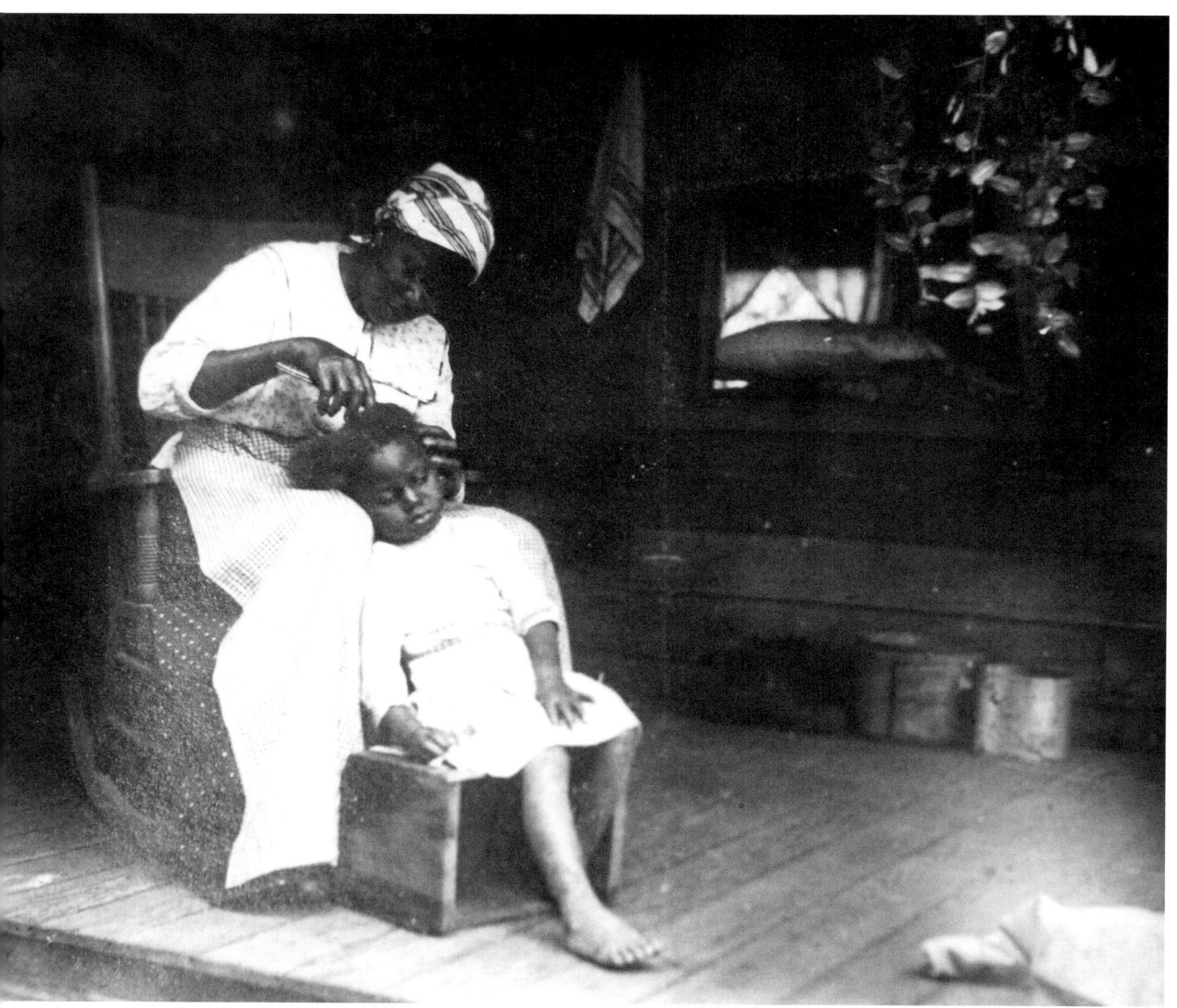

Plate 33.

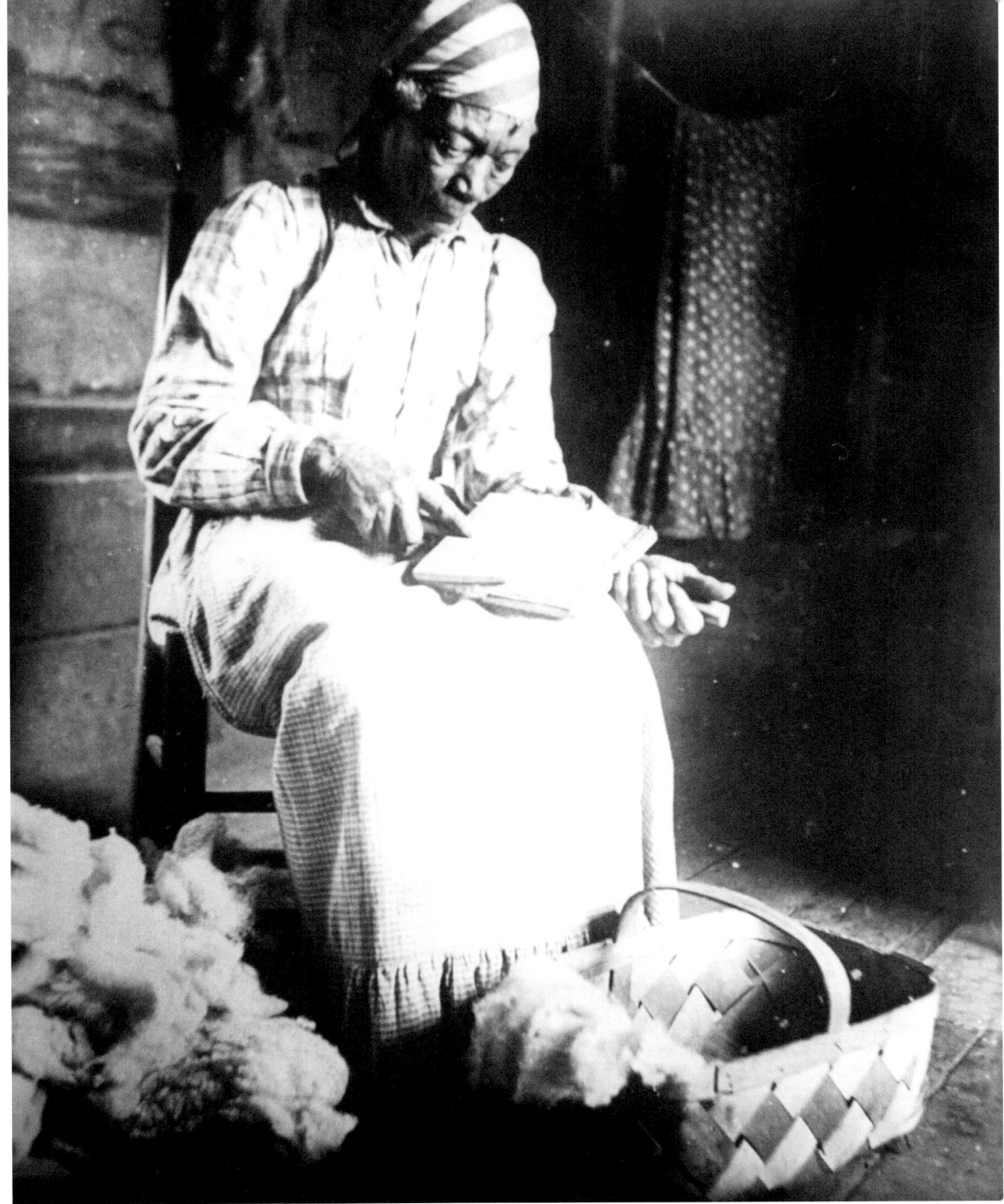

Plate 34.

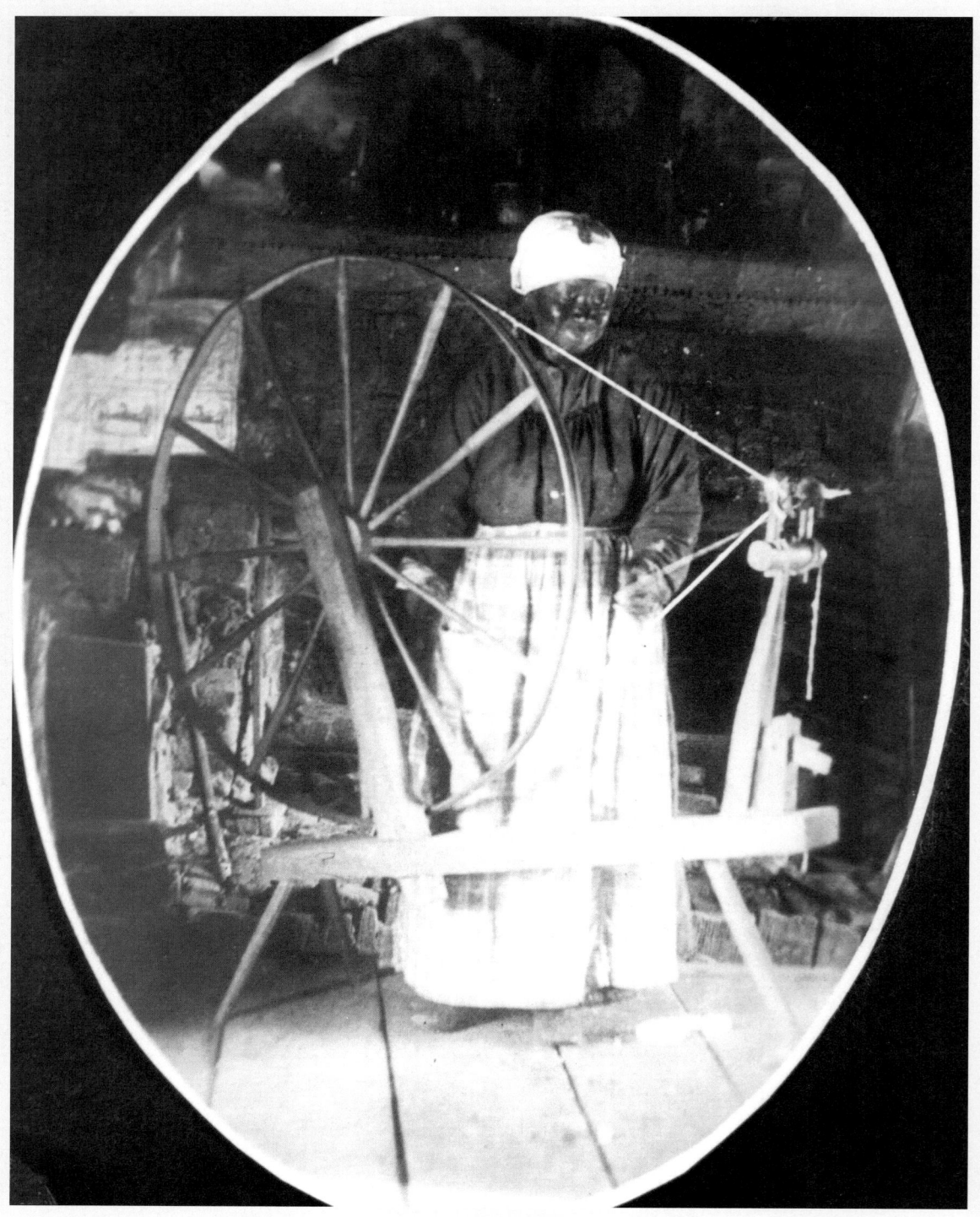

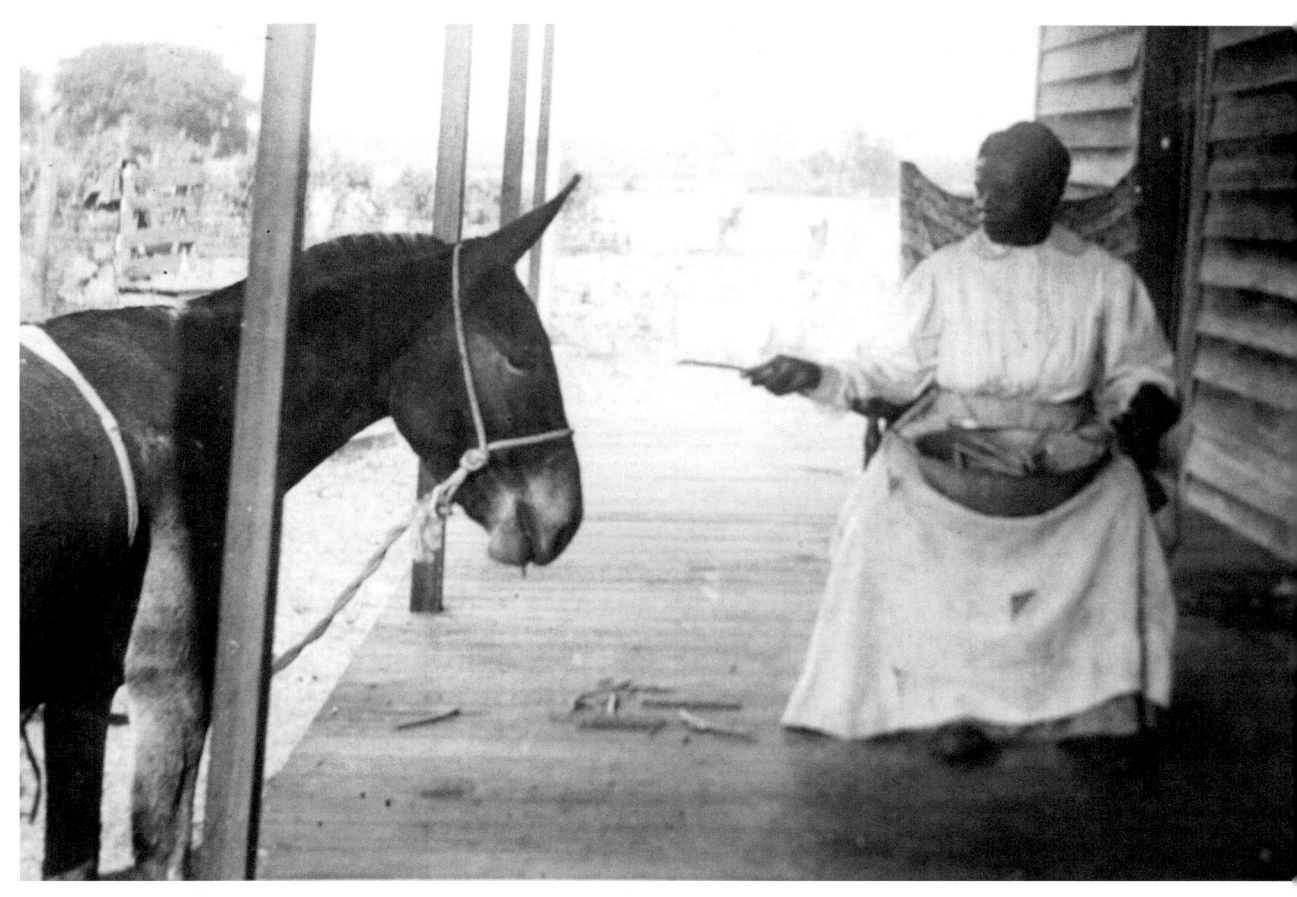

Opposite, Plate 35, spinning thread.
Above, Plate 36, shelling peas and feeding hulls to the mule.

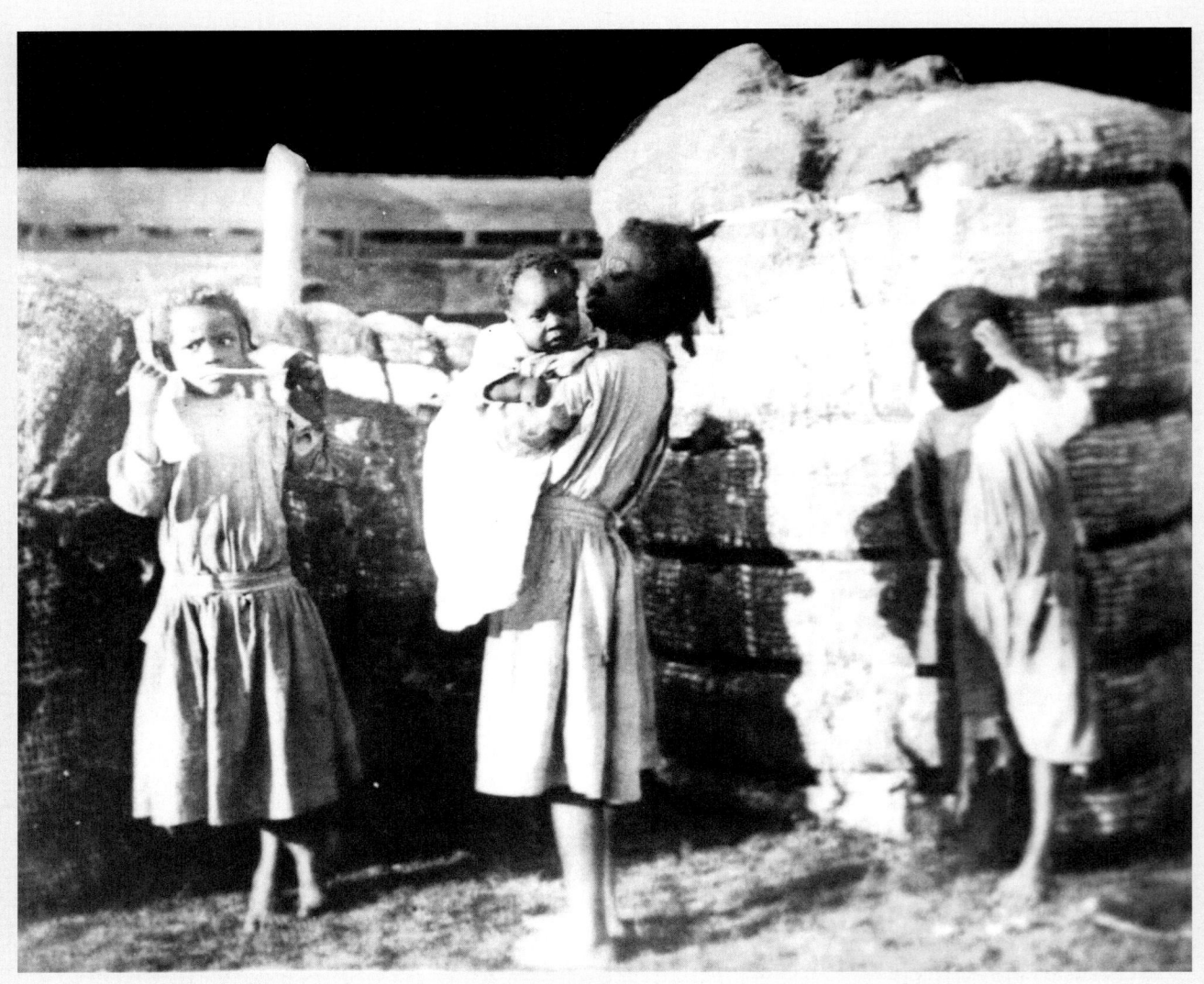

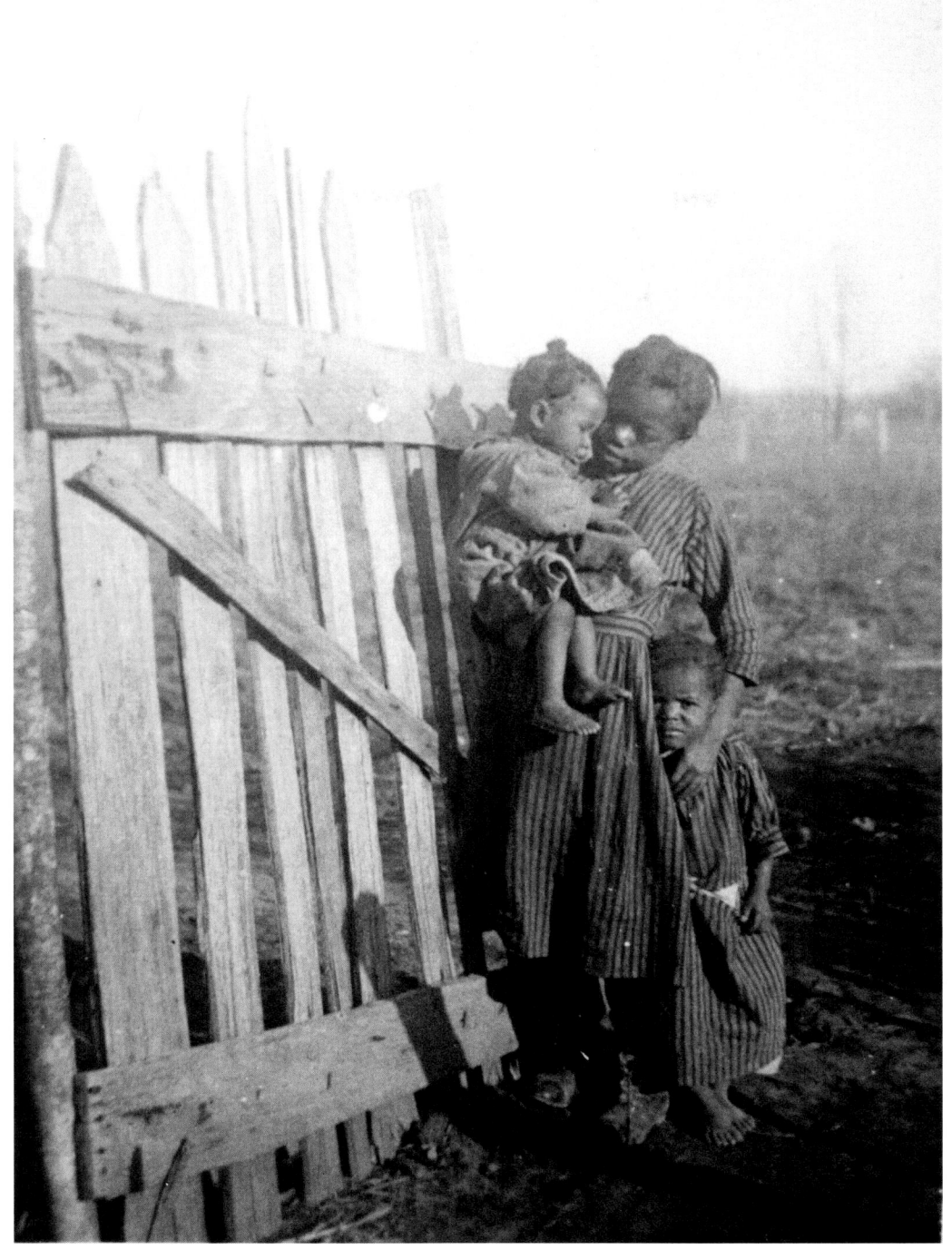

Opposite, Plate 37. Above, Plate 38.

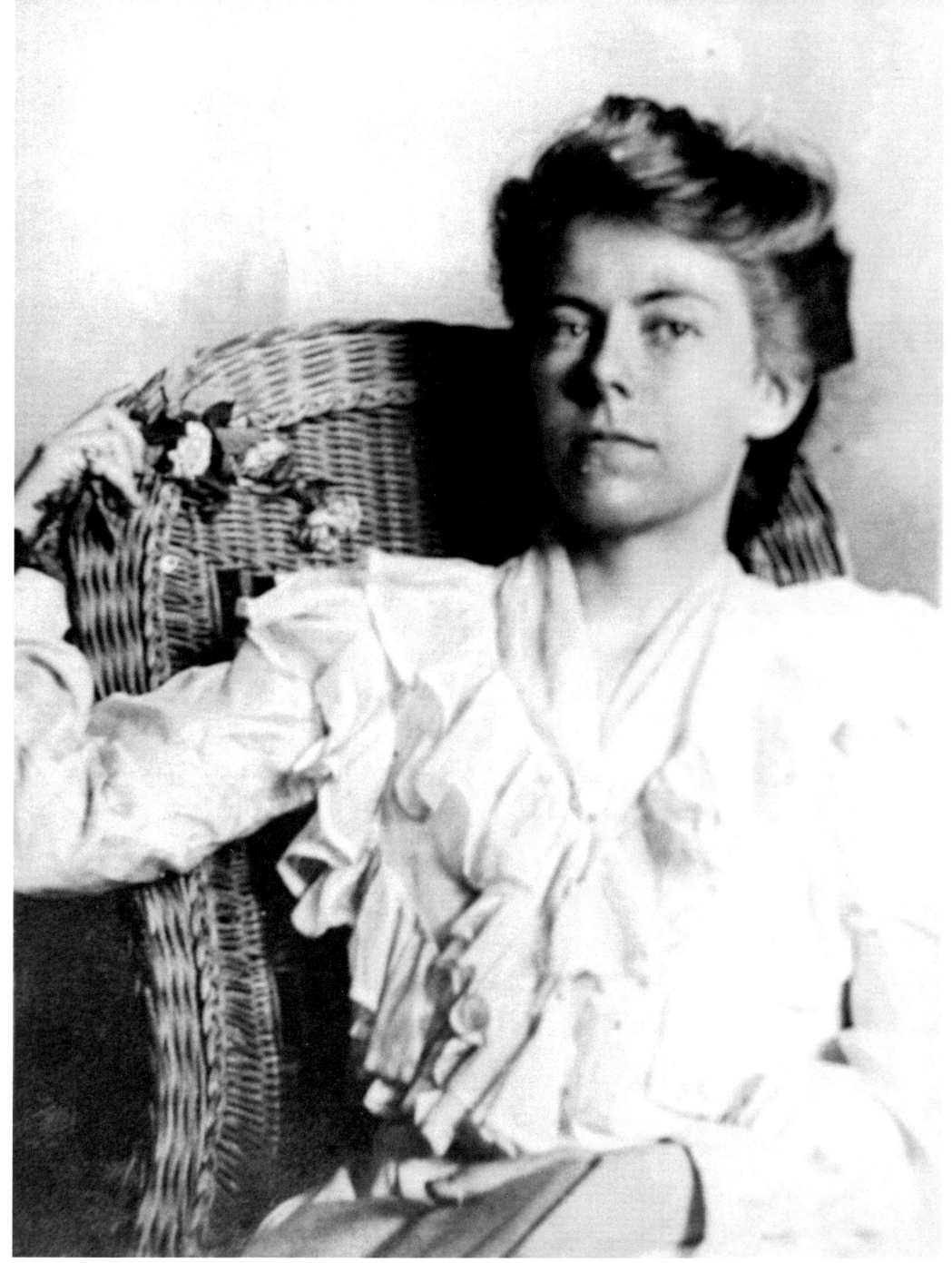

Above, Plate 39, Edith Morgan. Opposite, Plate 40.

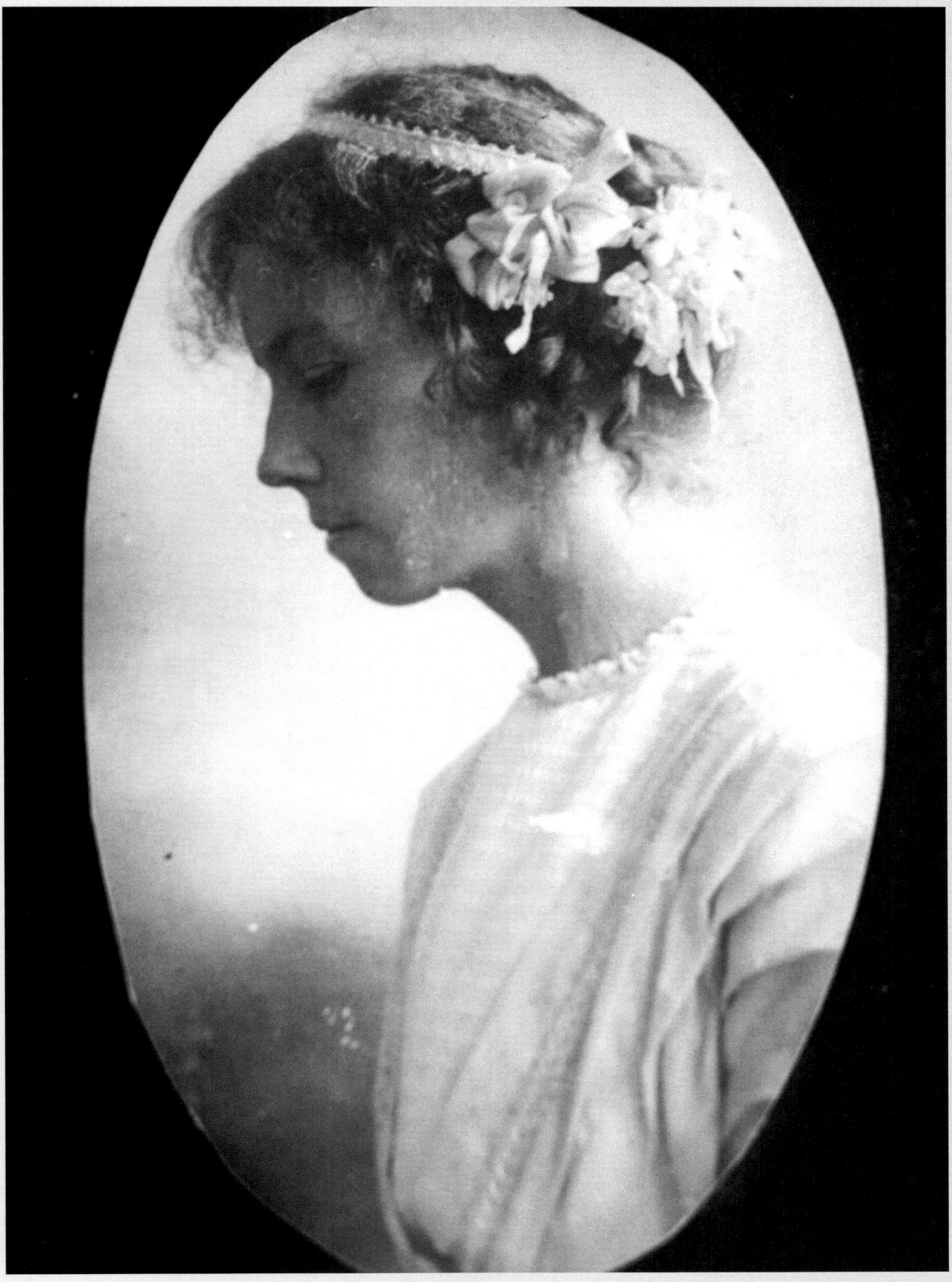

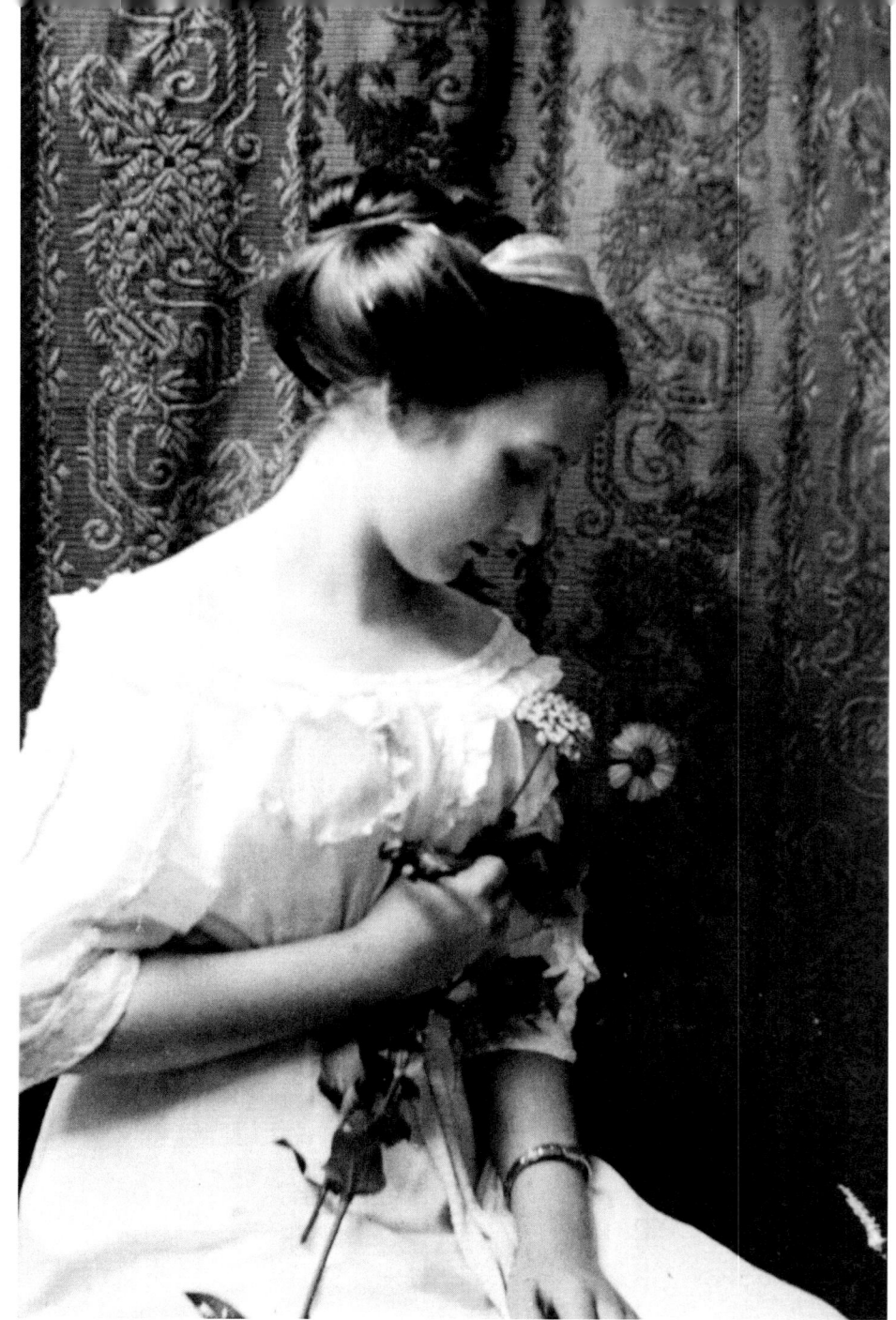

Above, Plate 41. Opposite, Plate 42.

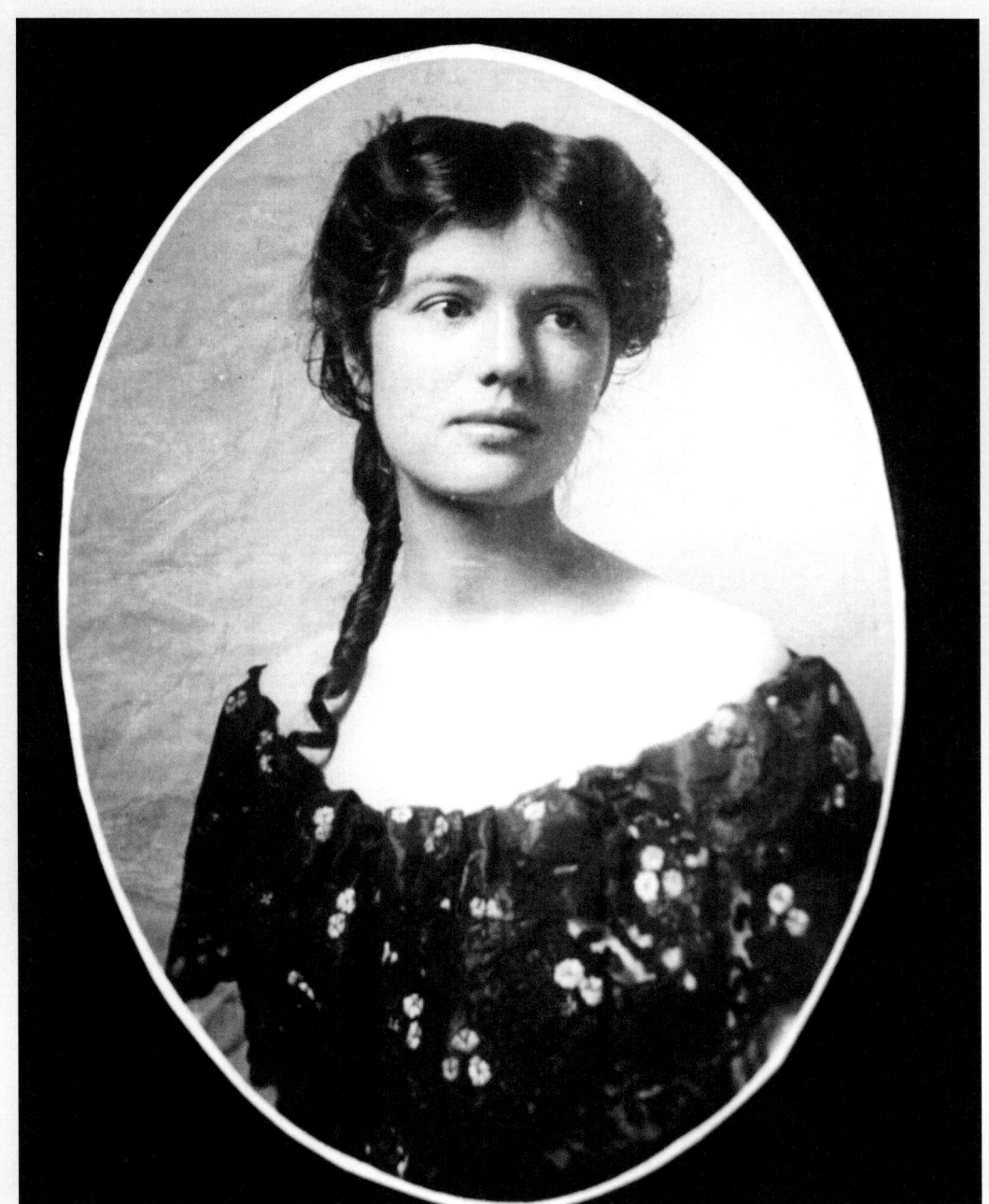

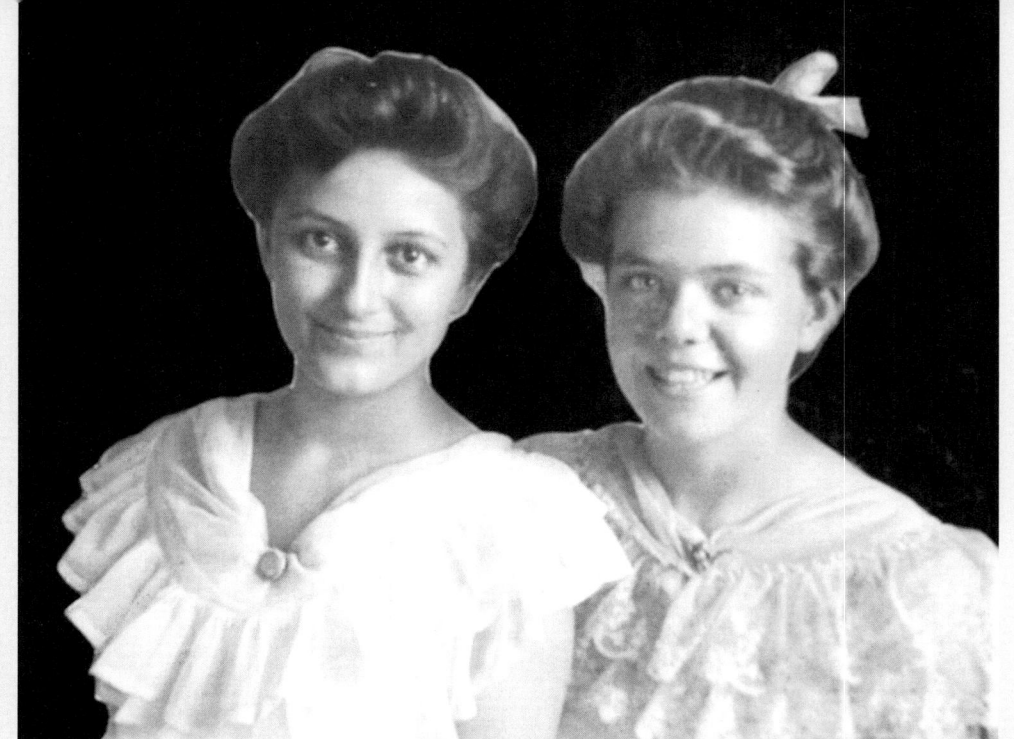

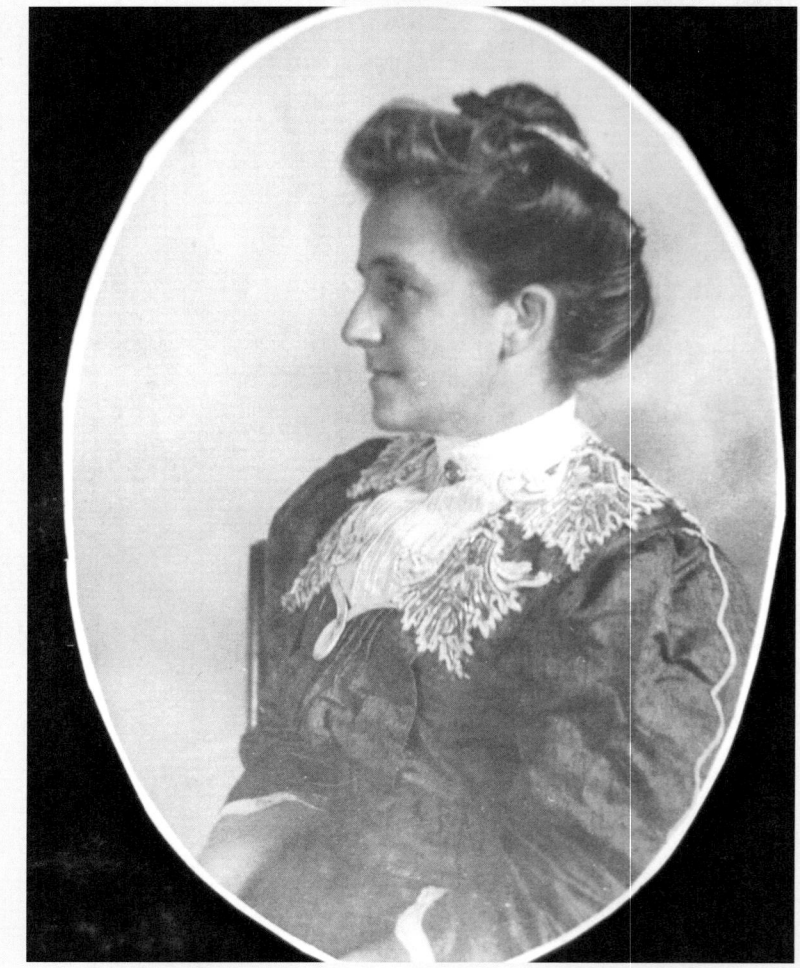

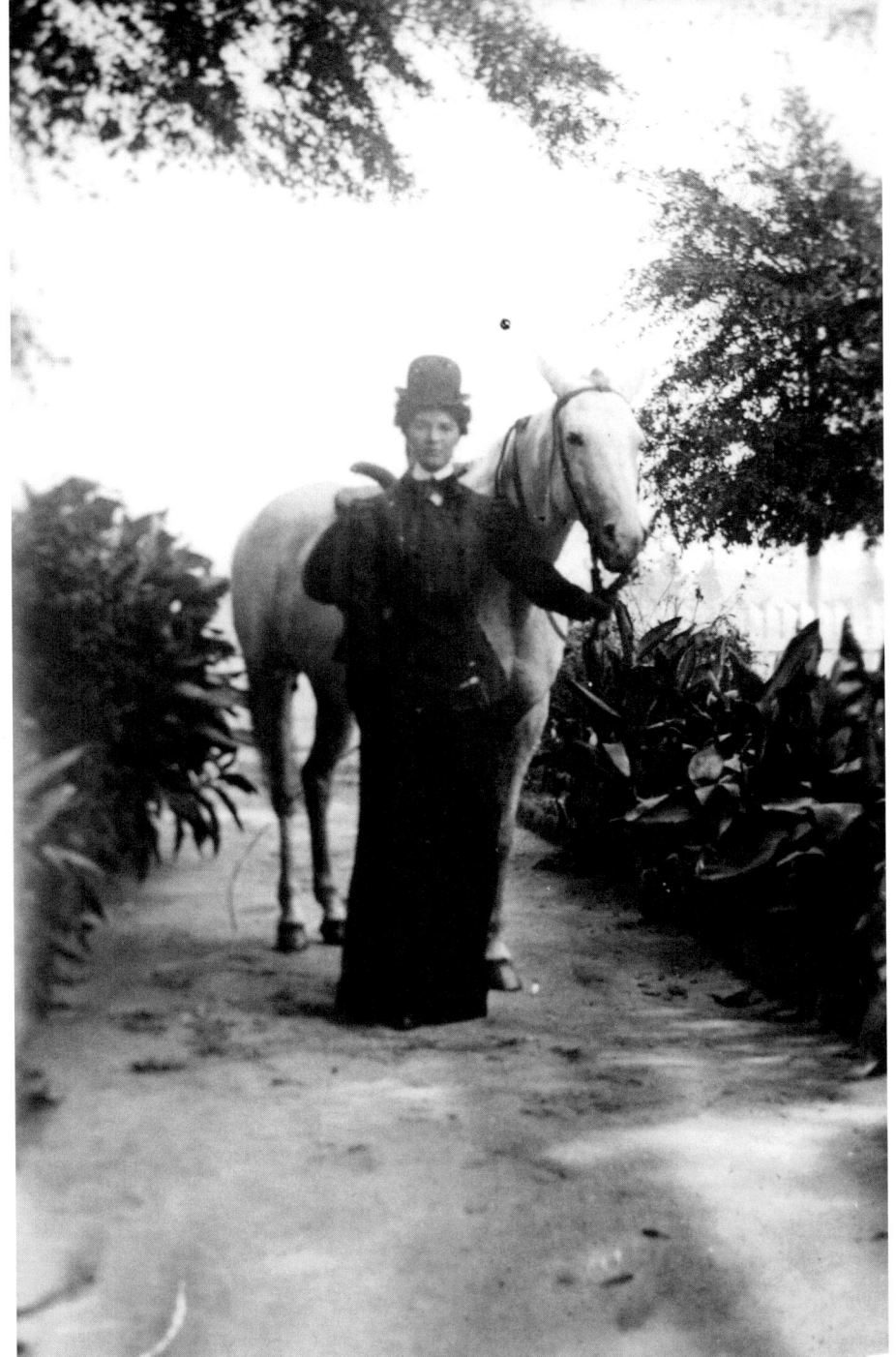

Opposite, Plates 43 and 44 (Mary Helen Rickey Liddell). Above, Plate 45.

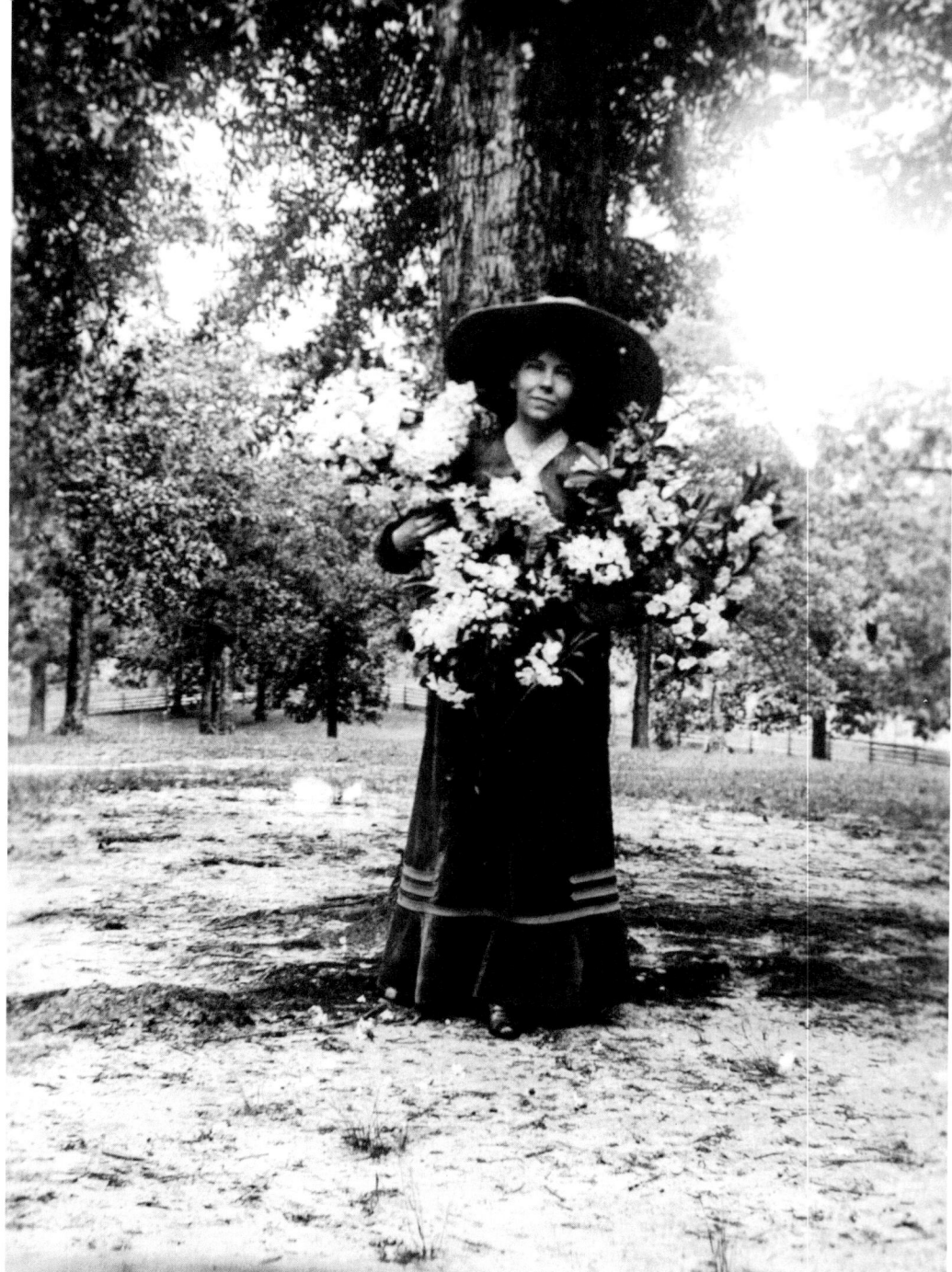

Plate 46.

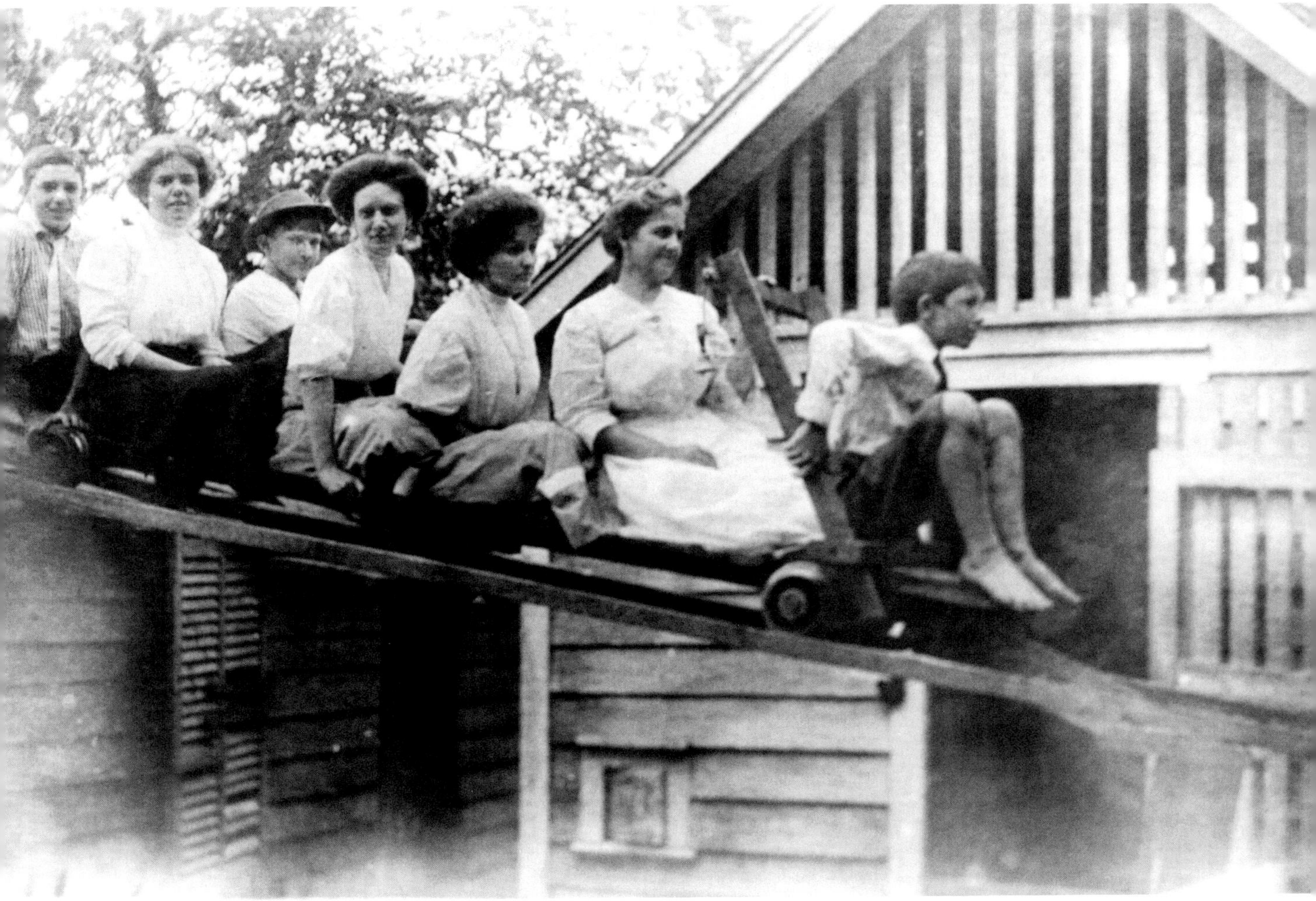

Plate 47.

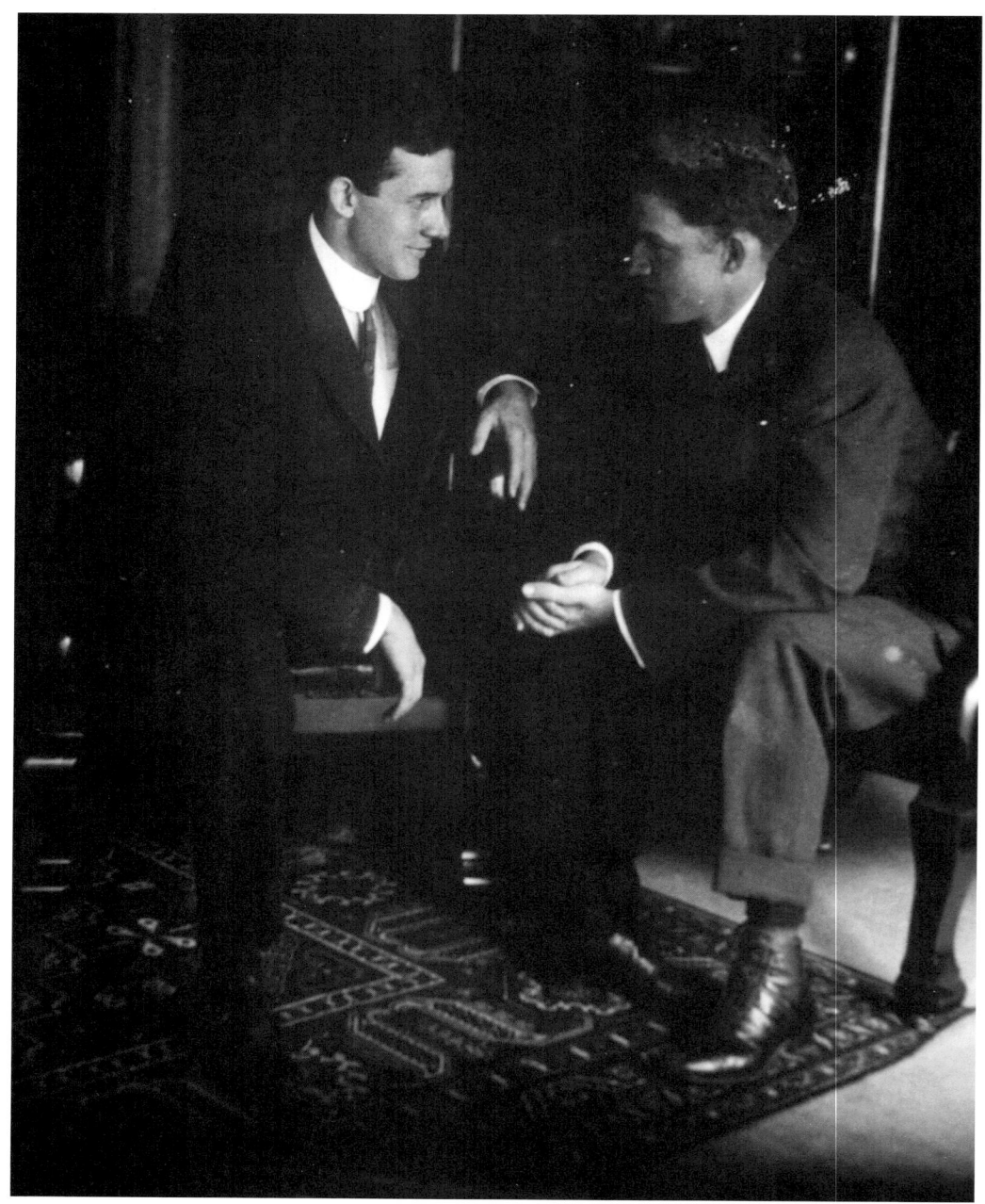

Plate 48, left, Roy Henderson Liddell; right, his son, John Russell Liddell.

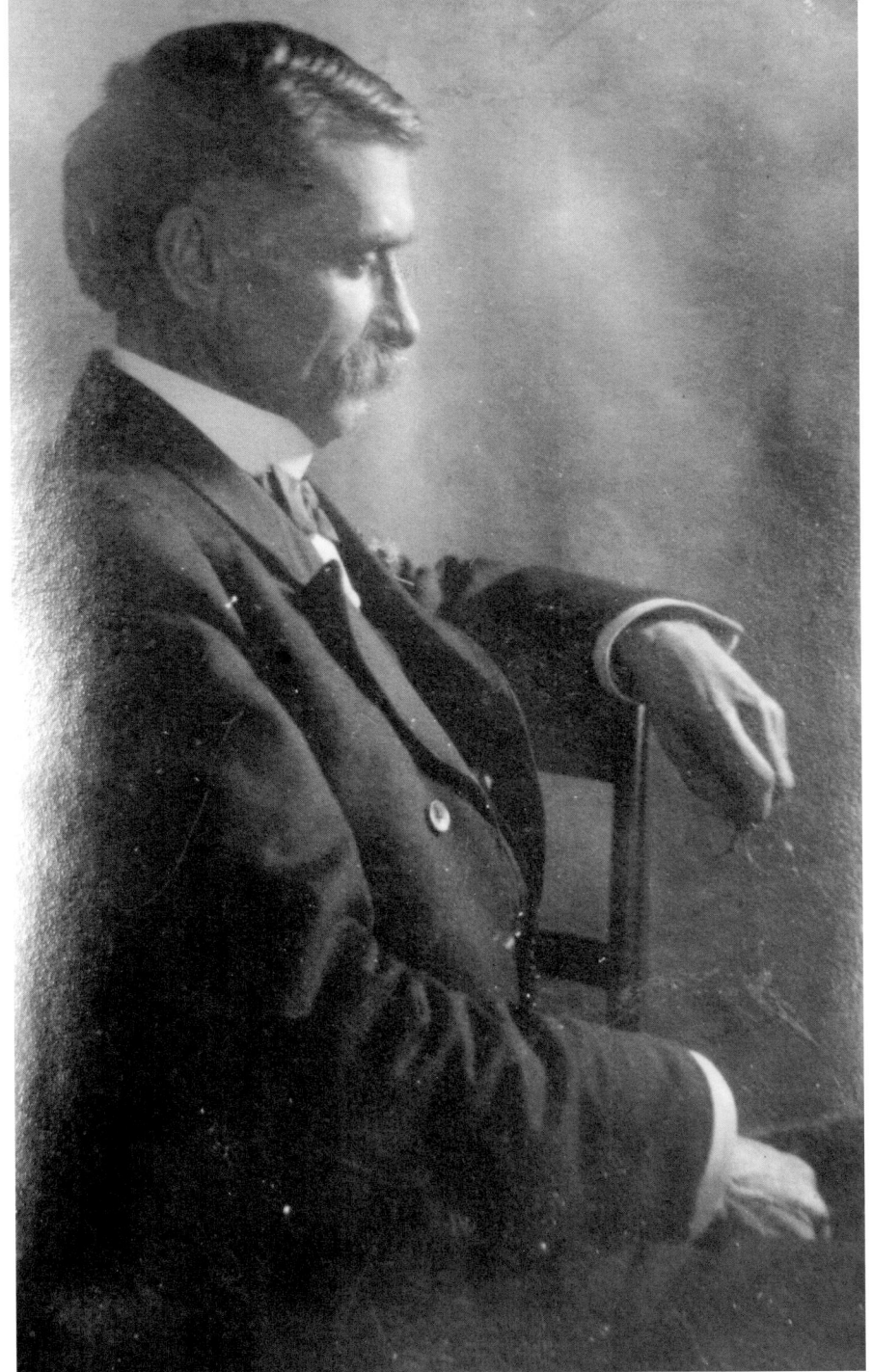

Plate 49.

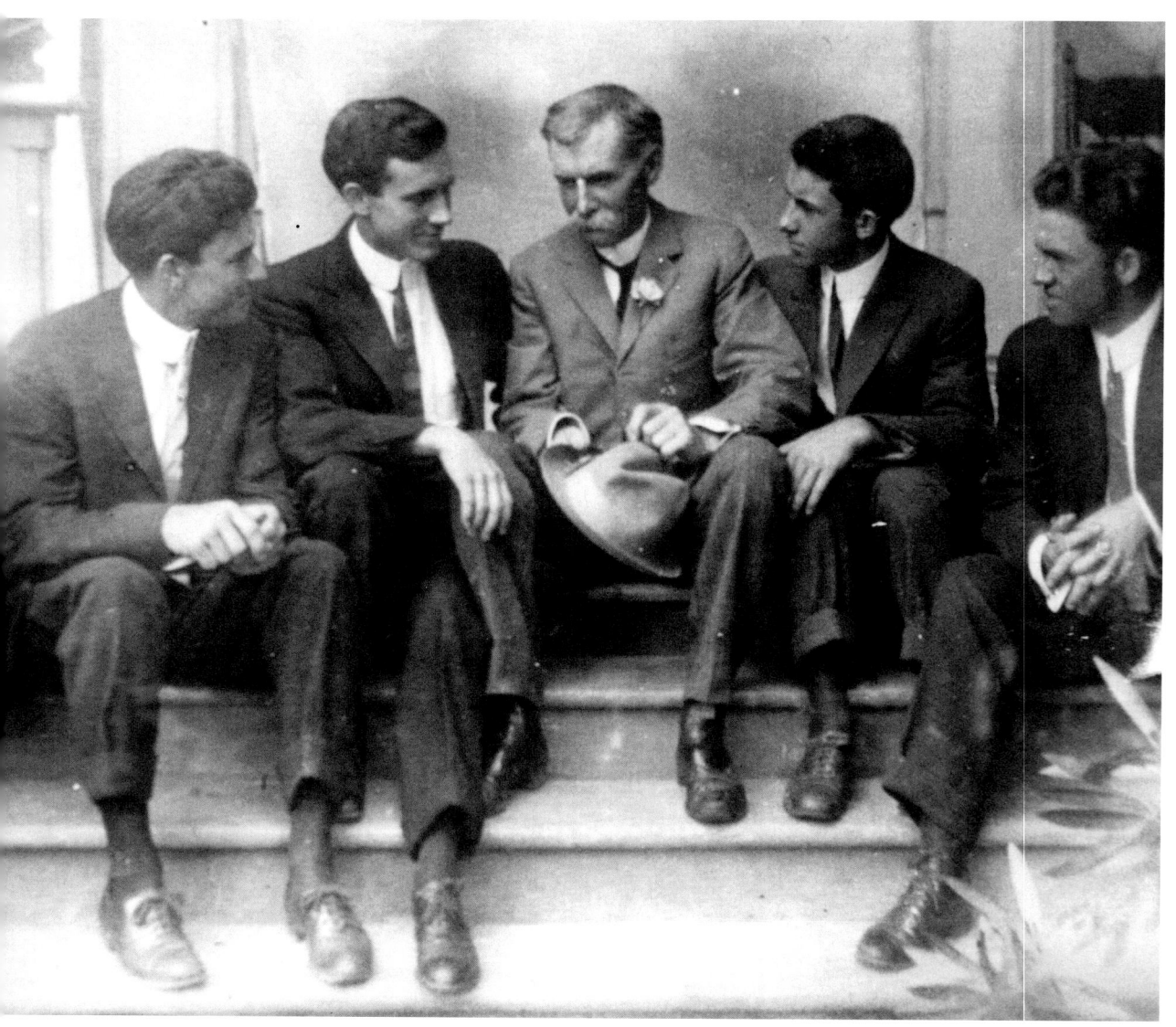

Plate 50, from left, Glen David Liddell, Roy Henderson Liddell, John Russell Liddell Sr. (the father), William Lithgow Liddell, and John Russell Liddell Jr.

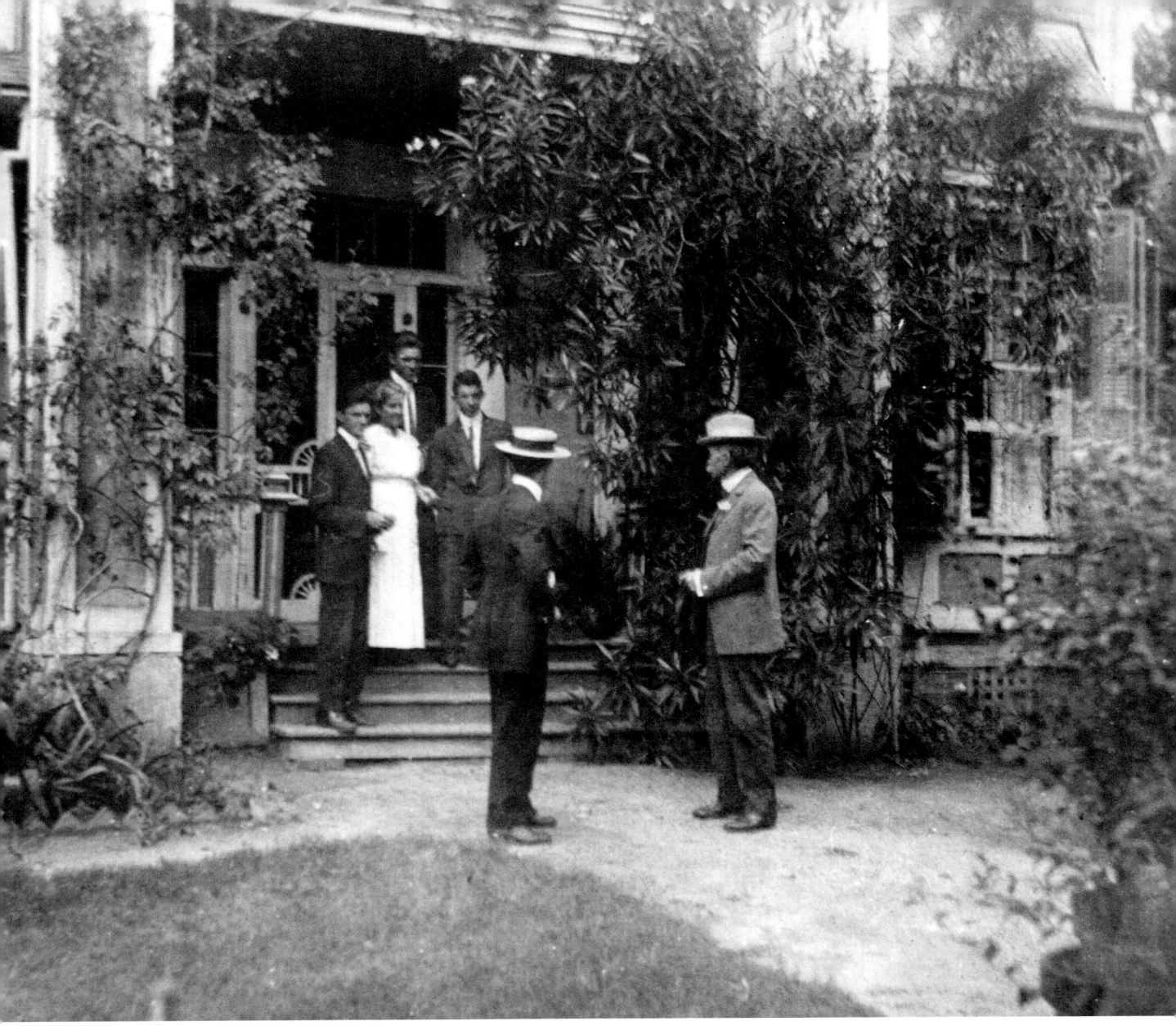

Plate 51, from left, Glen David Liddell, Mary Helen Rickey Liddell, John Russell Liddell Jr., William Lithgow Liddell, Roy Henderson Liddell, and John Russell Liddell Sr.

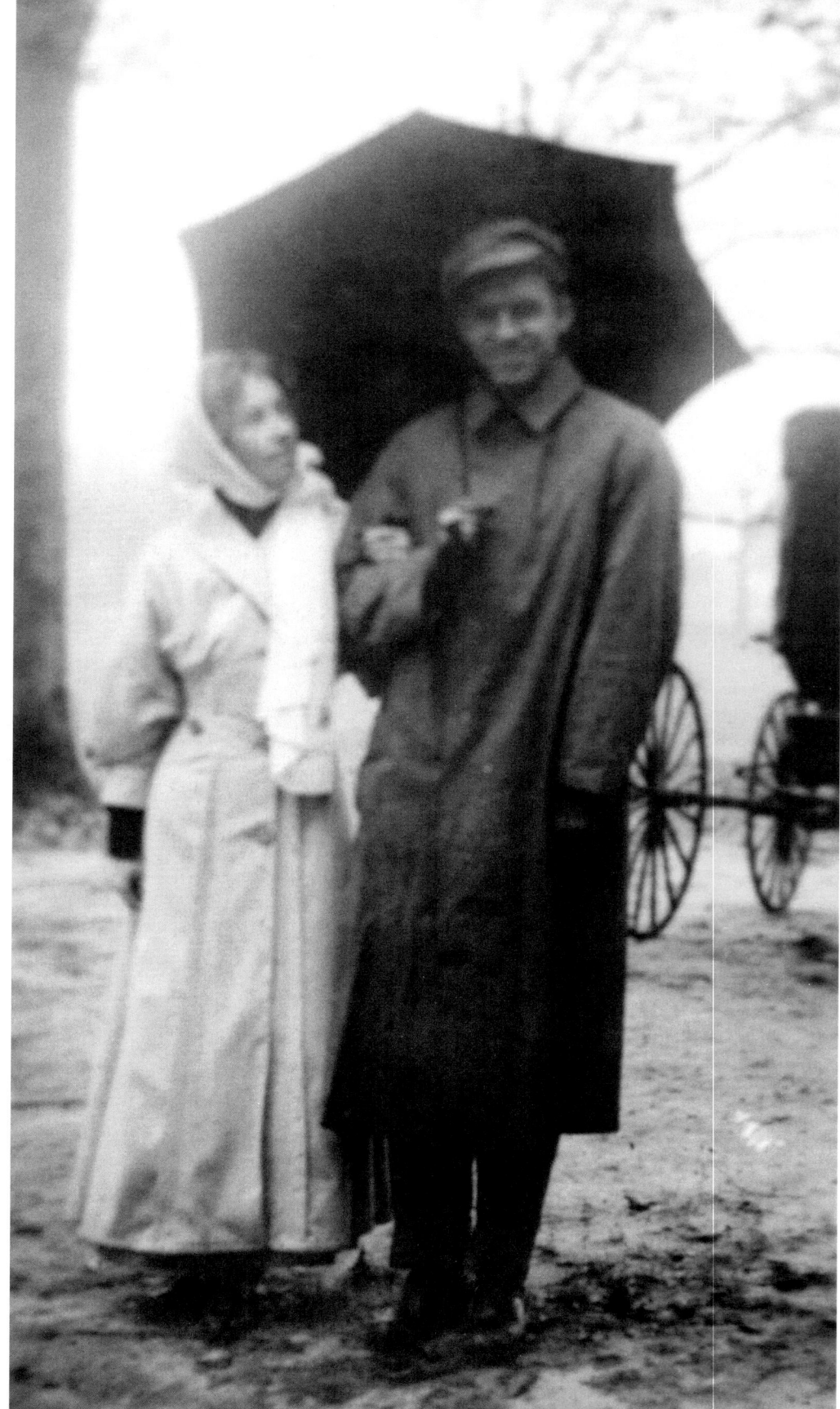

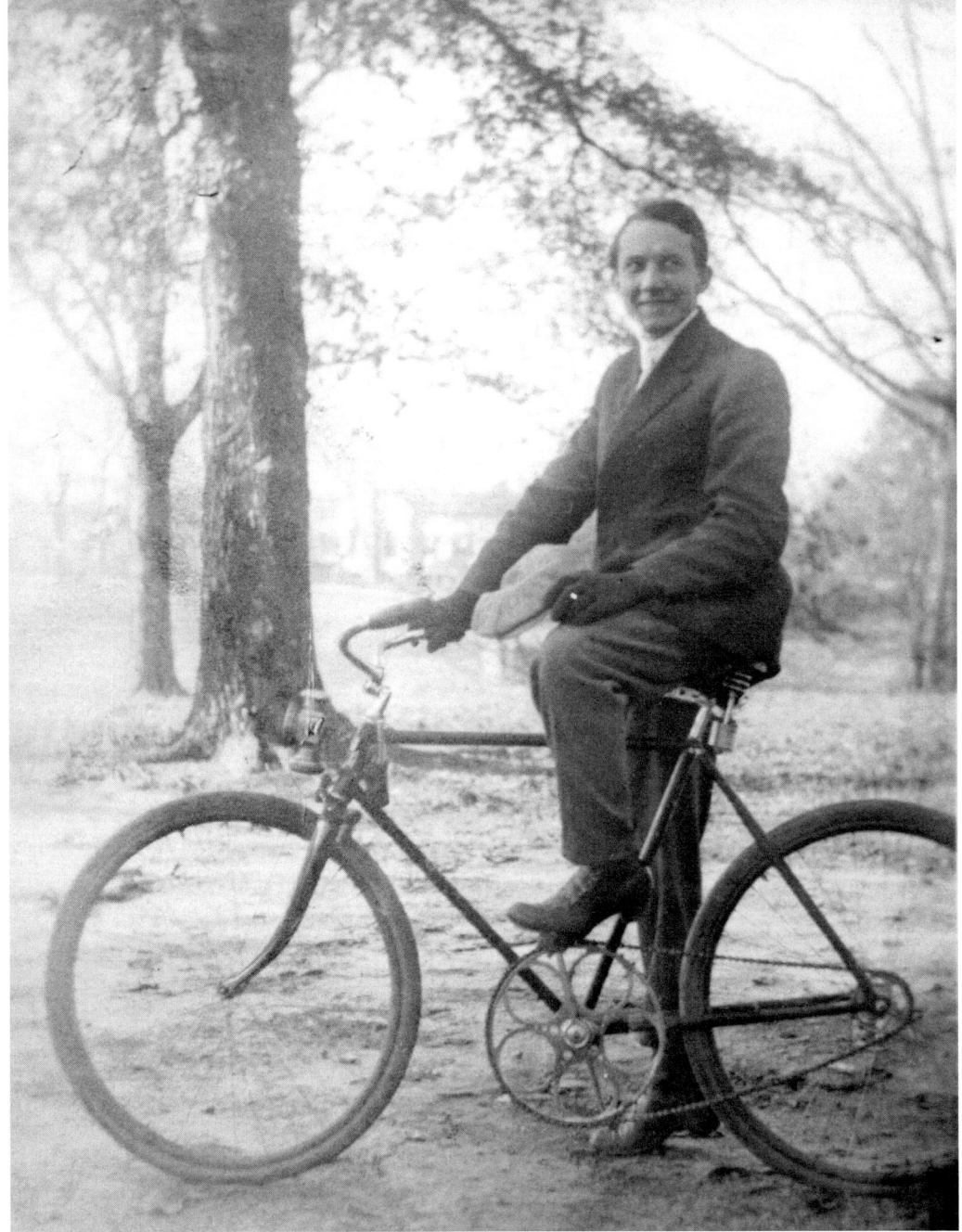

Opposite, Plate 52, unidentified woman with John Russell Liddell Jr.
Above, Plate 53.

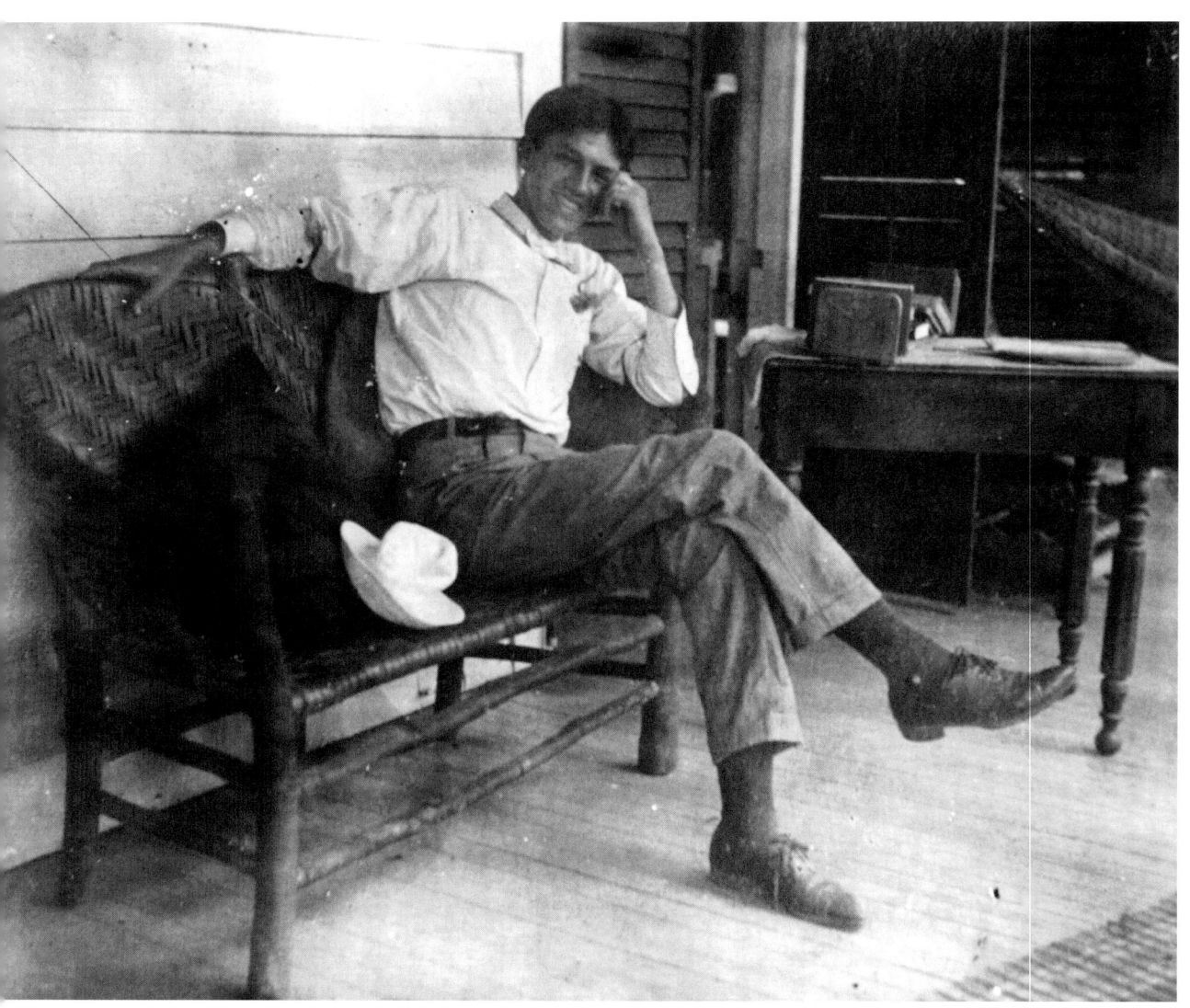

Plate 54, John Russell Liddell Jr.

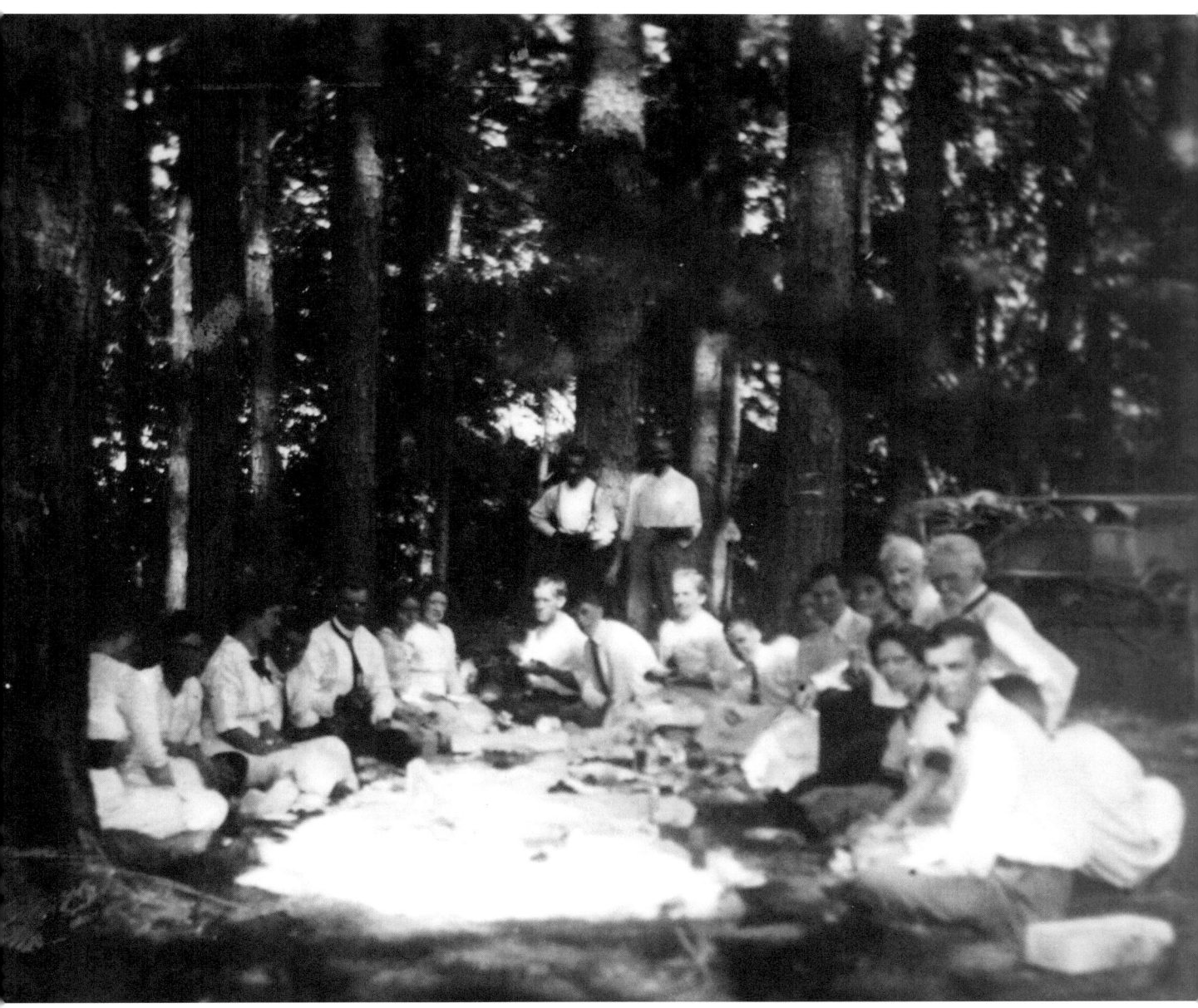

Plate 55.

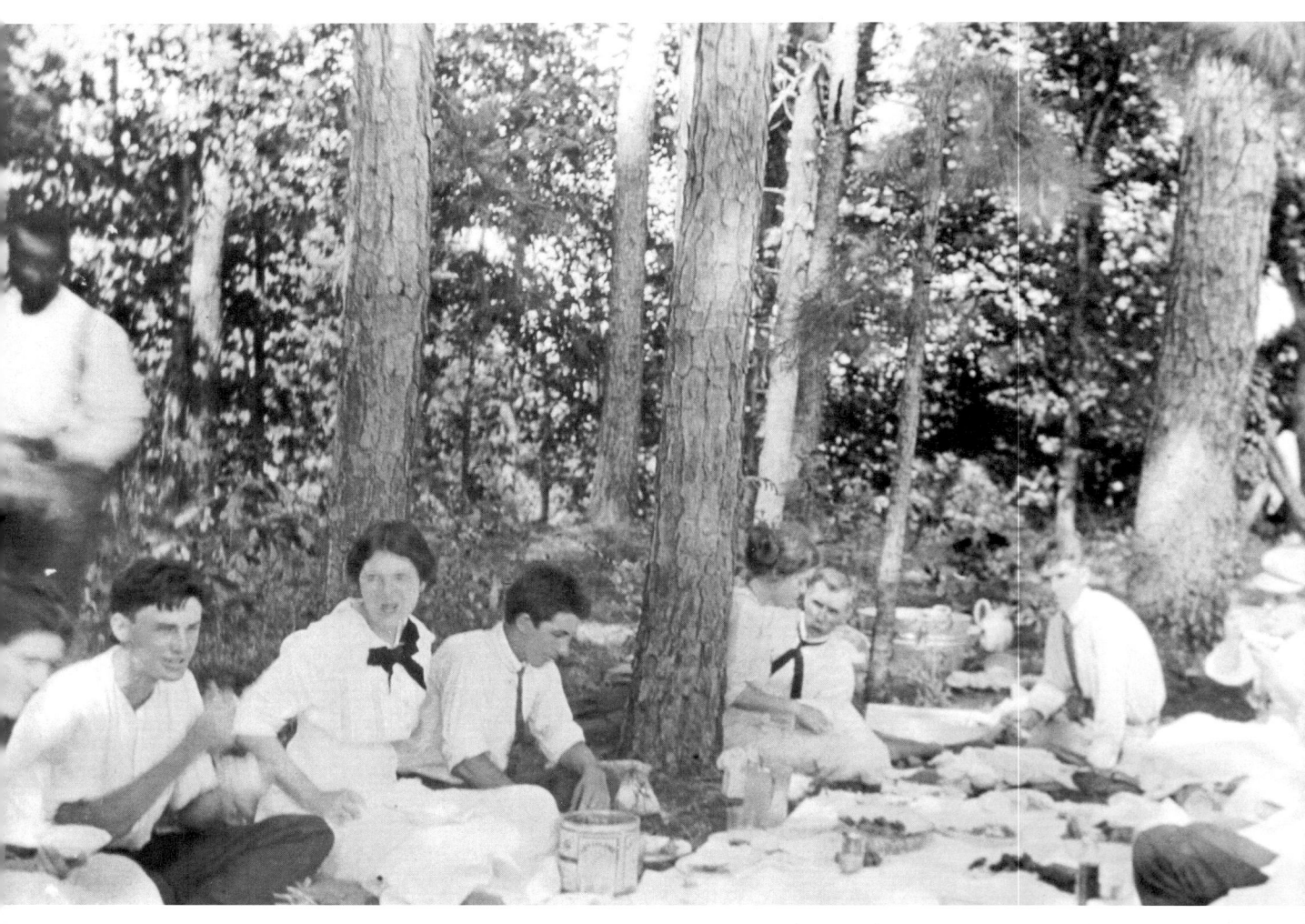

Above, Plate 56. Opposite, Plate 57.

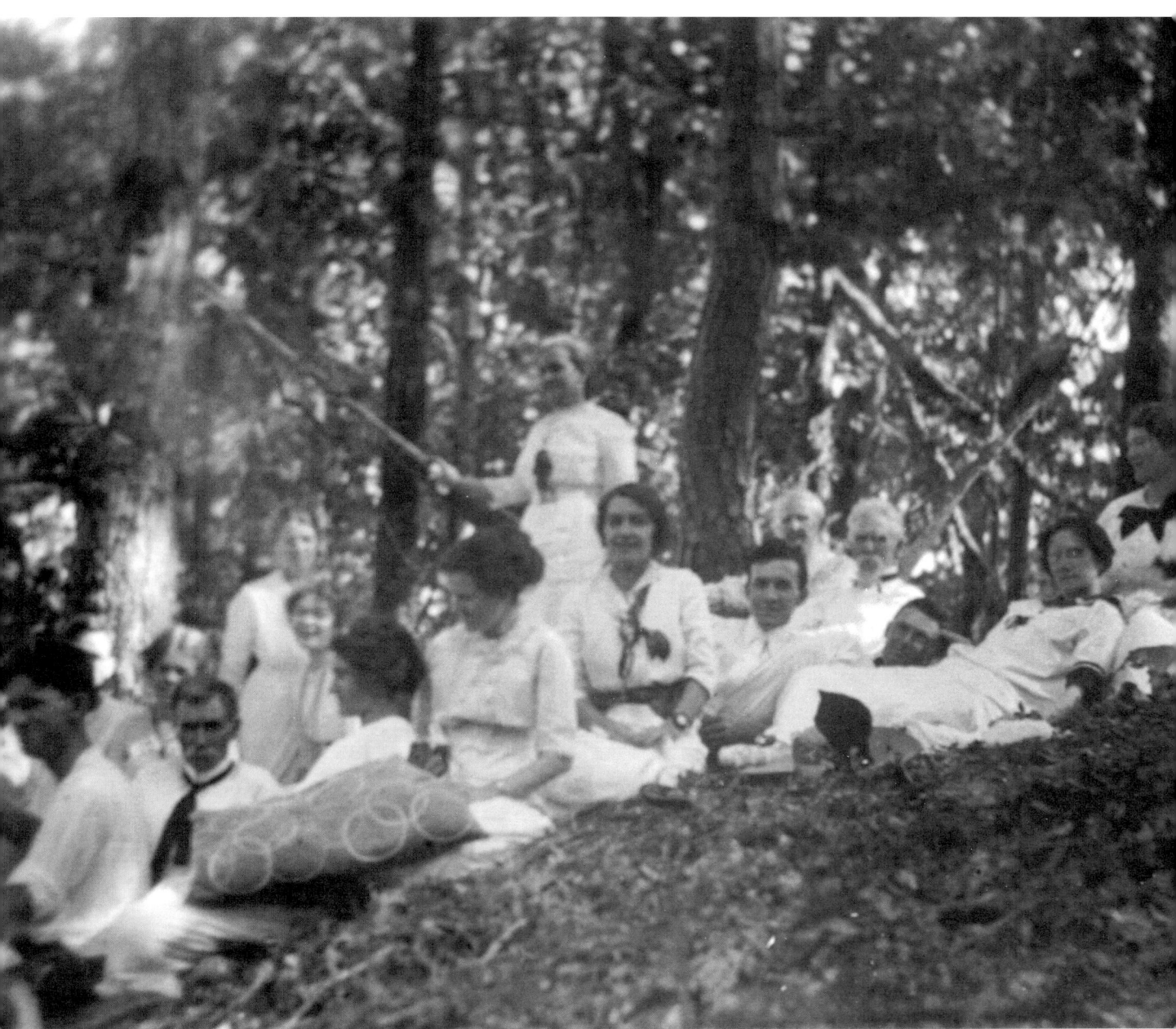

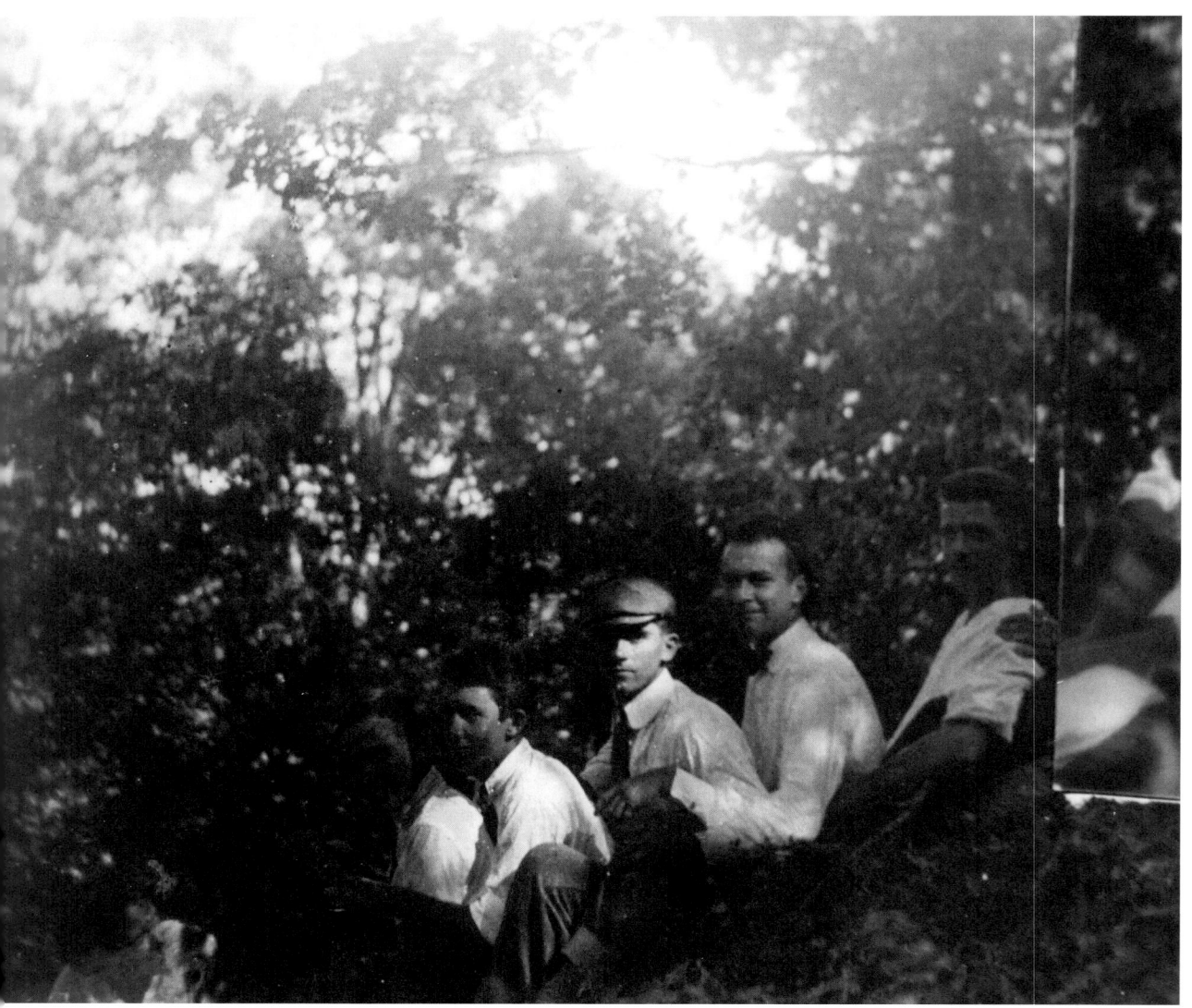

Plate 58.

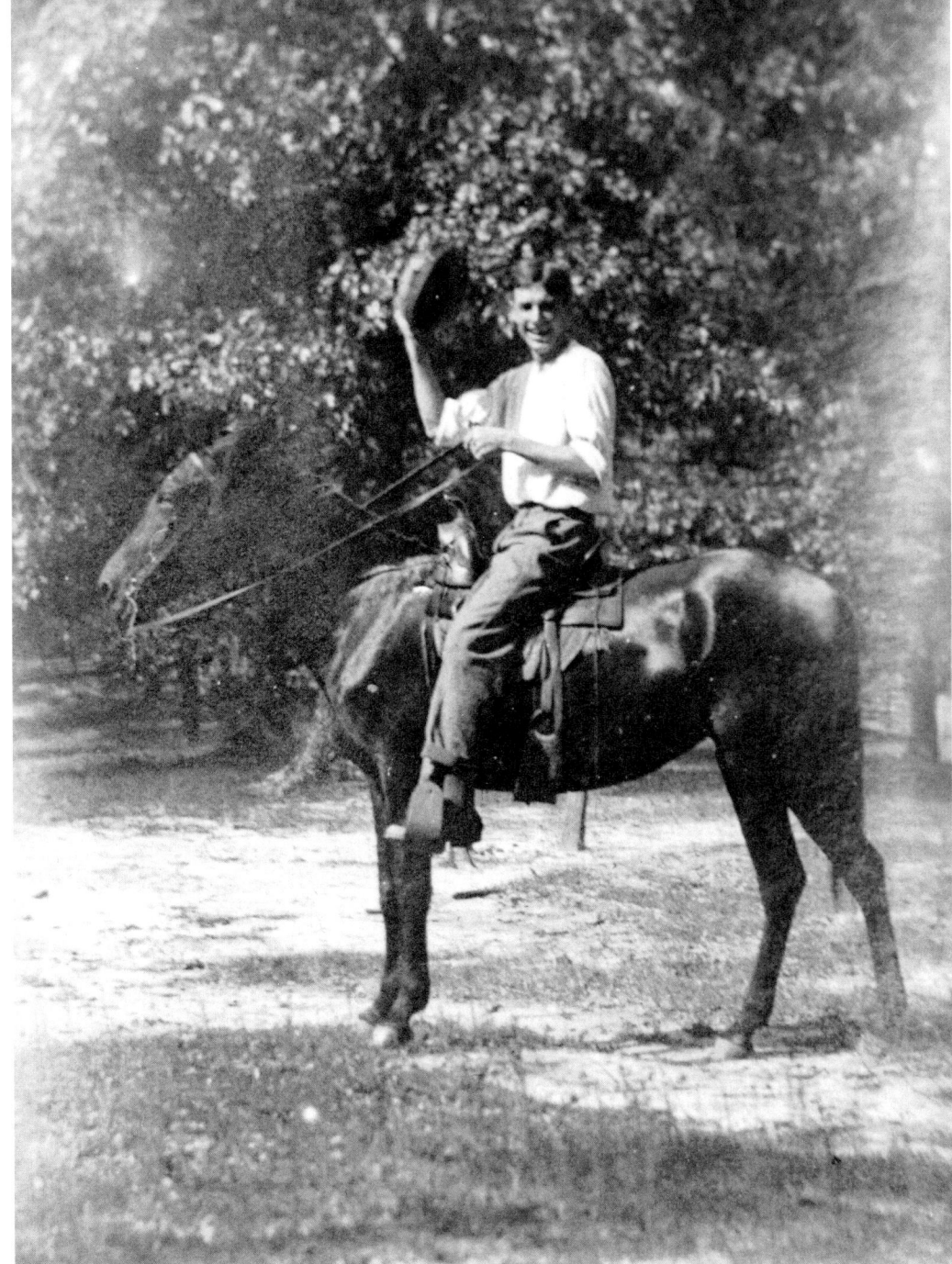

Plate 59.

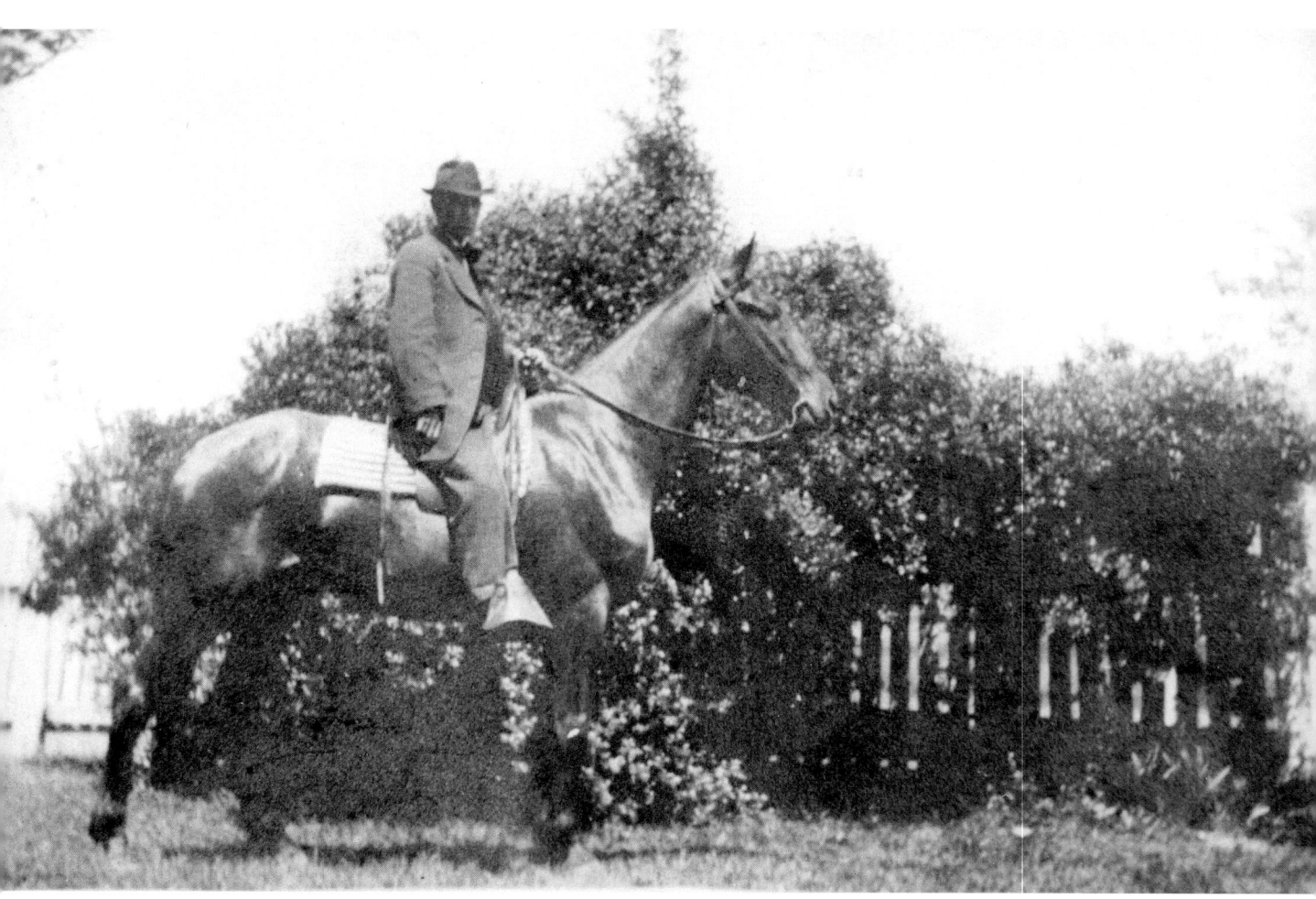

Plate 60.

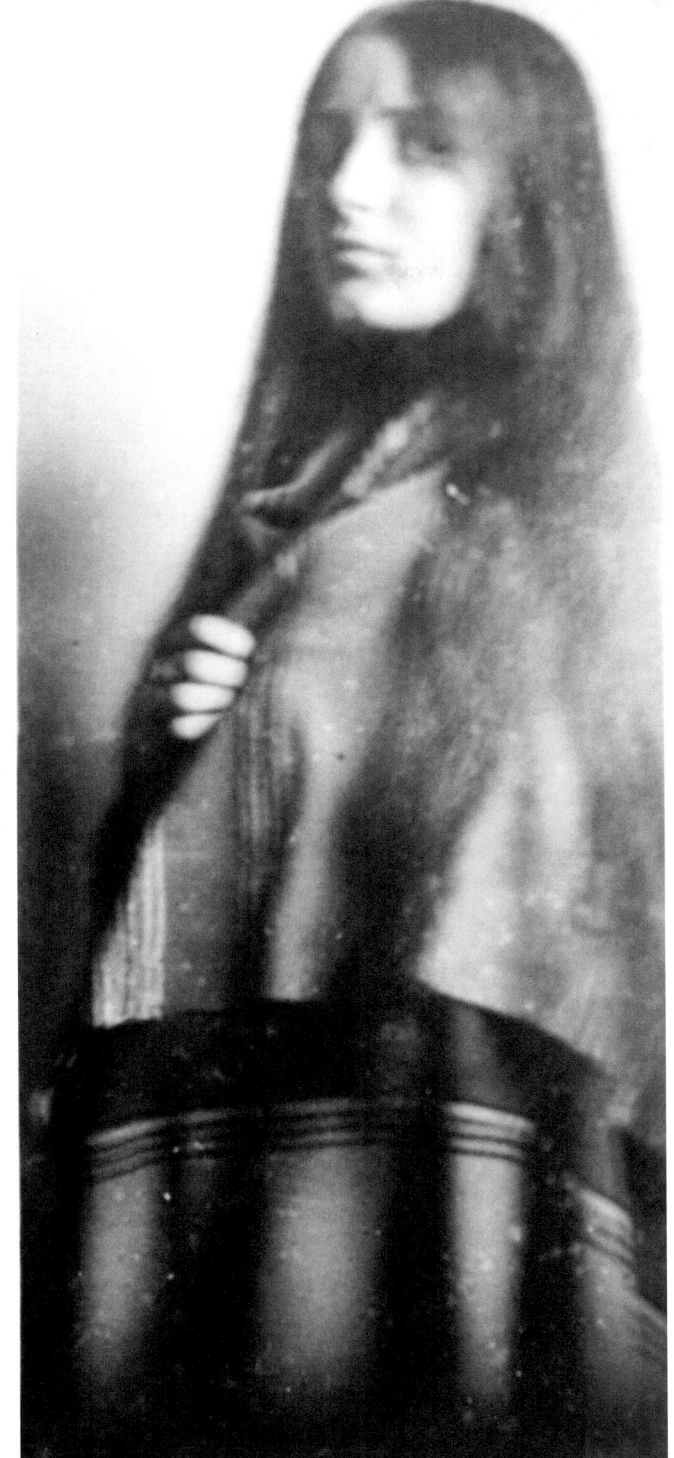

Plate 61.

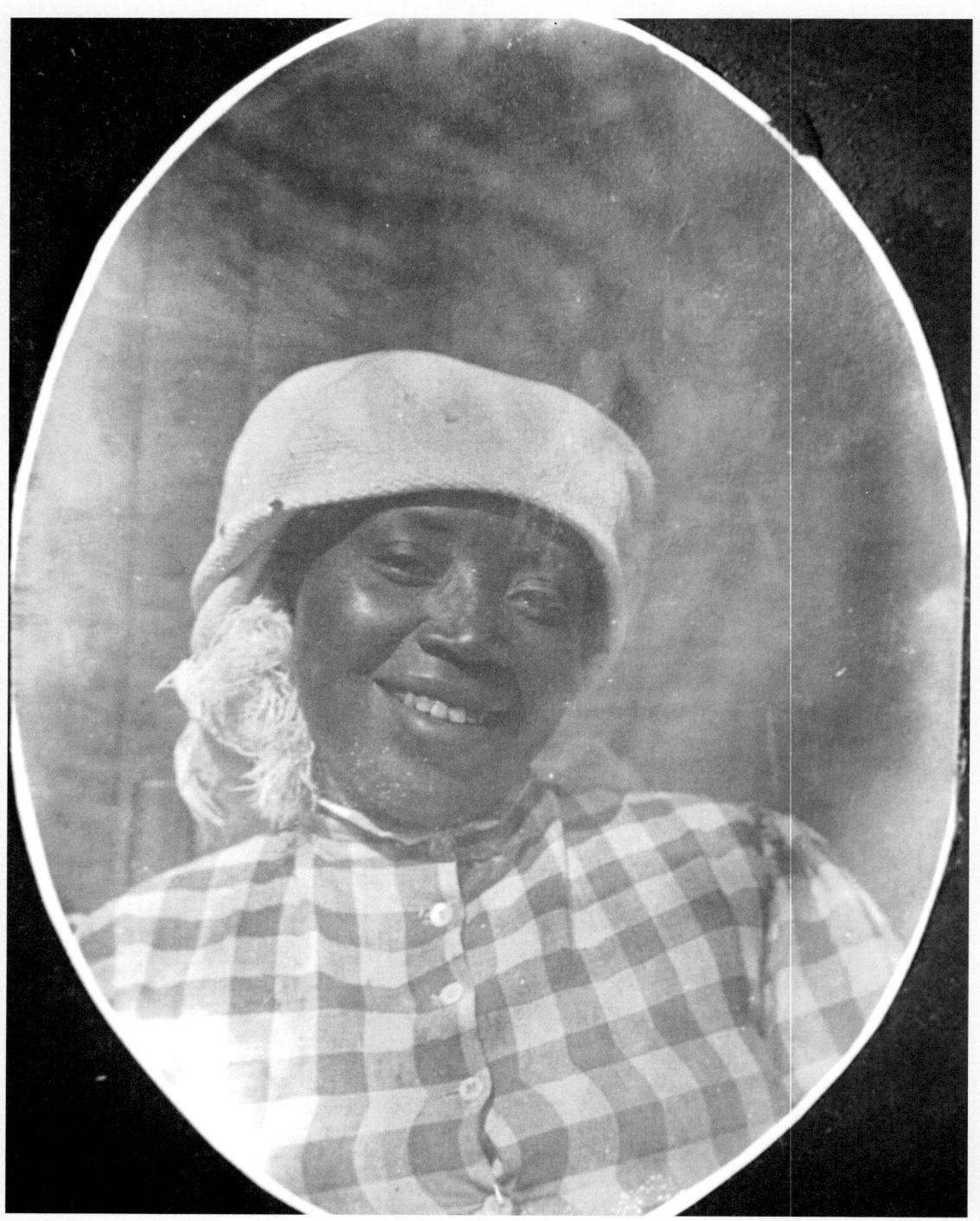

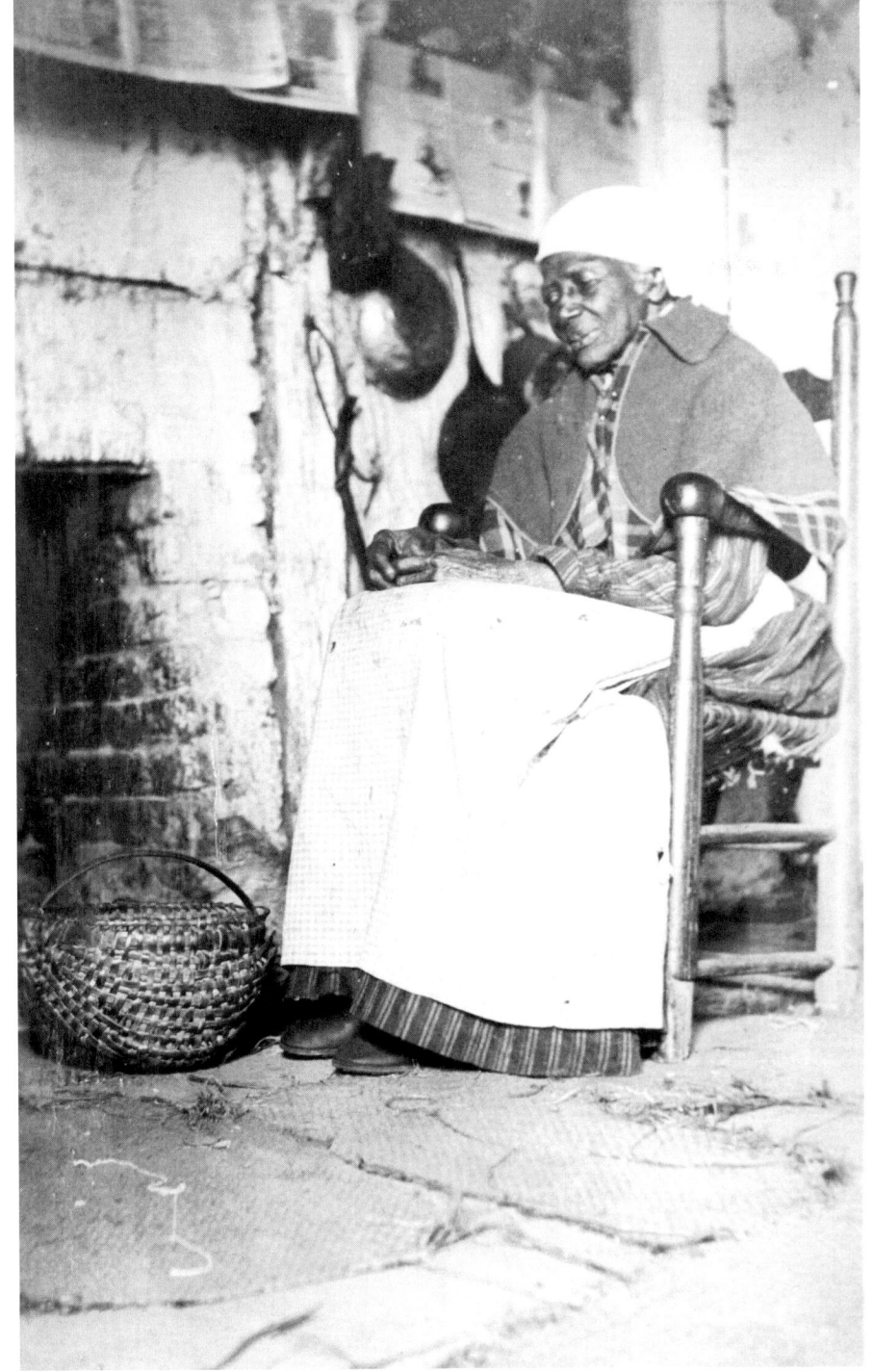

Opposite, Plate 62. Above, Plate 63.

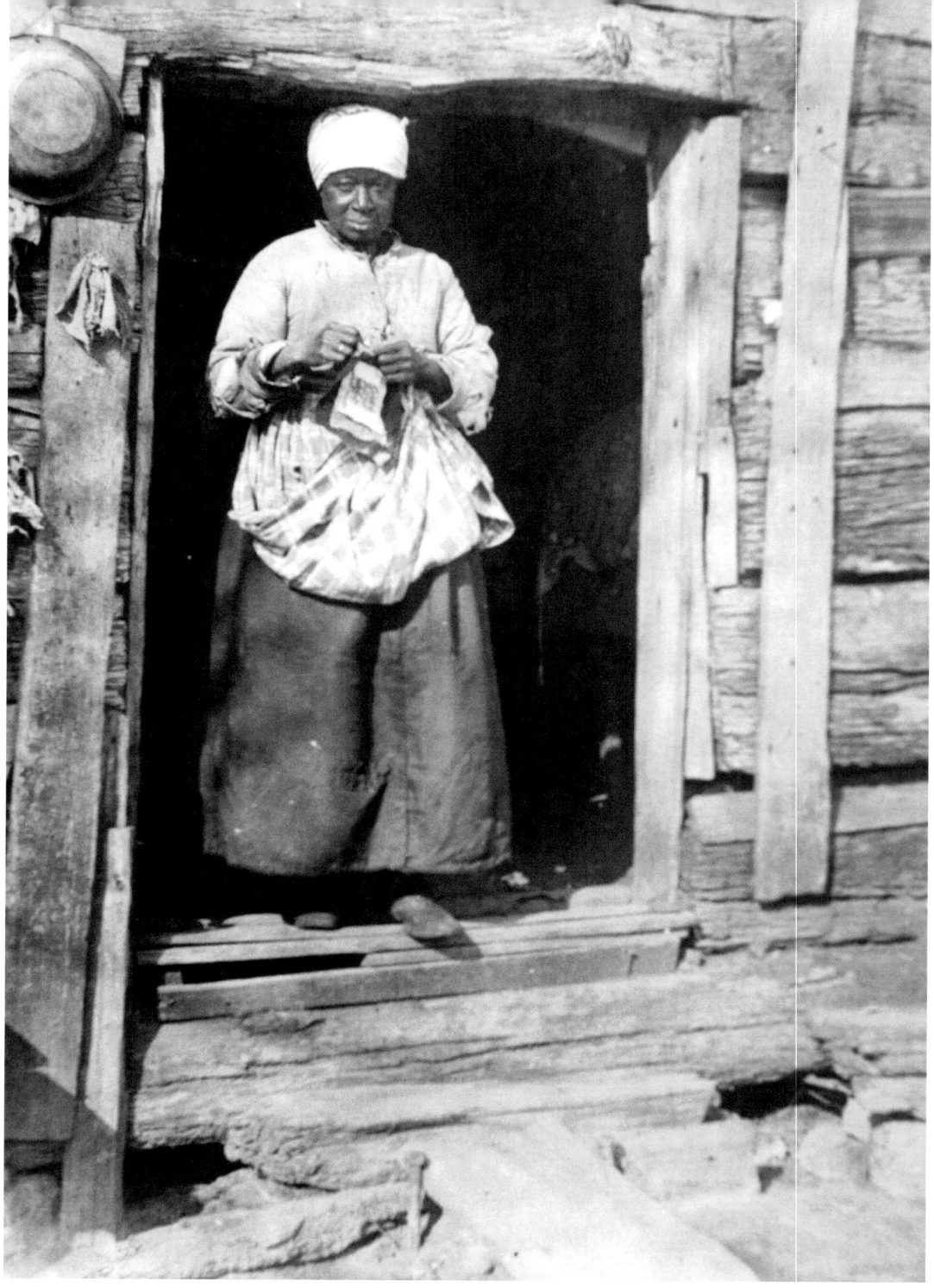

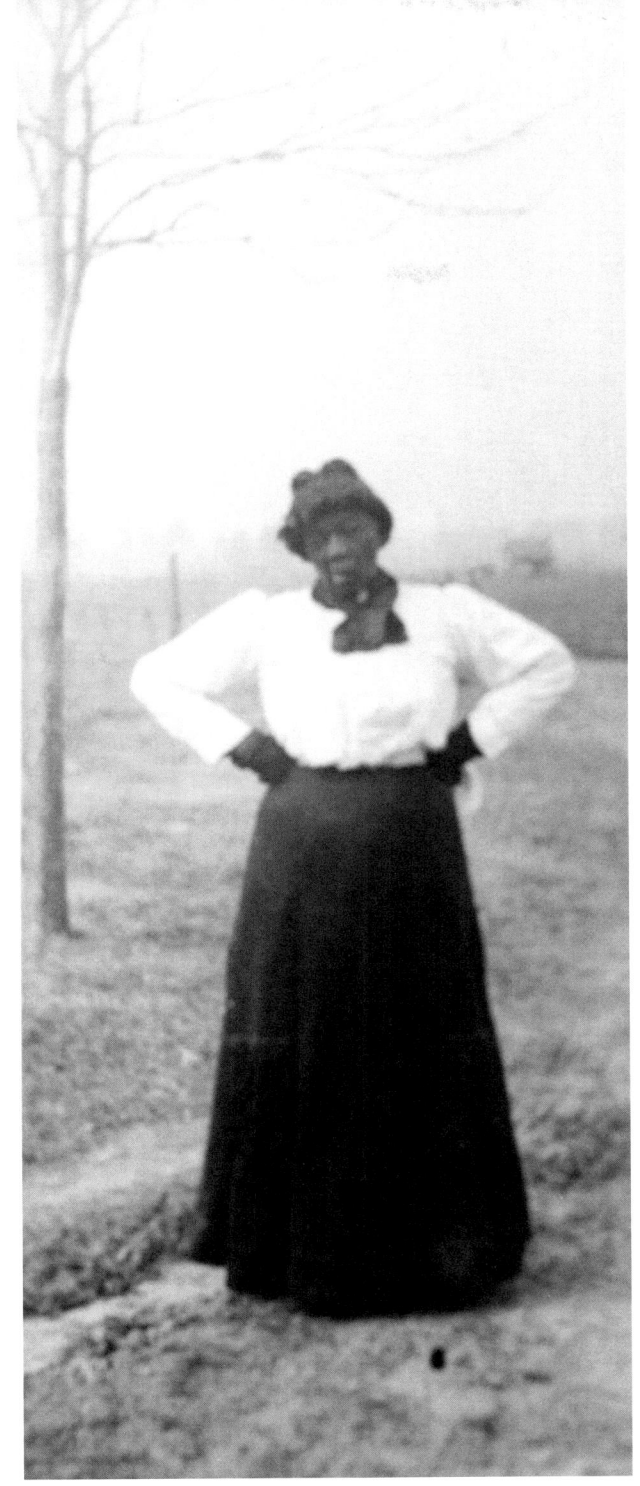

Opposite, Plate 64.
Left, Plate 65.

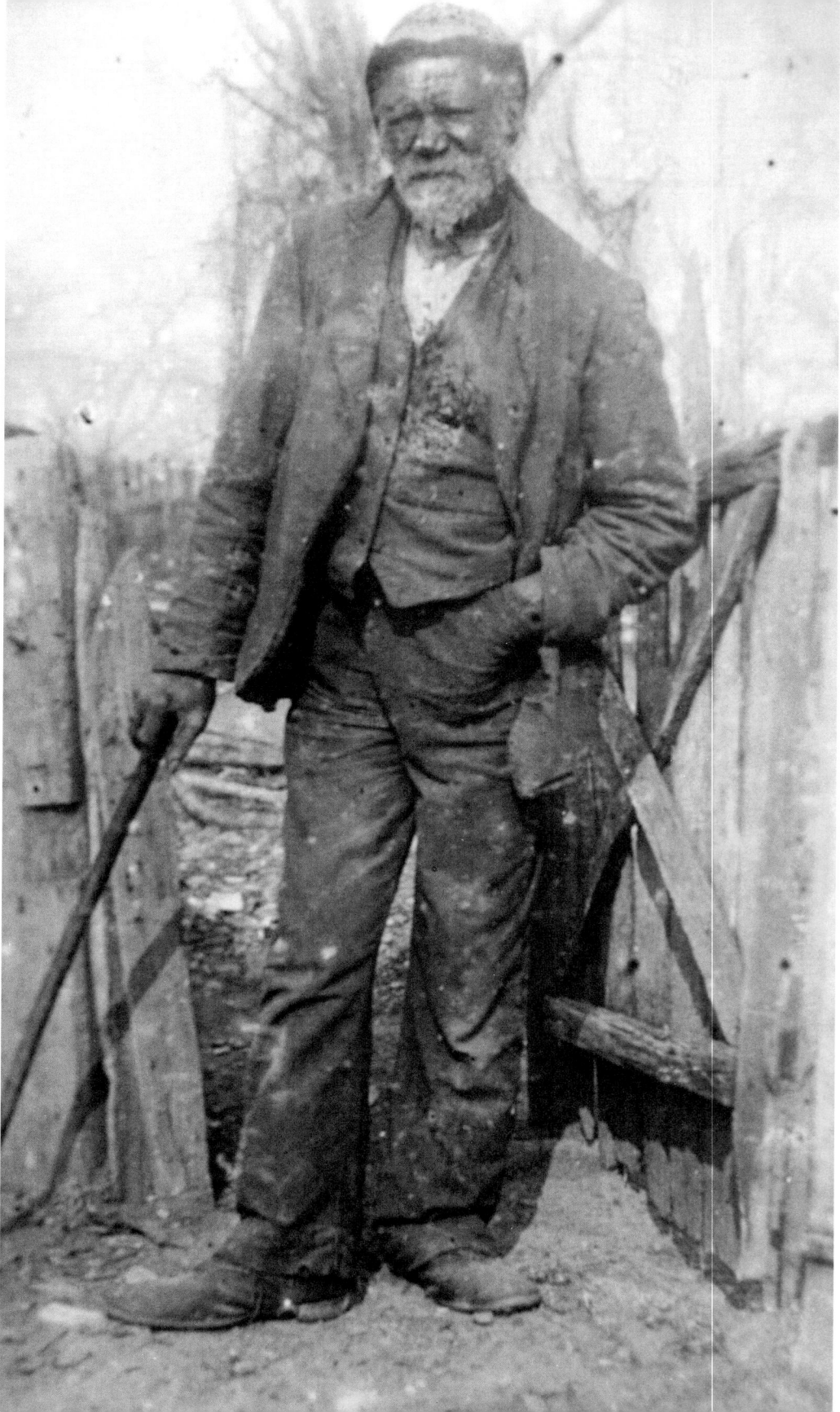

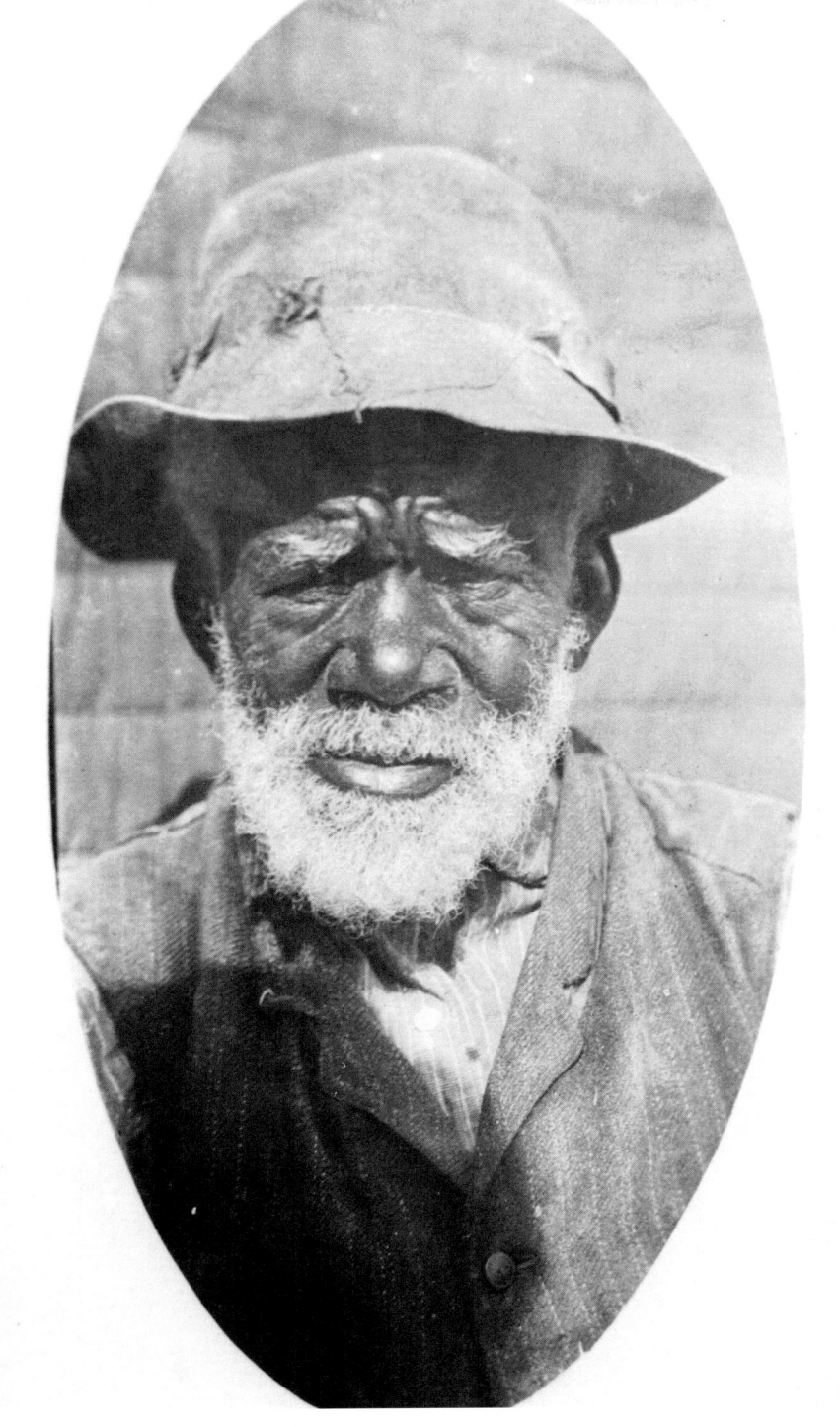

Opposite, Plate 66. Above, Plate 67.

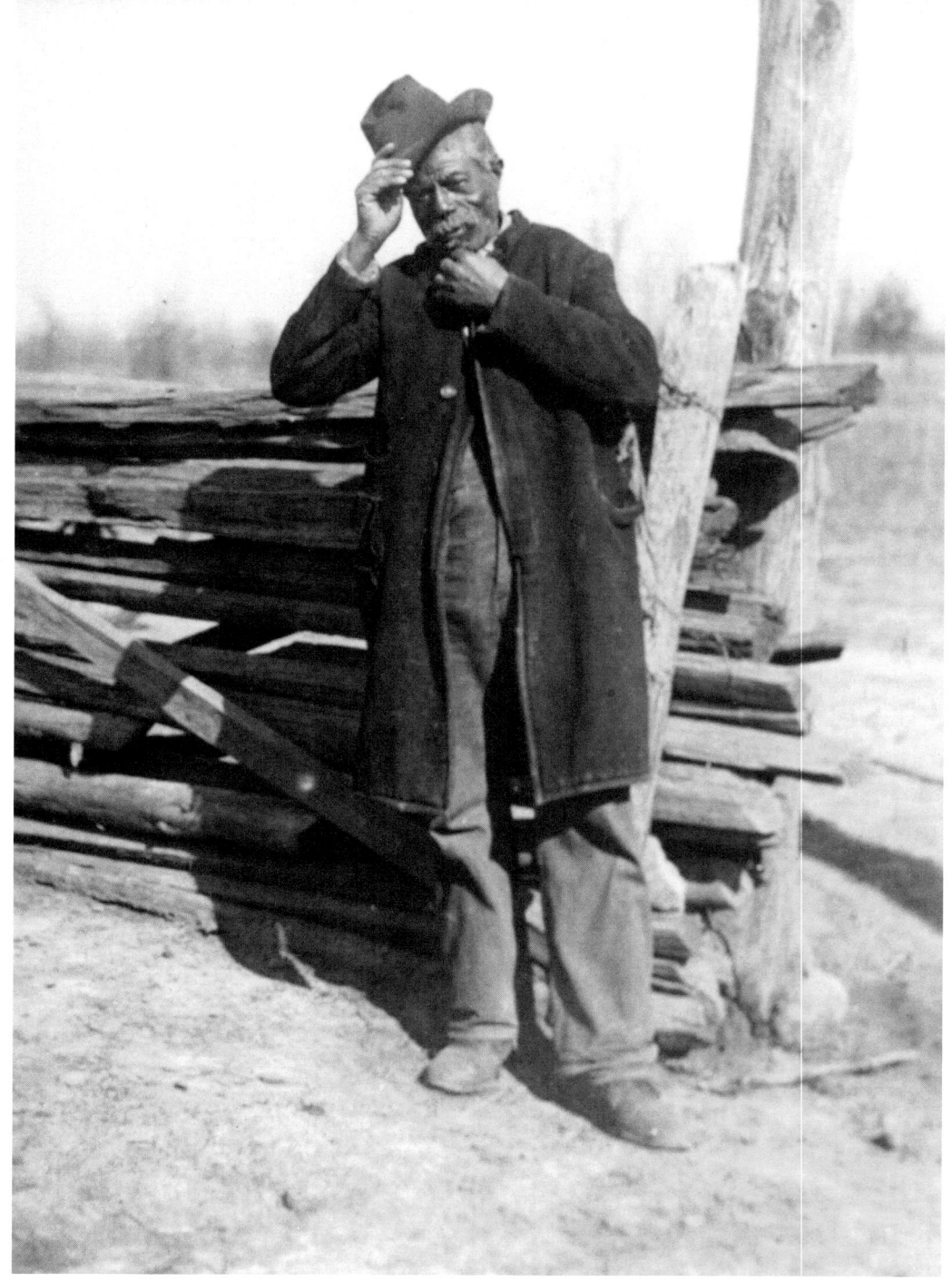

Above, Plate 68. Opposite, Plate 69.

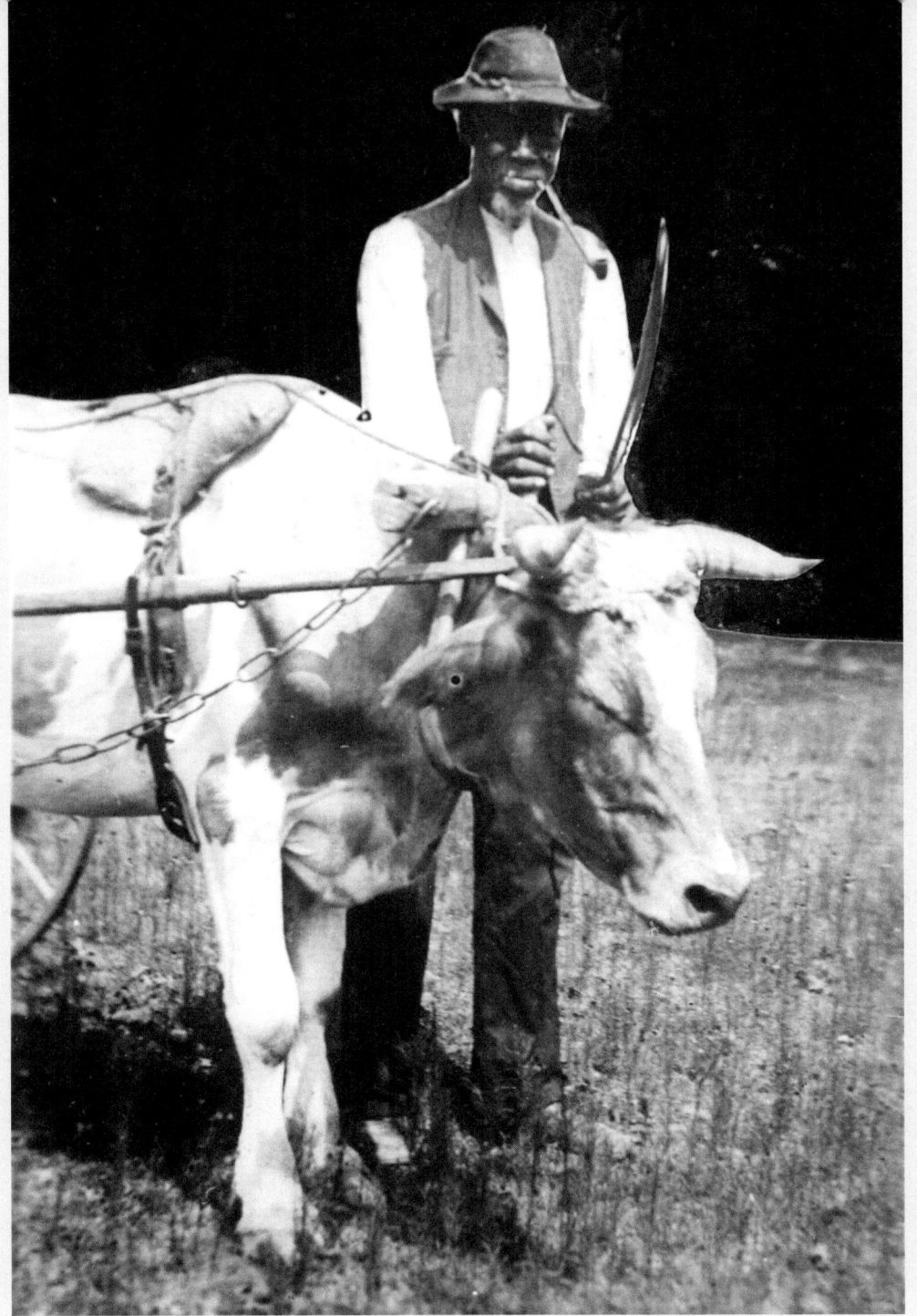

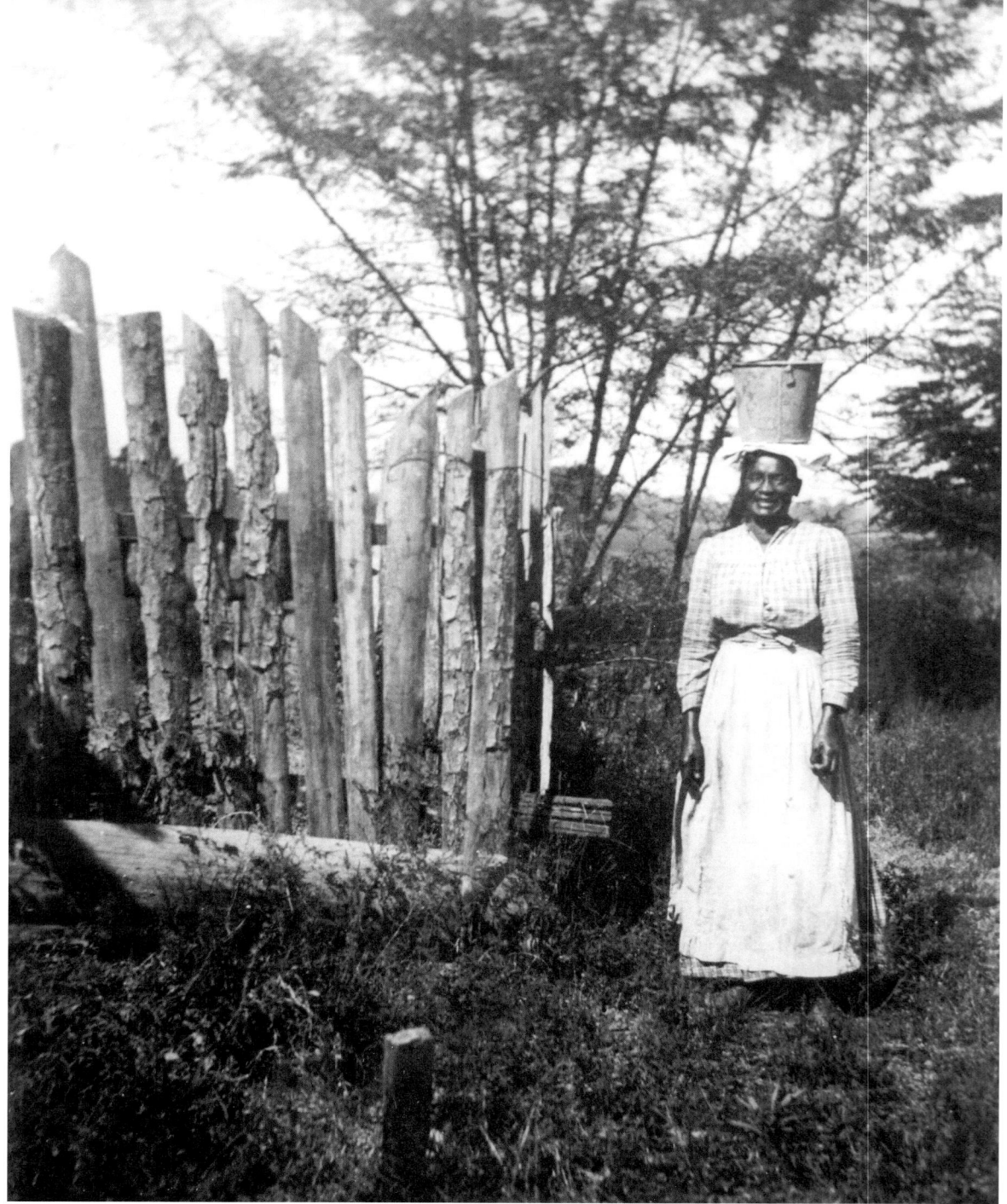

Plate 70.

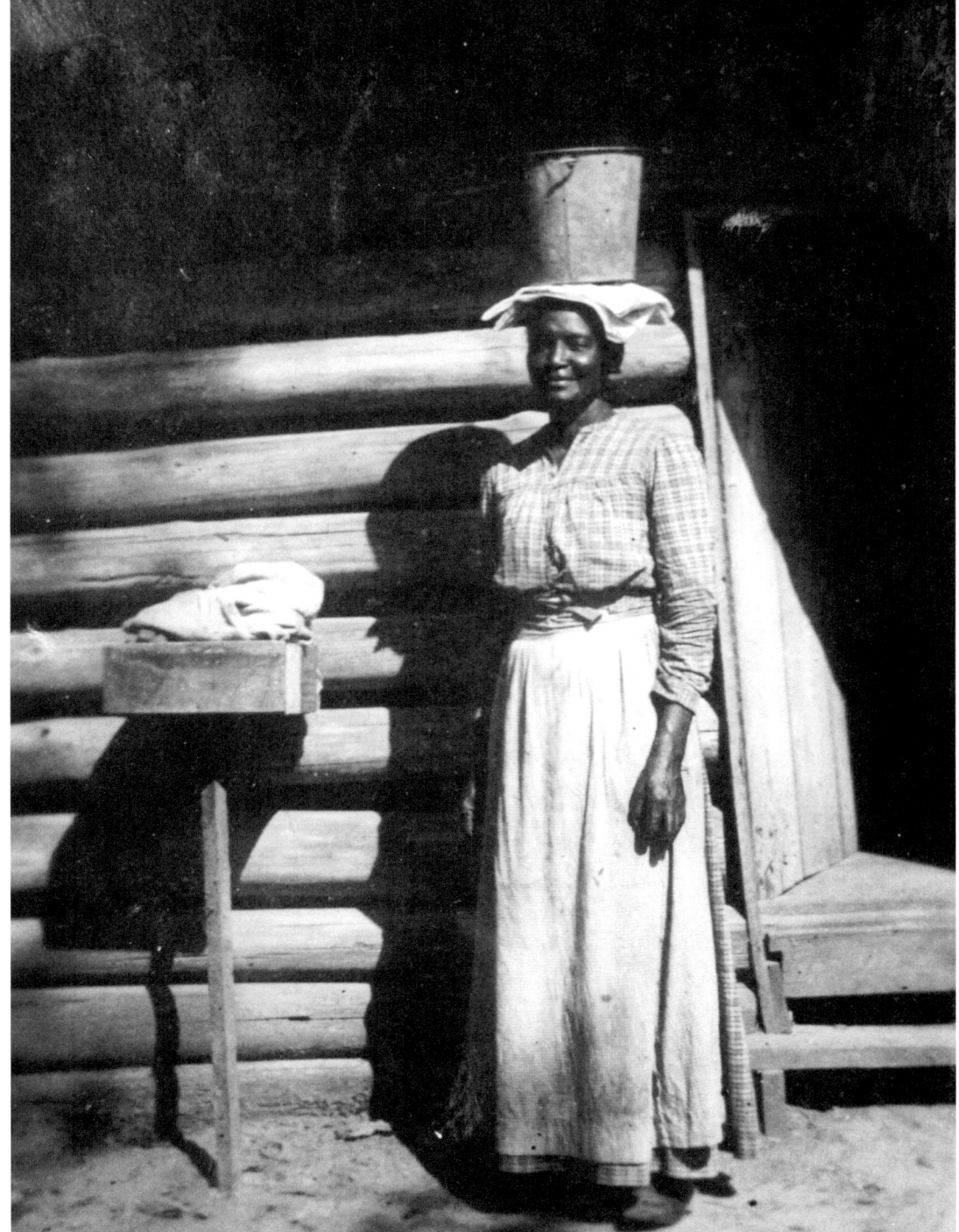

Plate 71.

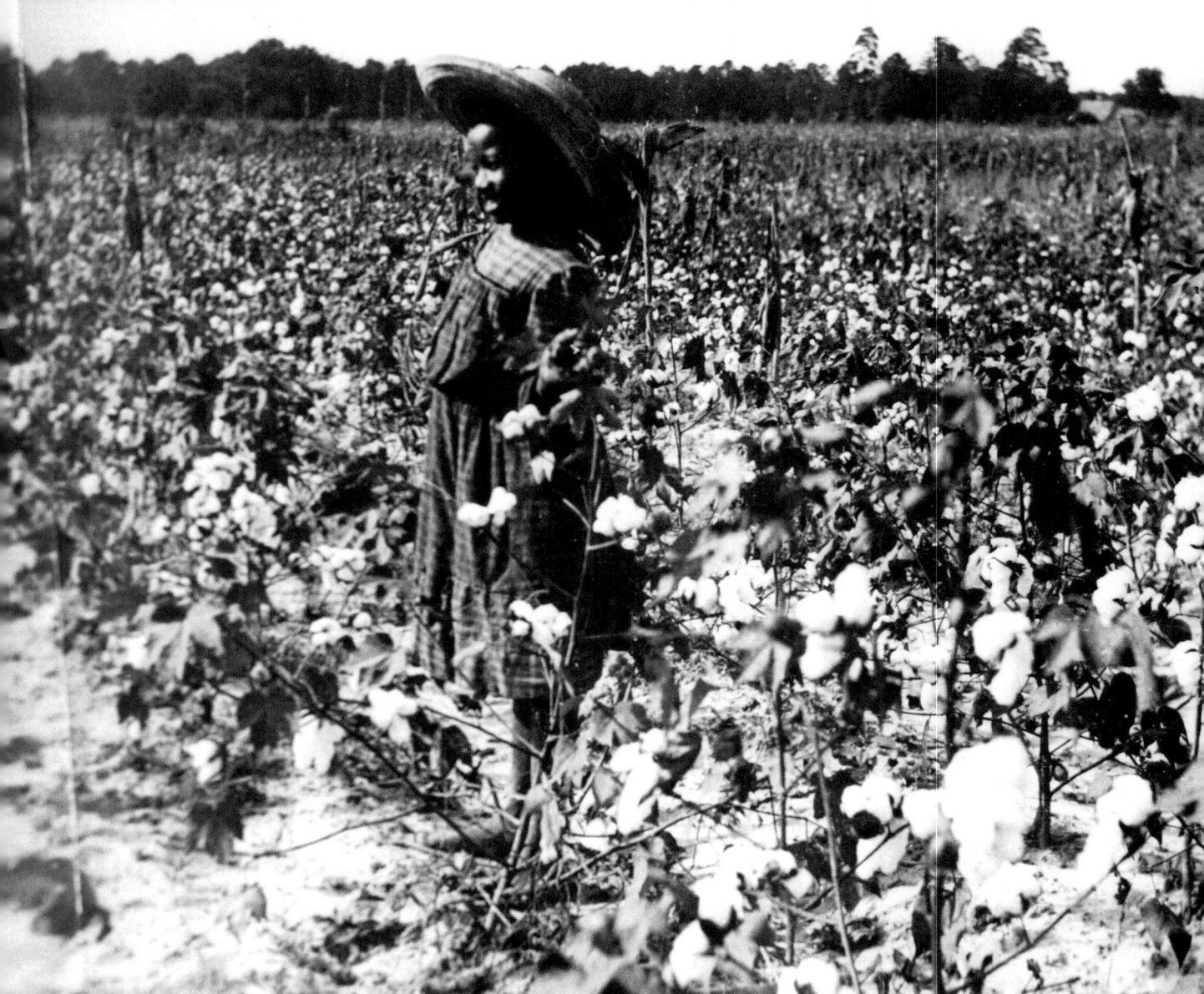

Plate 72.

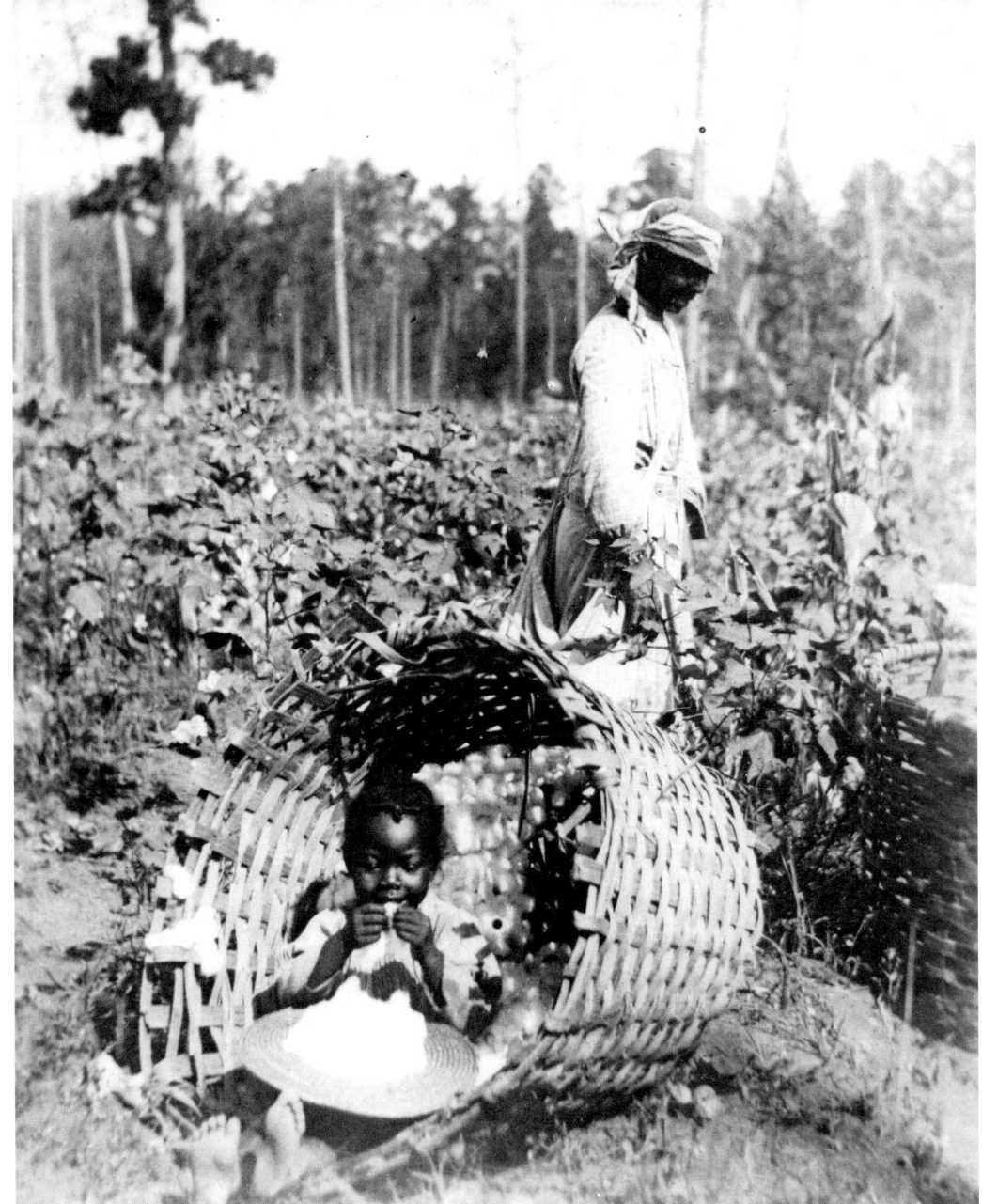

Plate 73.

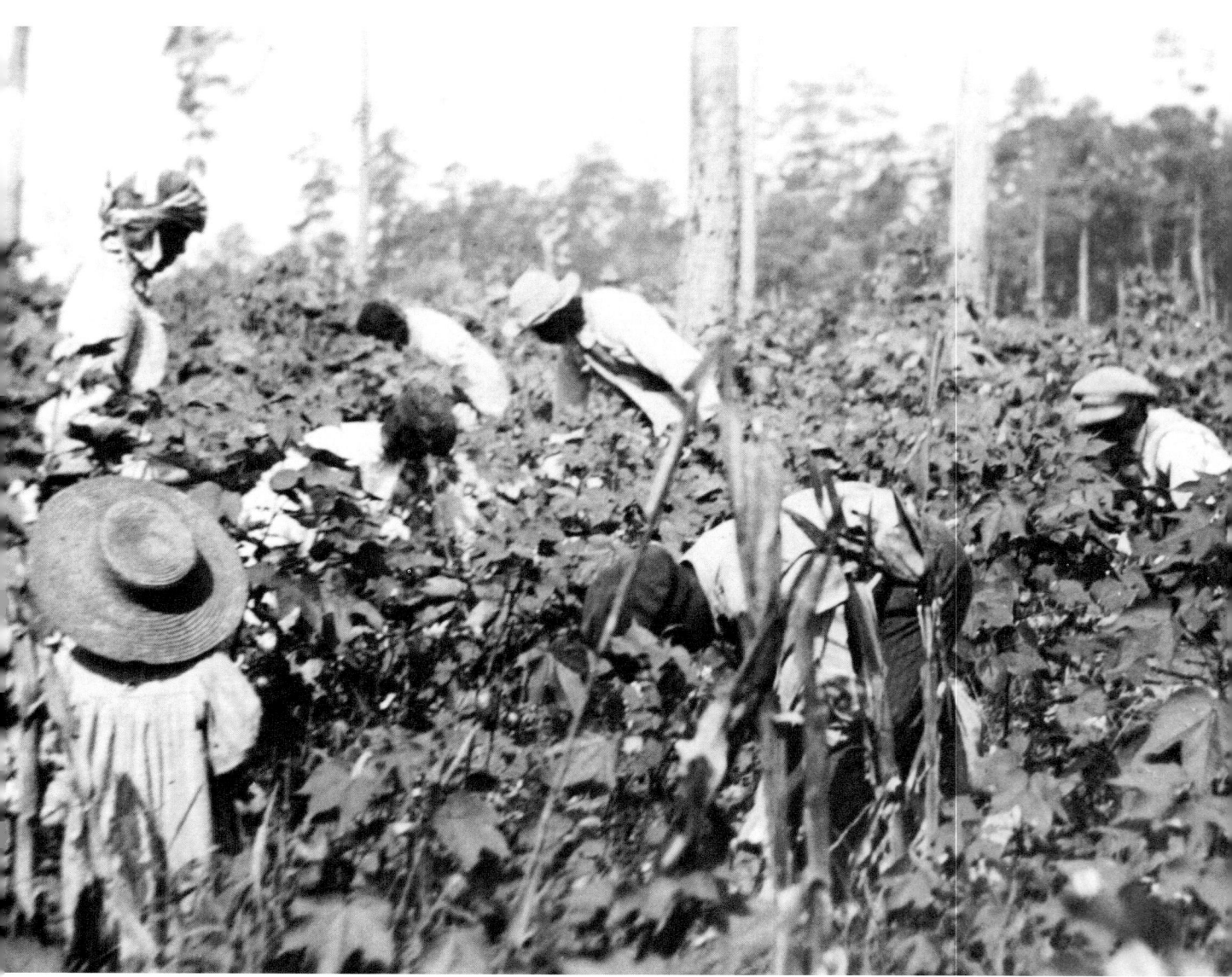

Above, Plate 74. Opposite, Plate 75.

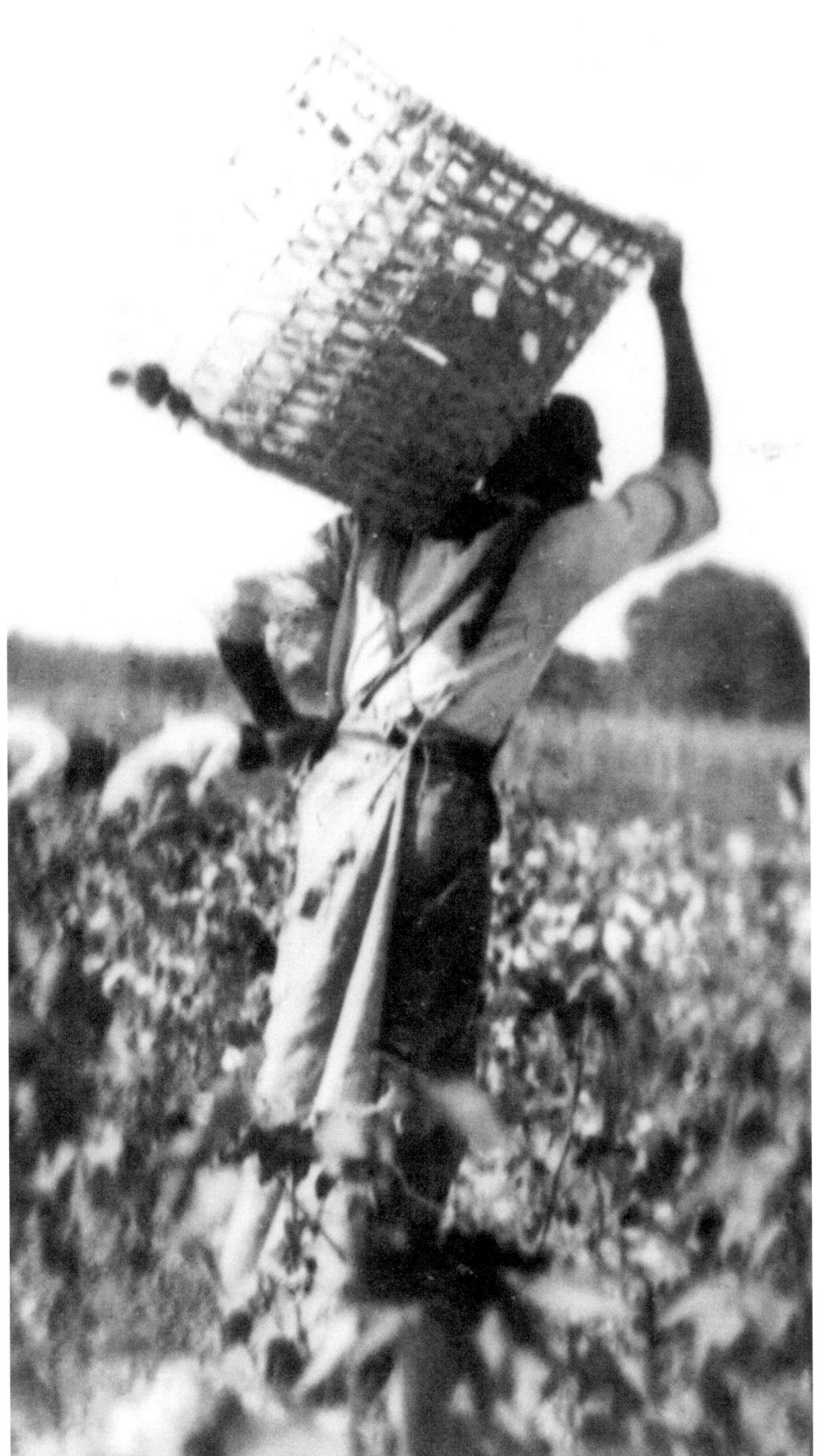

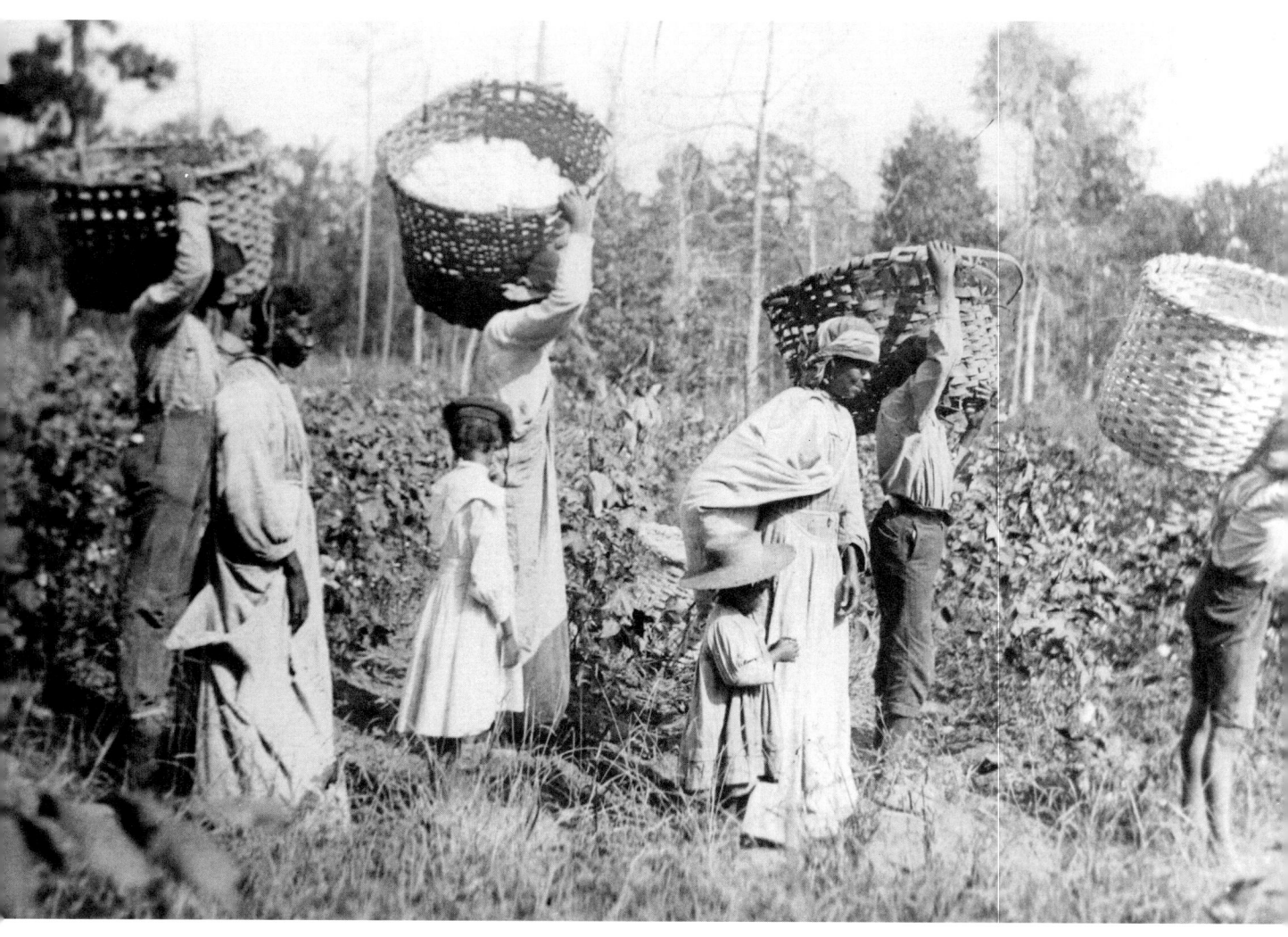

Plate 76.

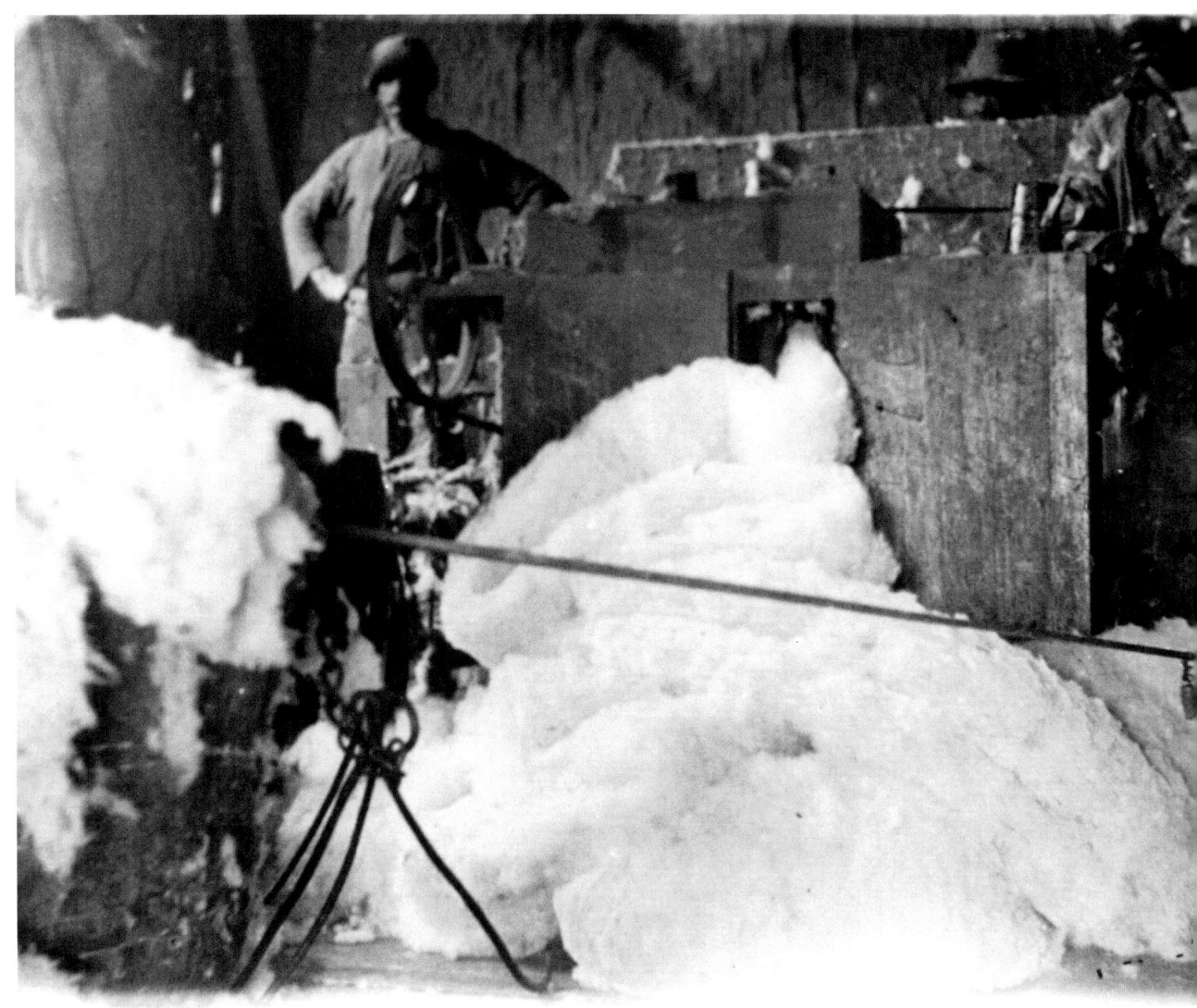

Plate 77.

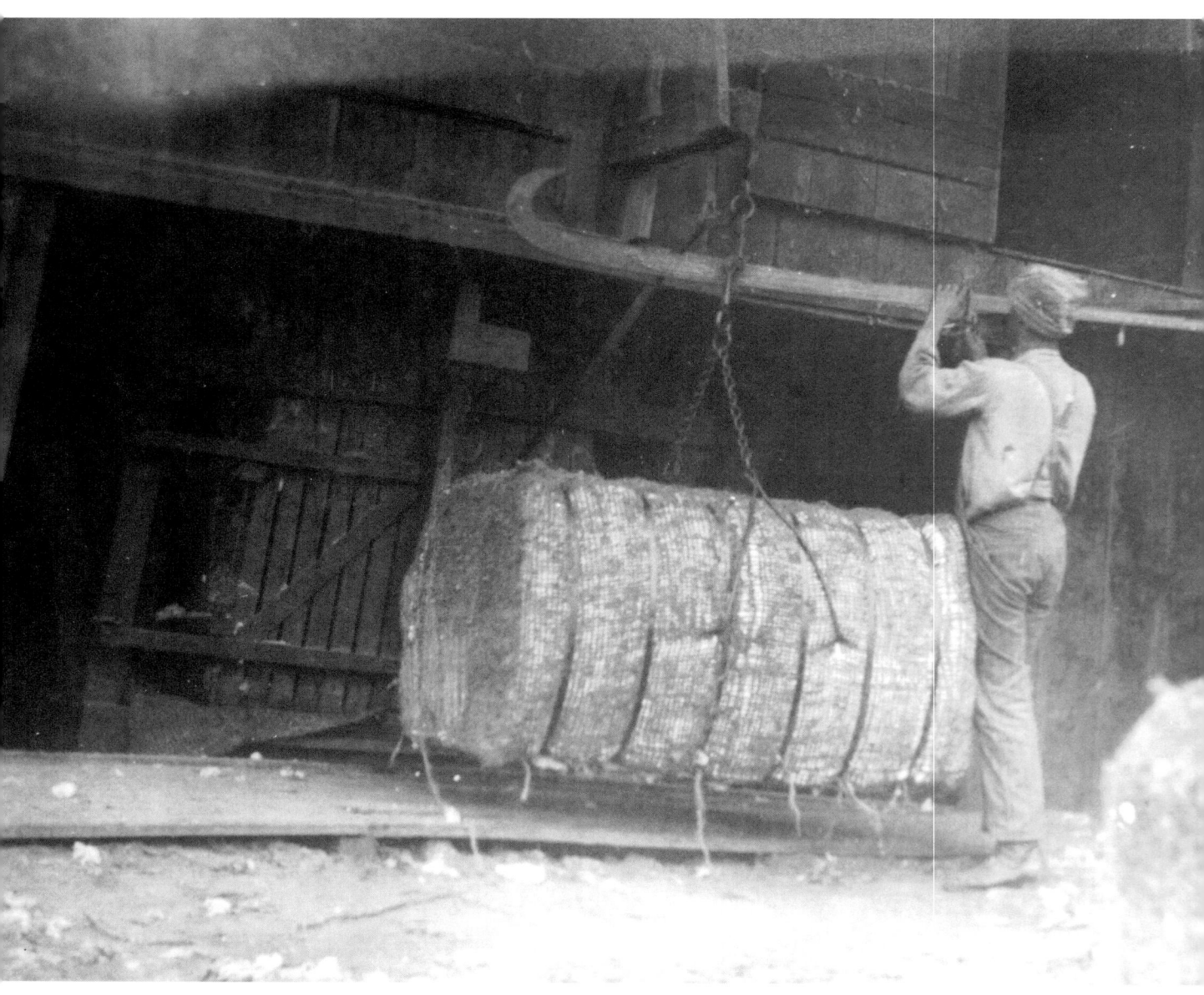

Above, Plate 78. Opposite, Plate 79.

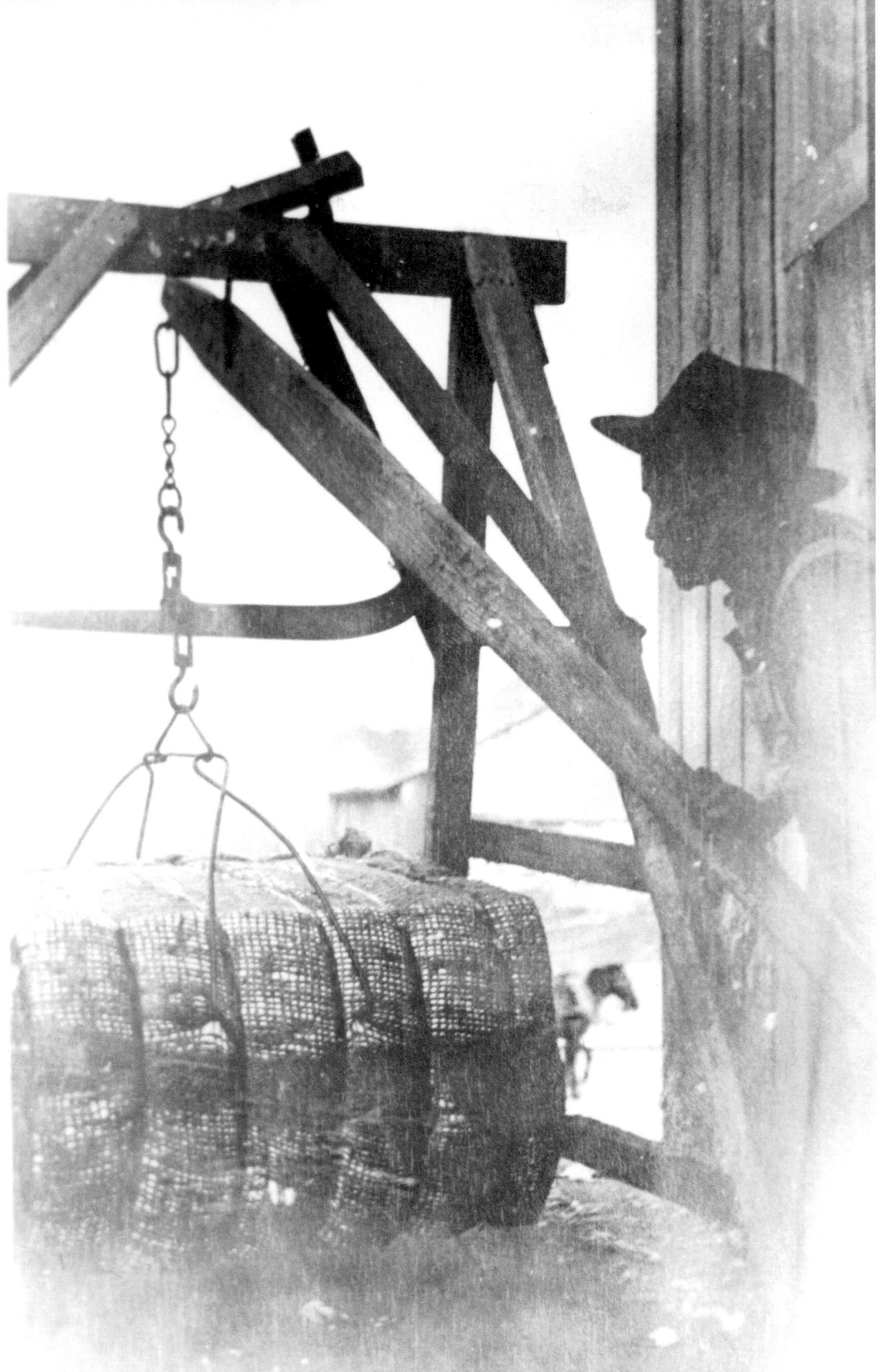

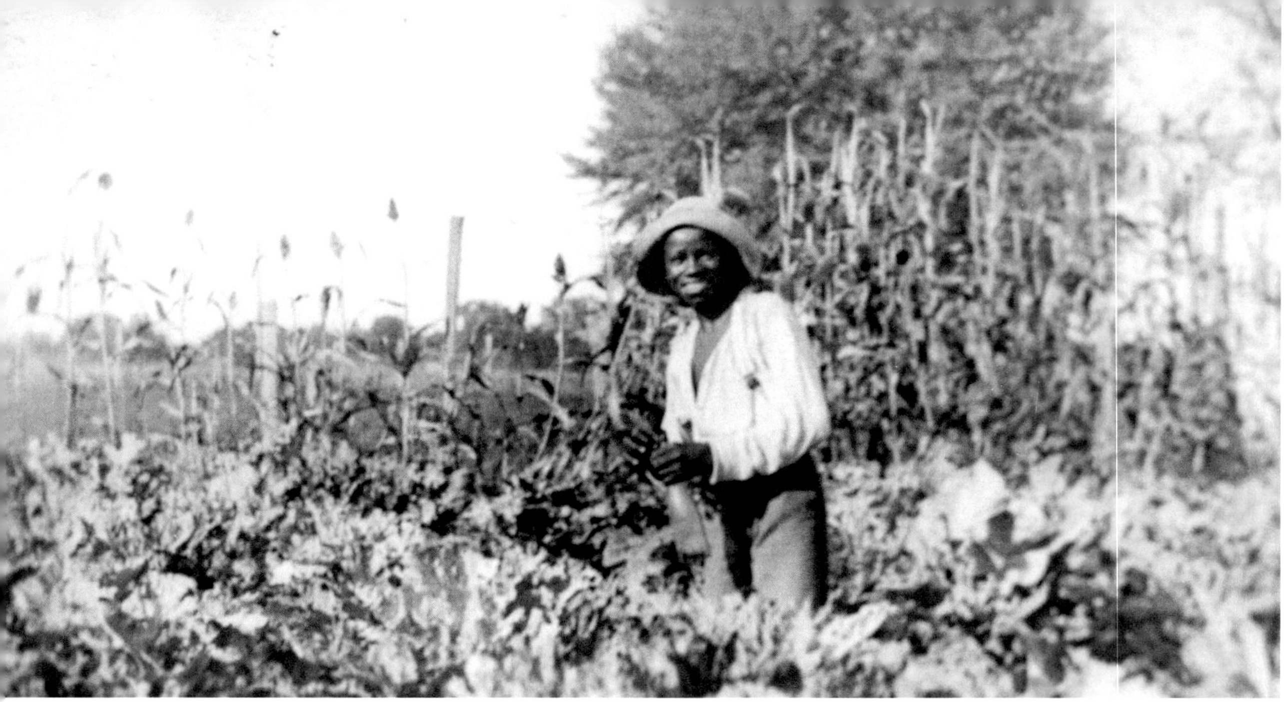

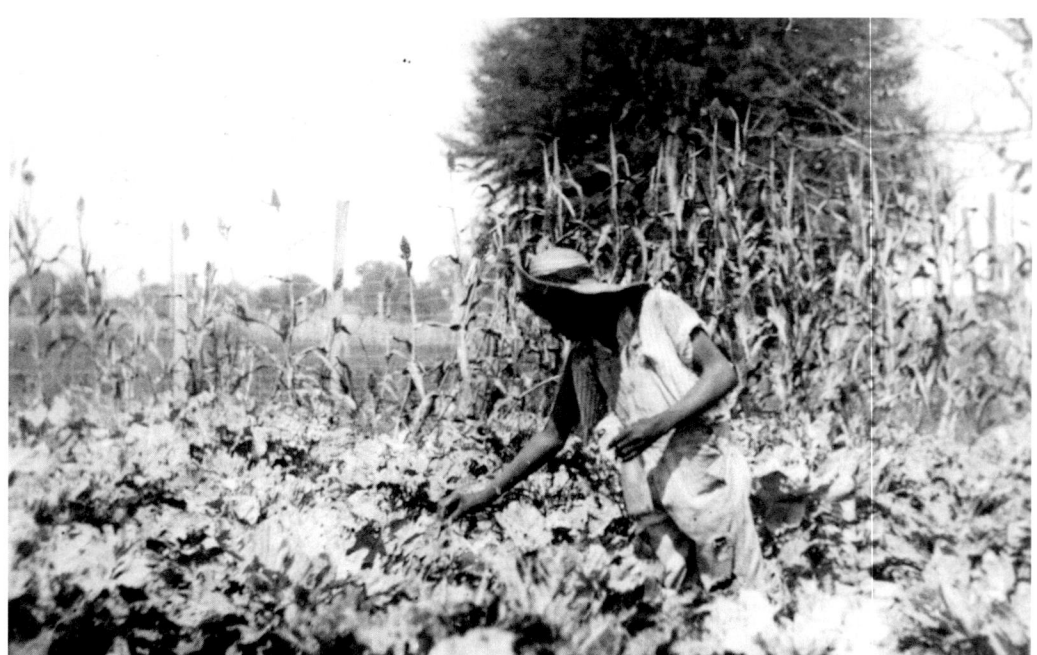

Plates 80 and 81.

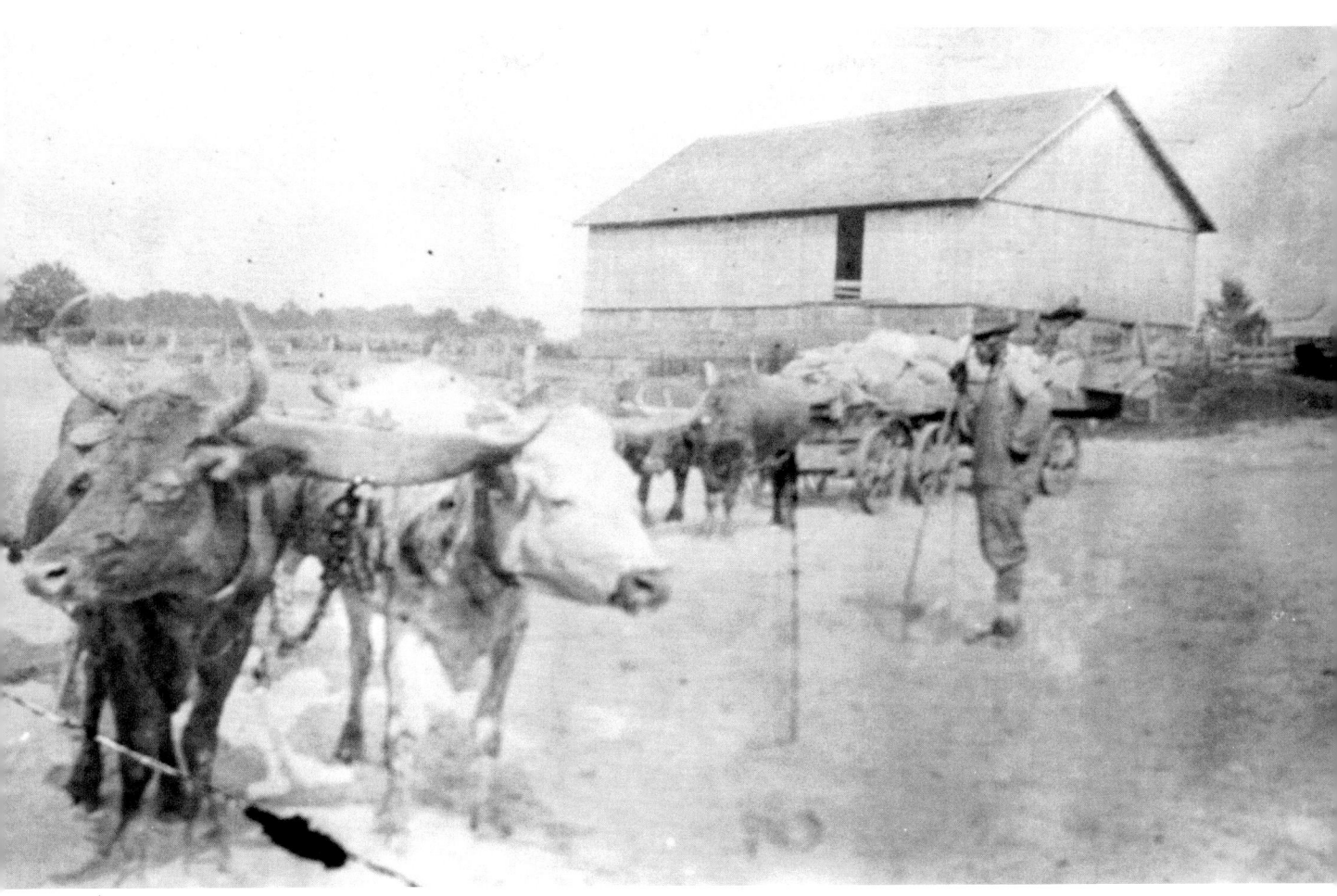

Plate 82.

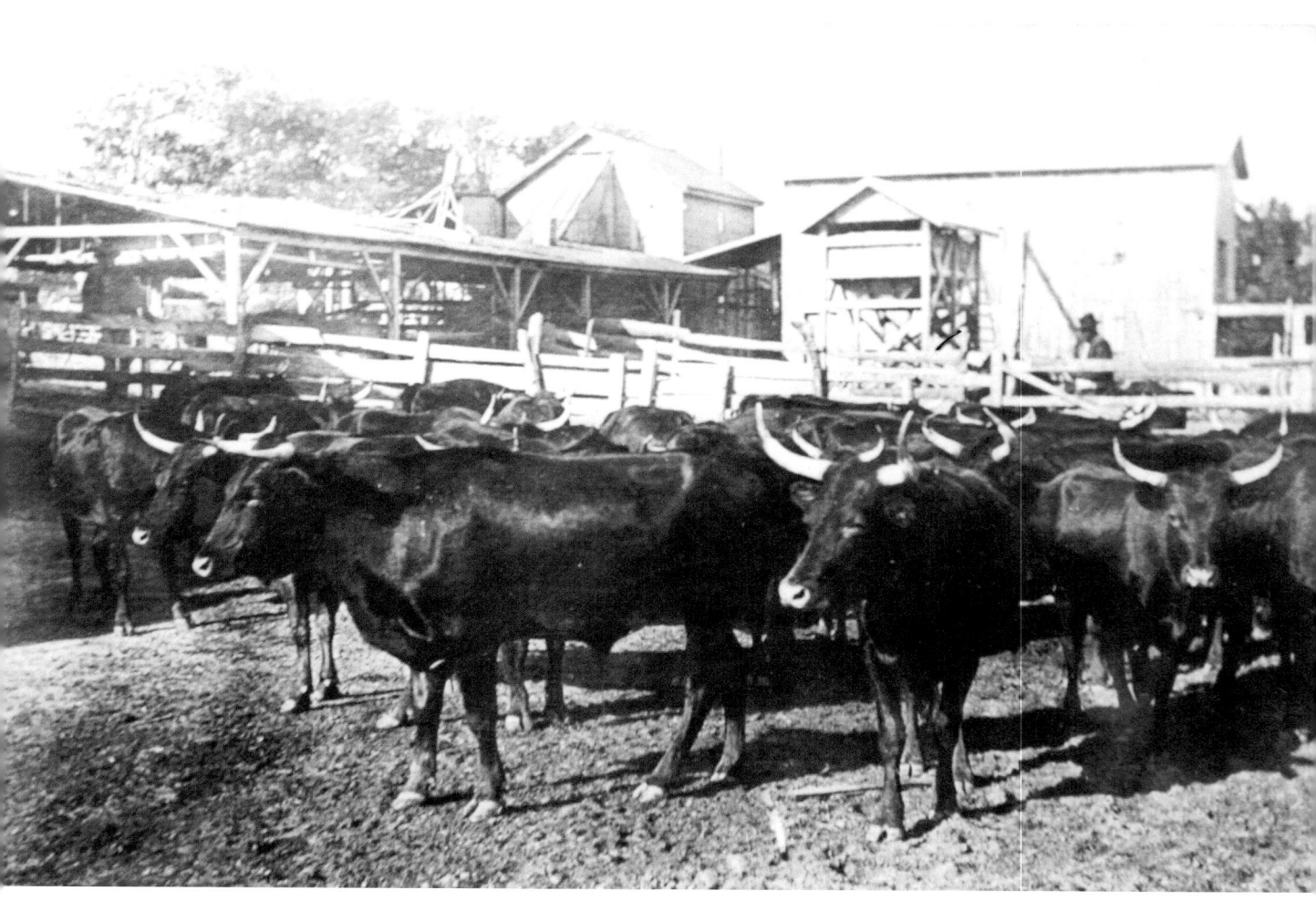

Plate 83.

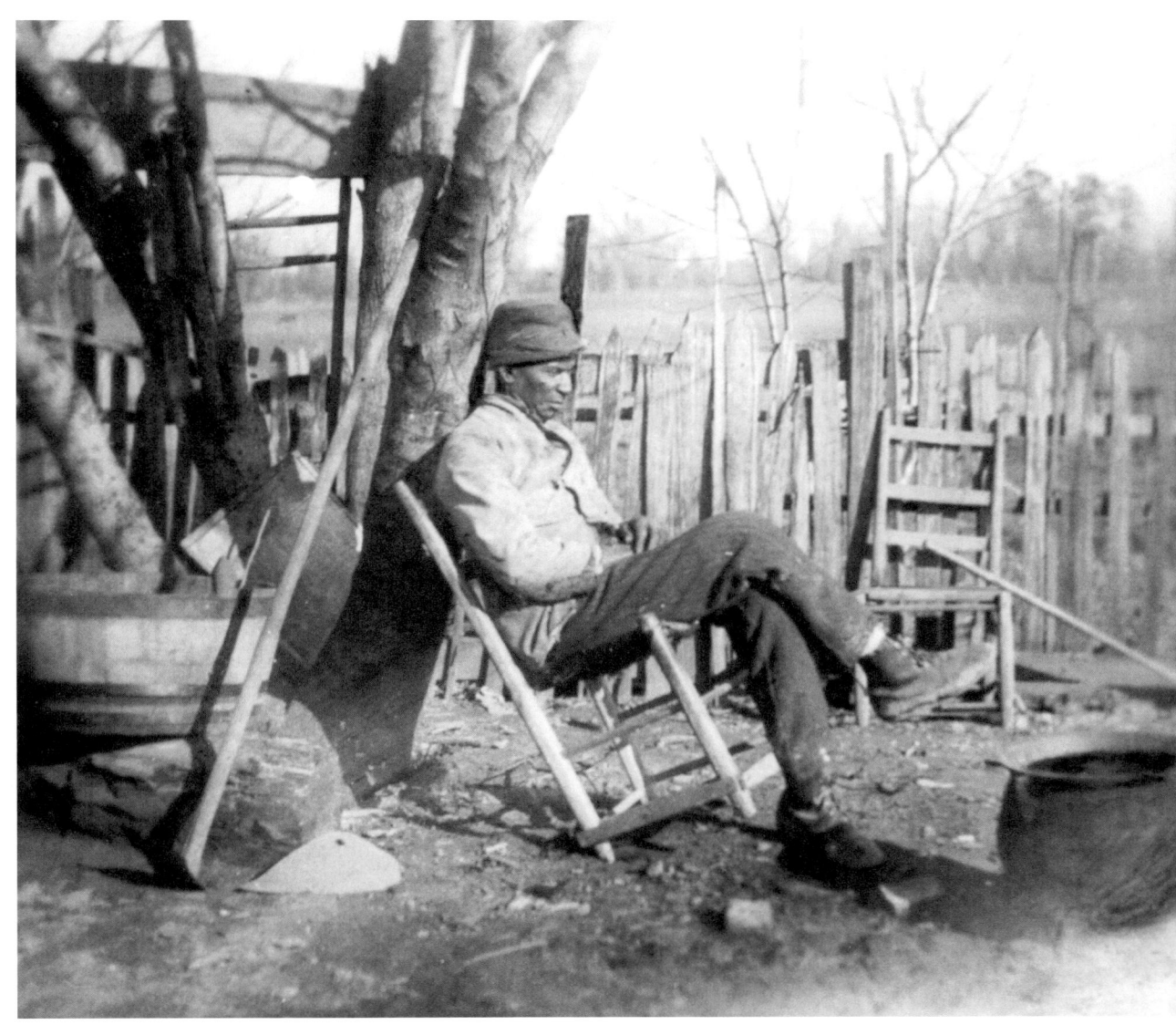

Plate 84.

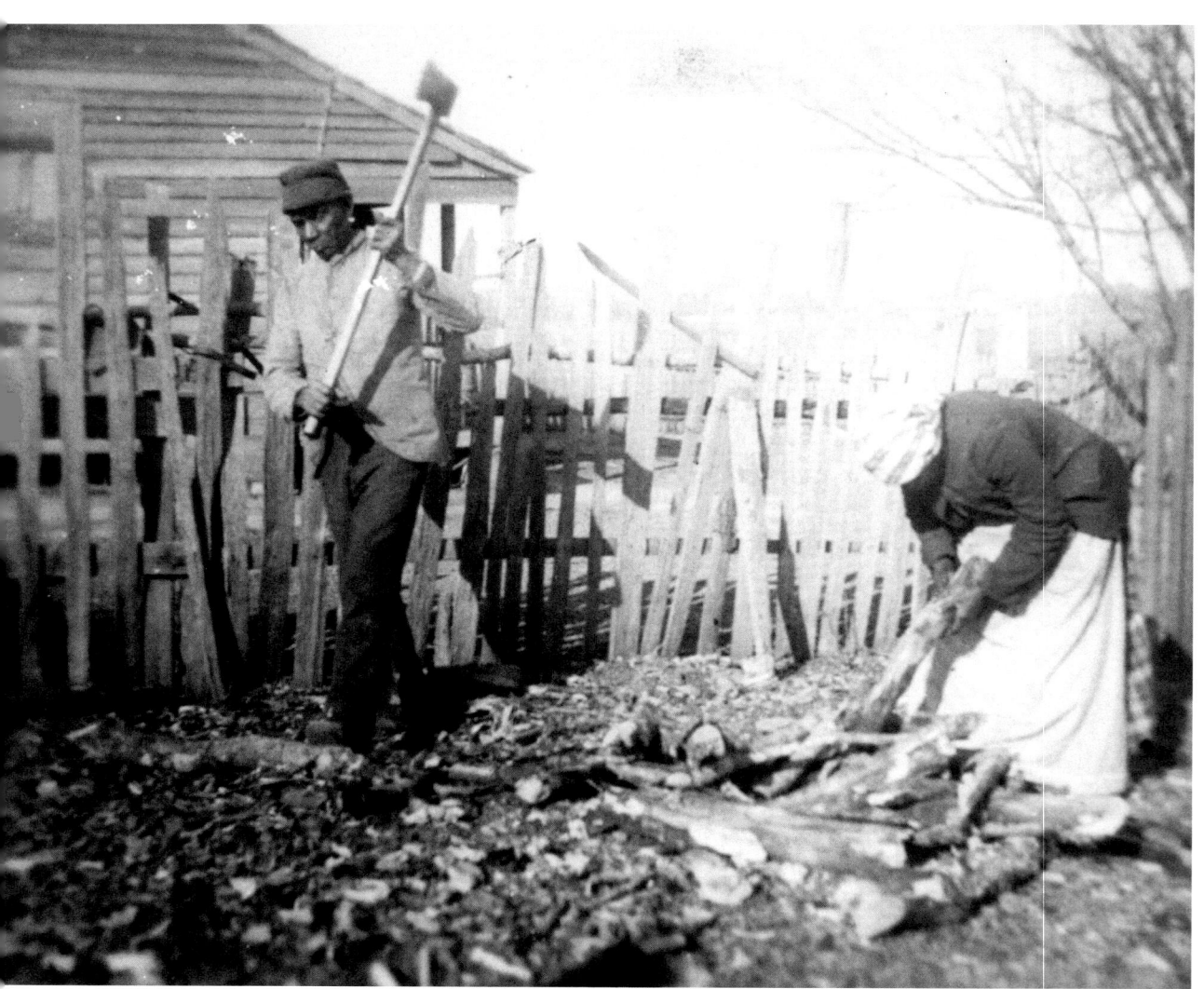

Plate 85.

114

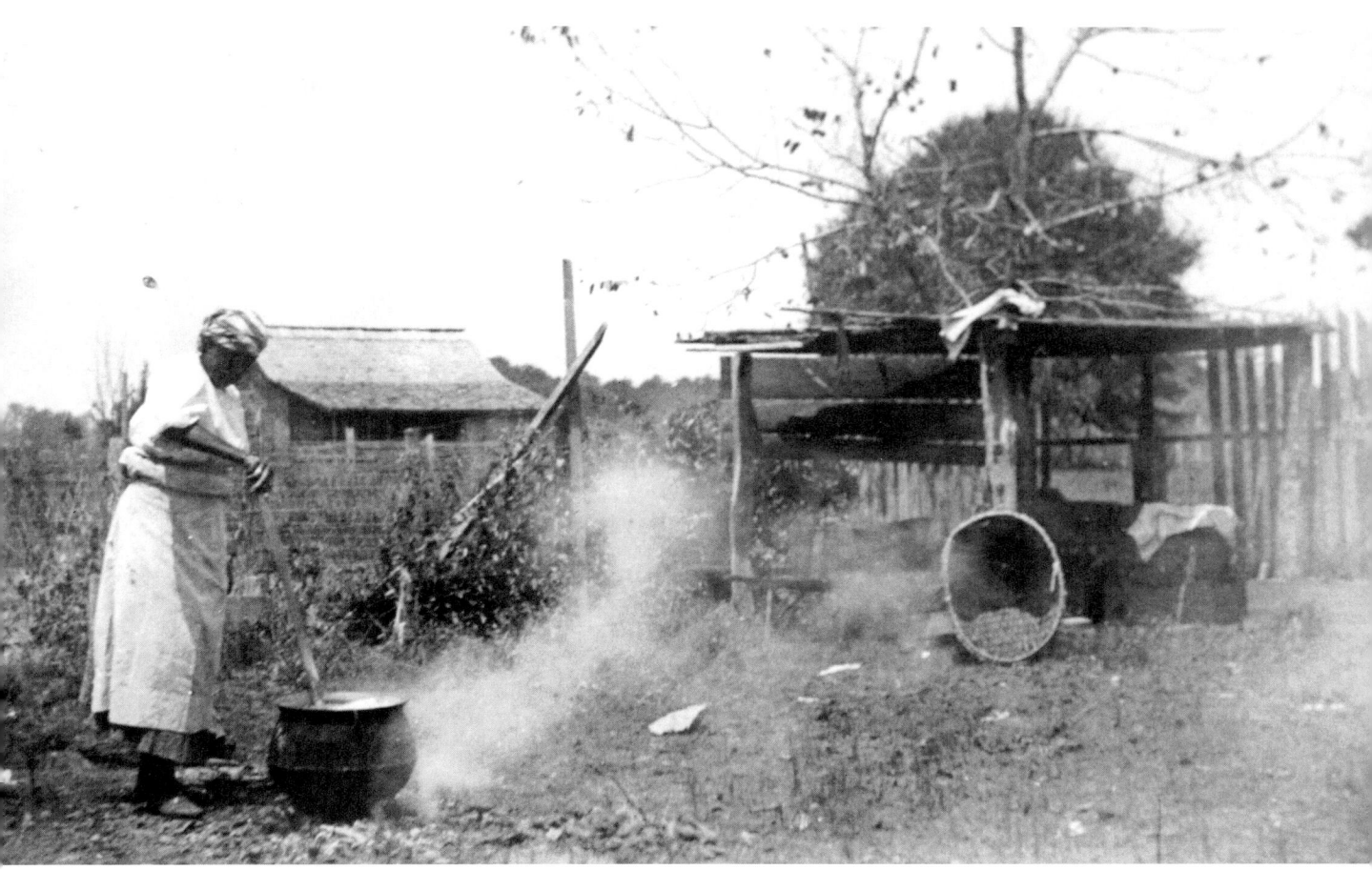

Plate 86.

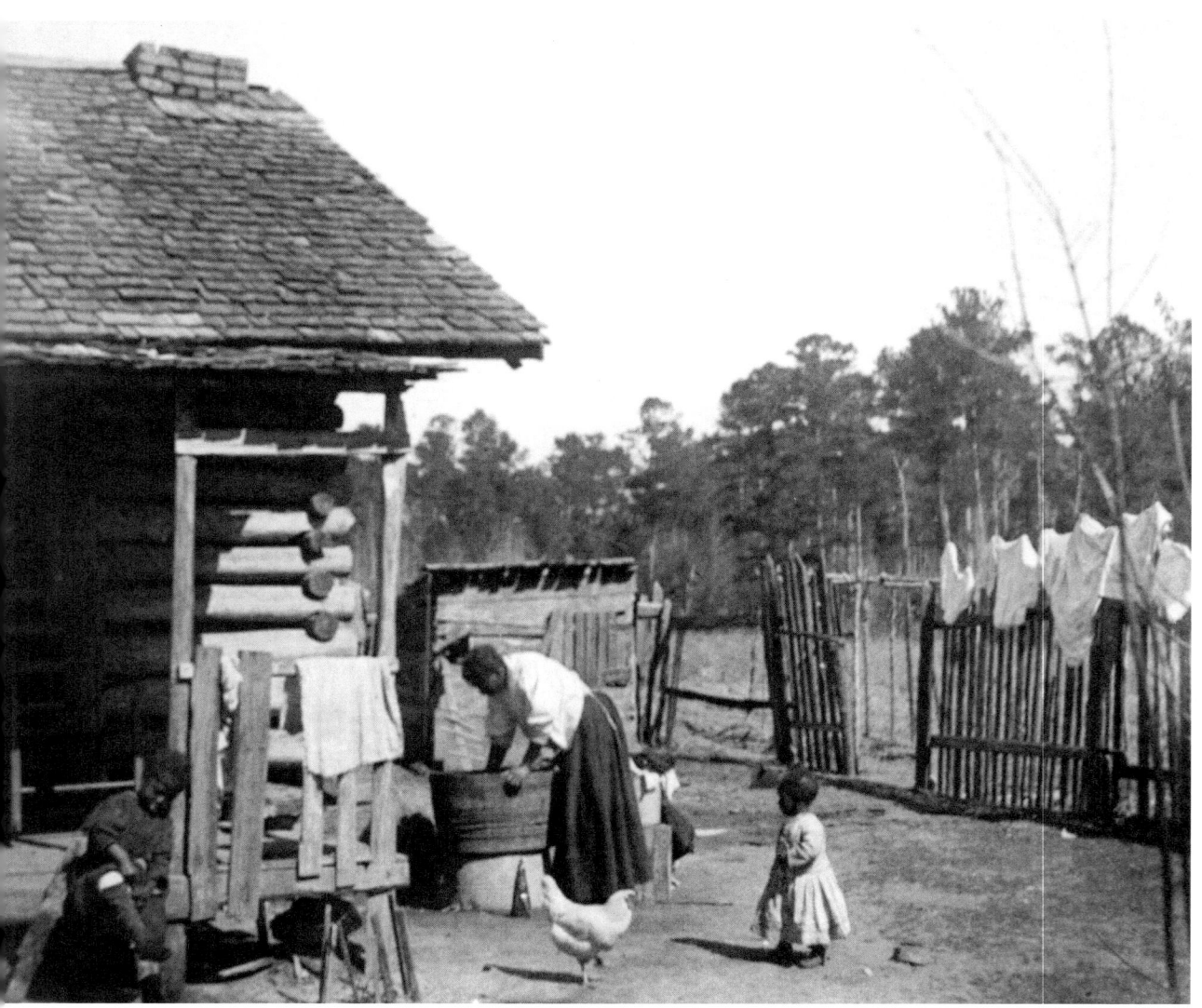

Plate 87.

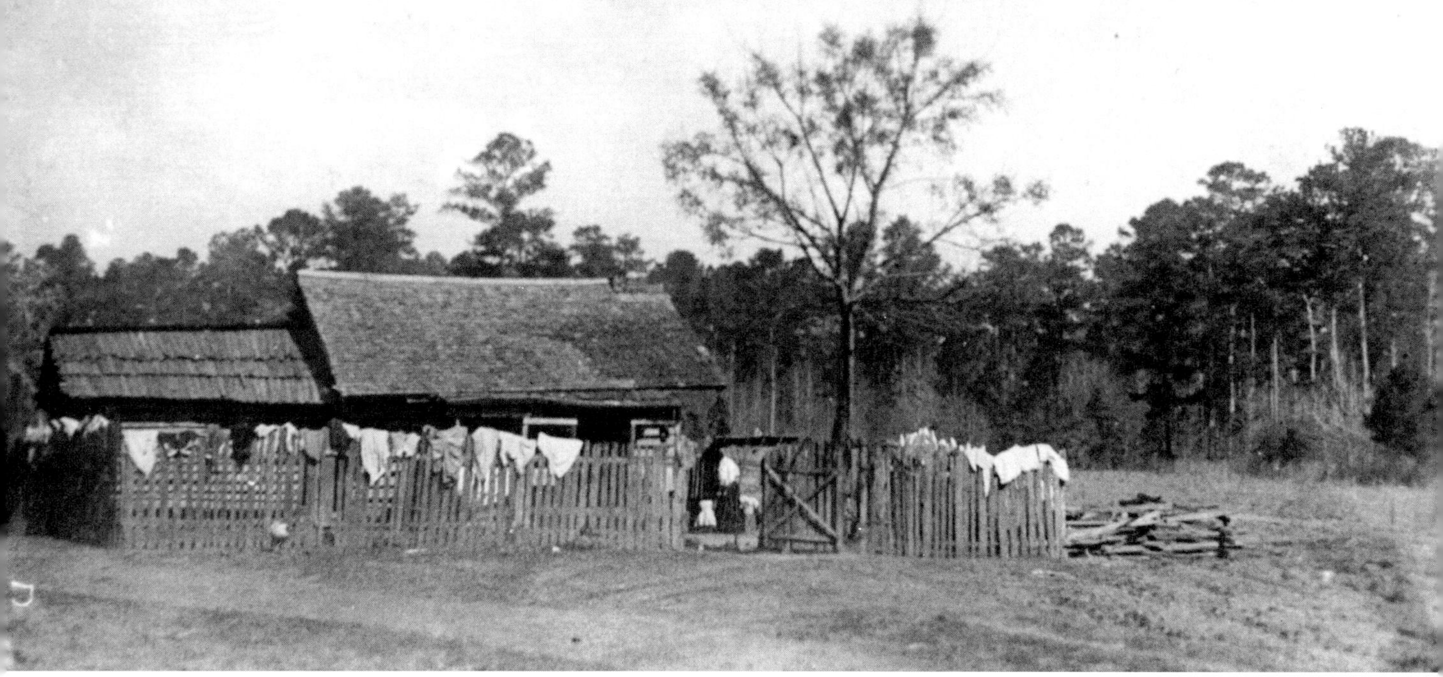

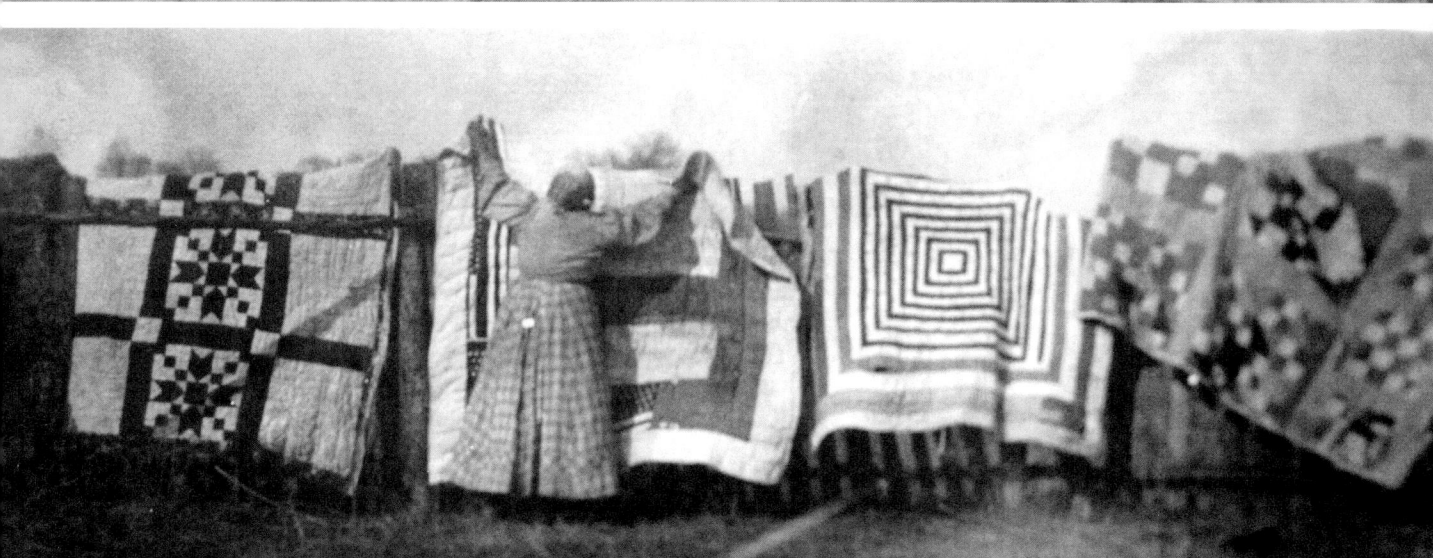

Plates 88 and 89.

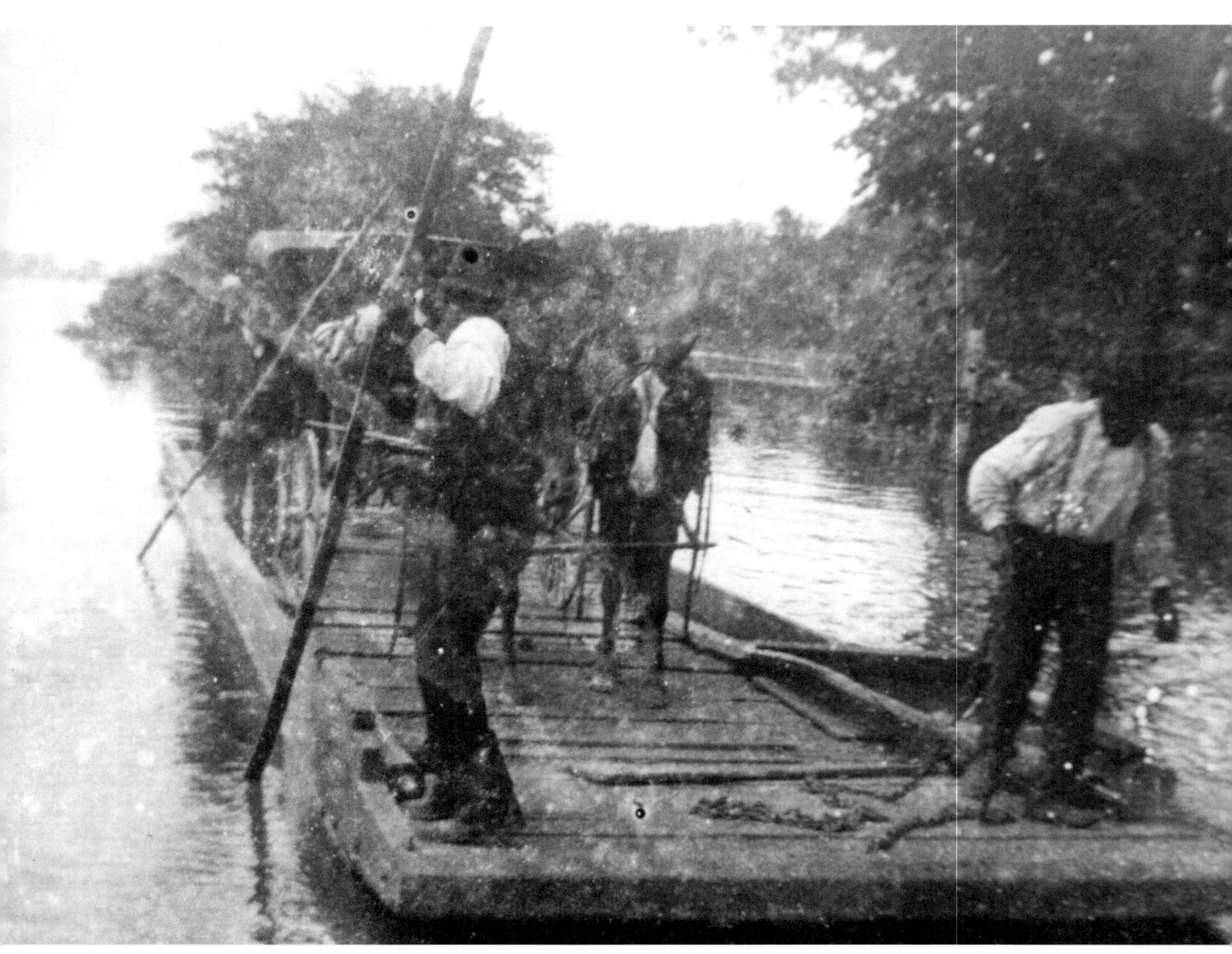

Plate 90, ferry across the Alabama River.

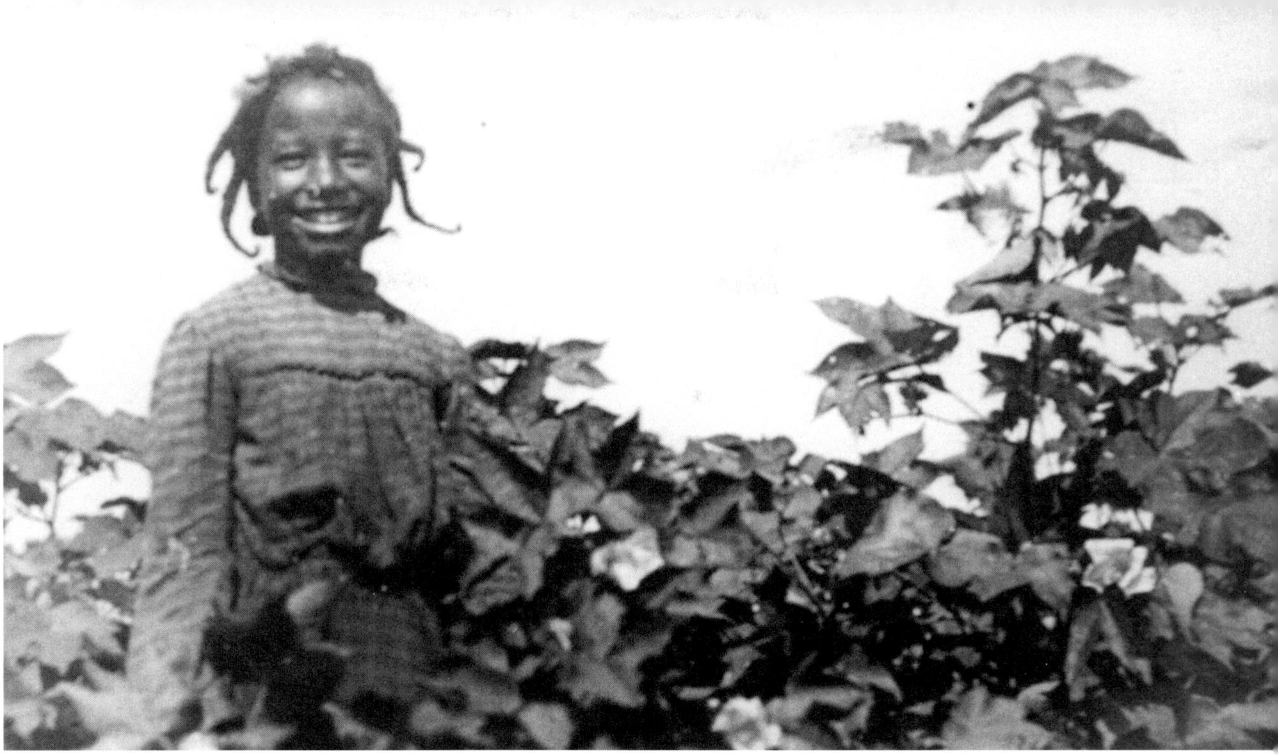

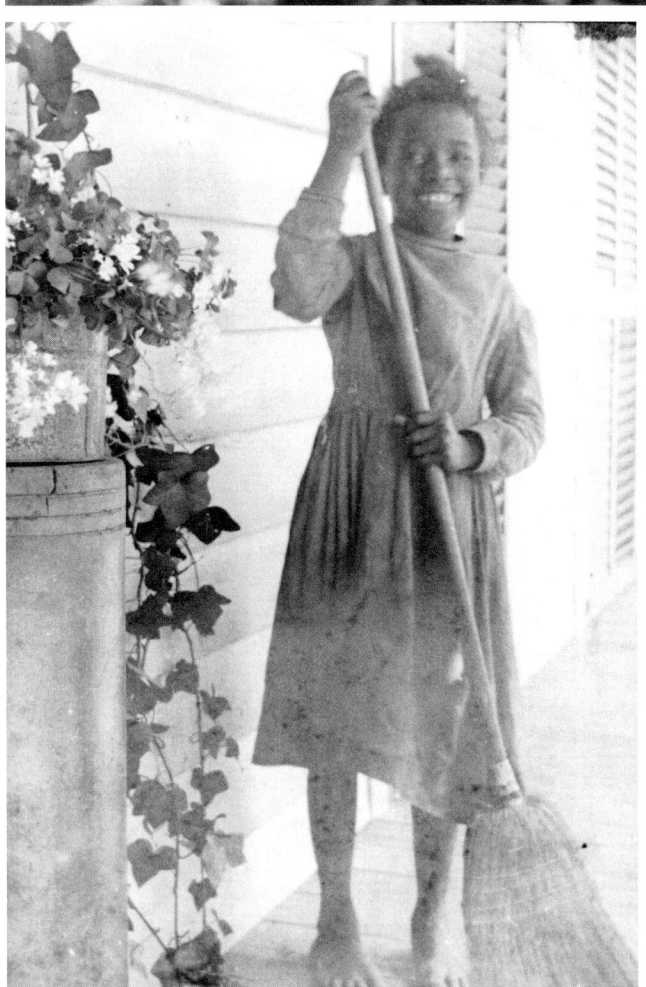

Plates 91, top, and 92, left.

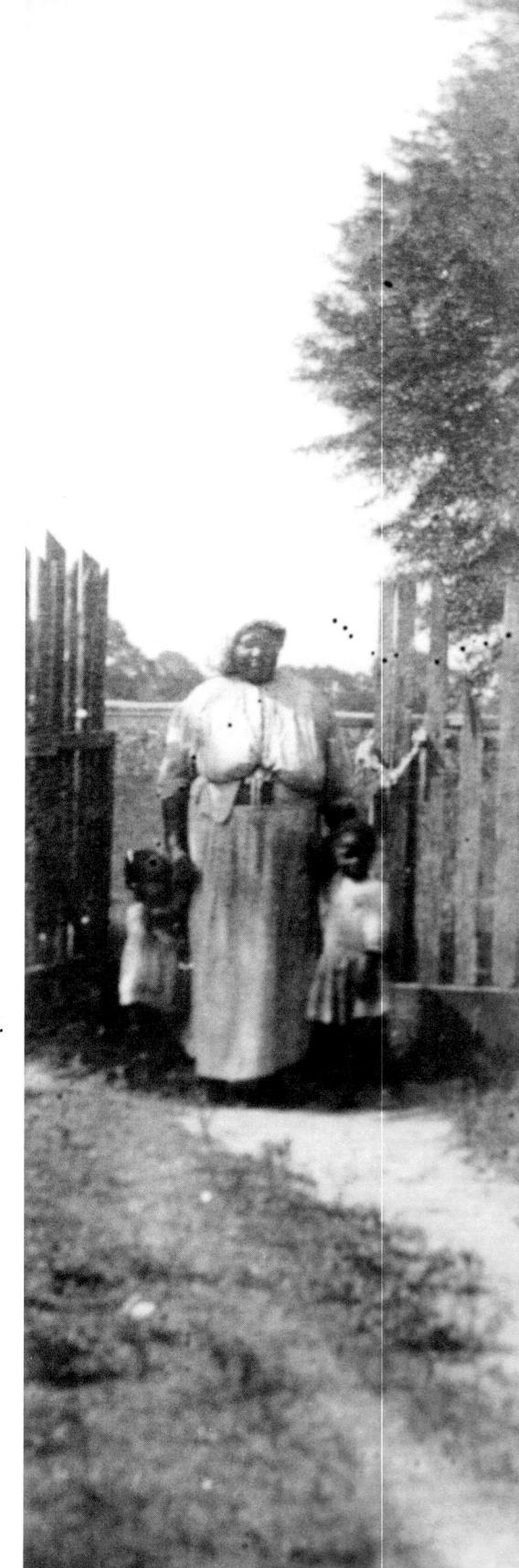

Plate 93.

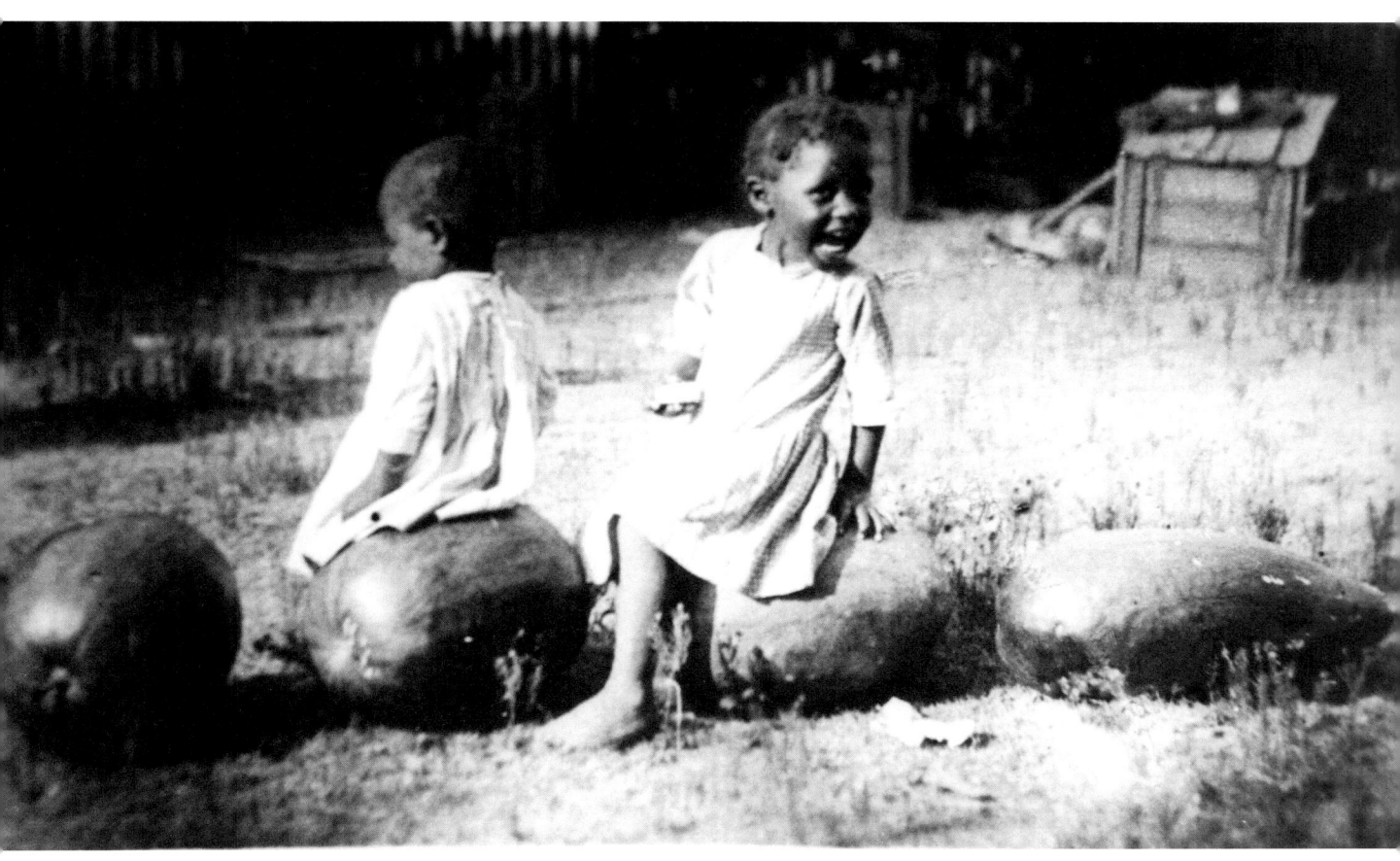

Plate 94.

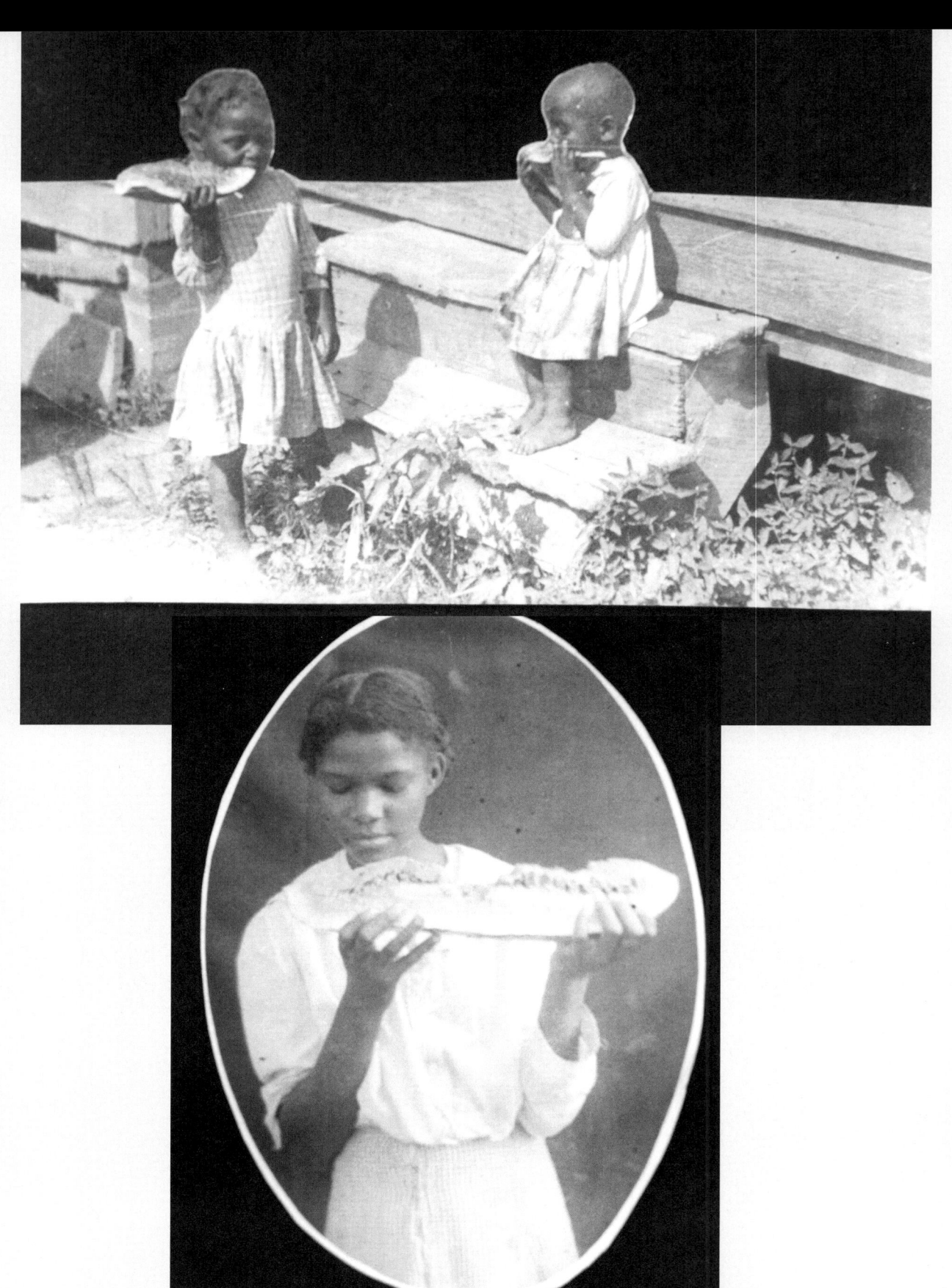

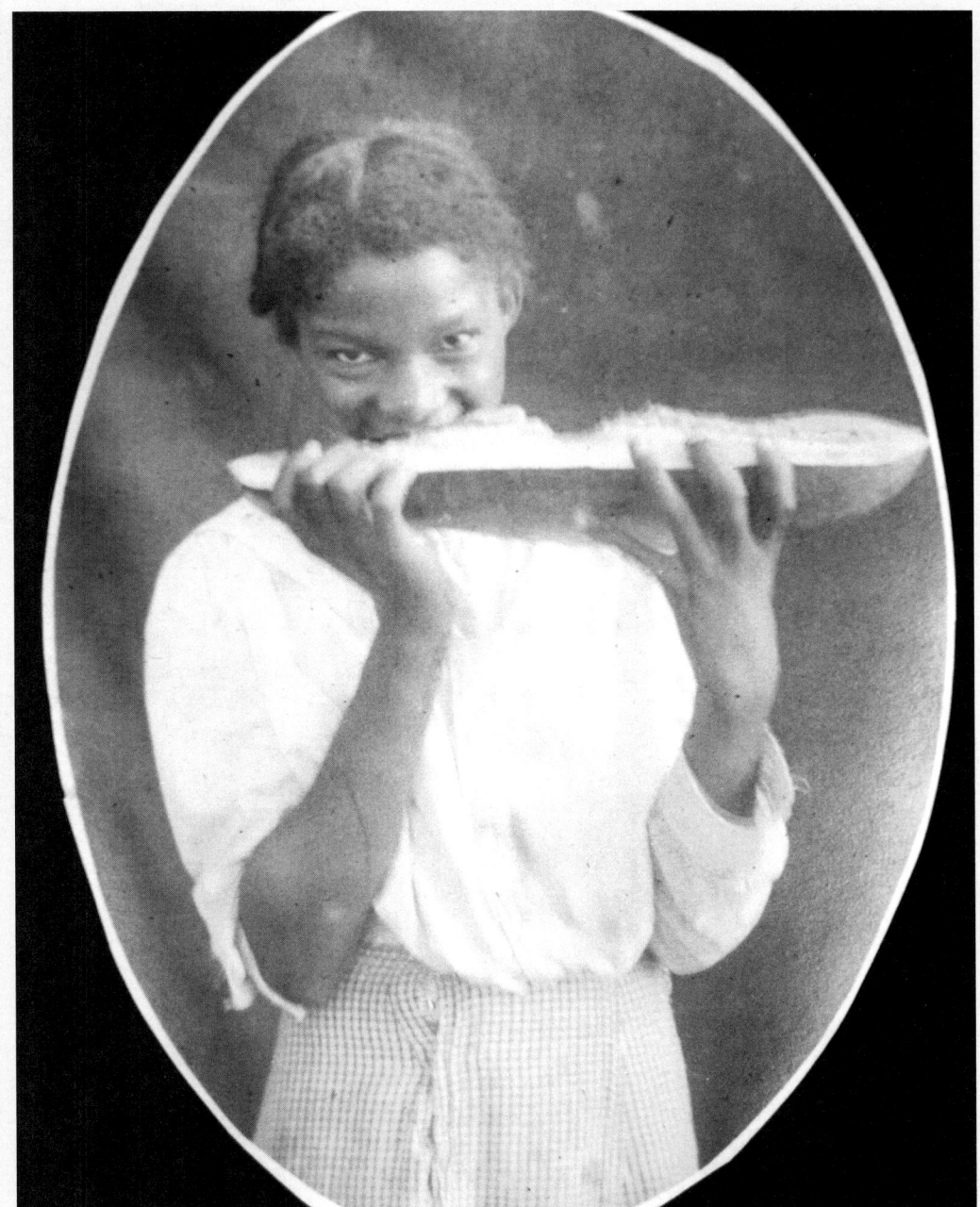

Opposite, top, Plate 95; bottom, Plate 96. Above, Plate 97.

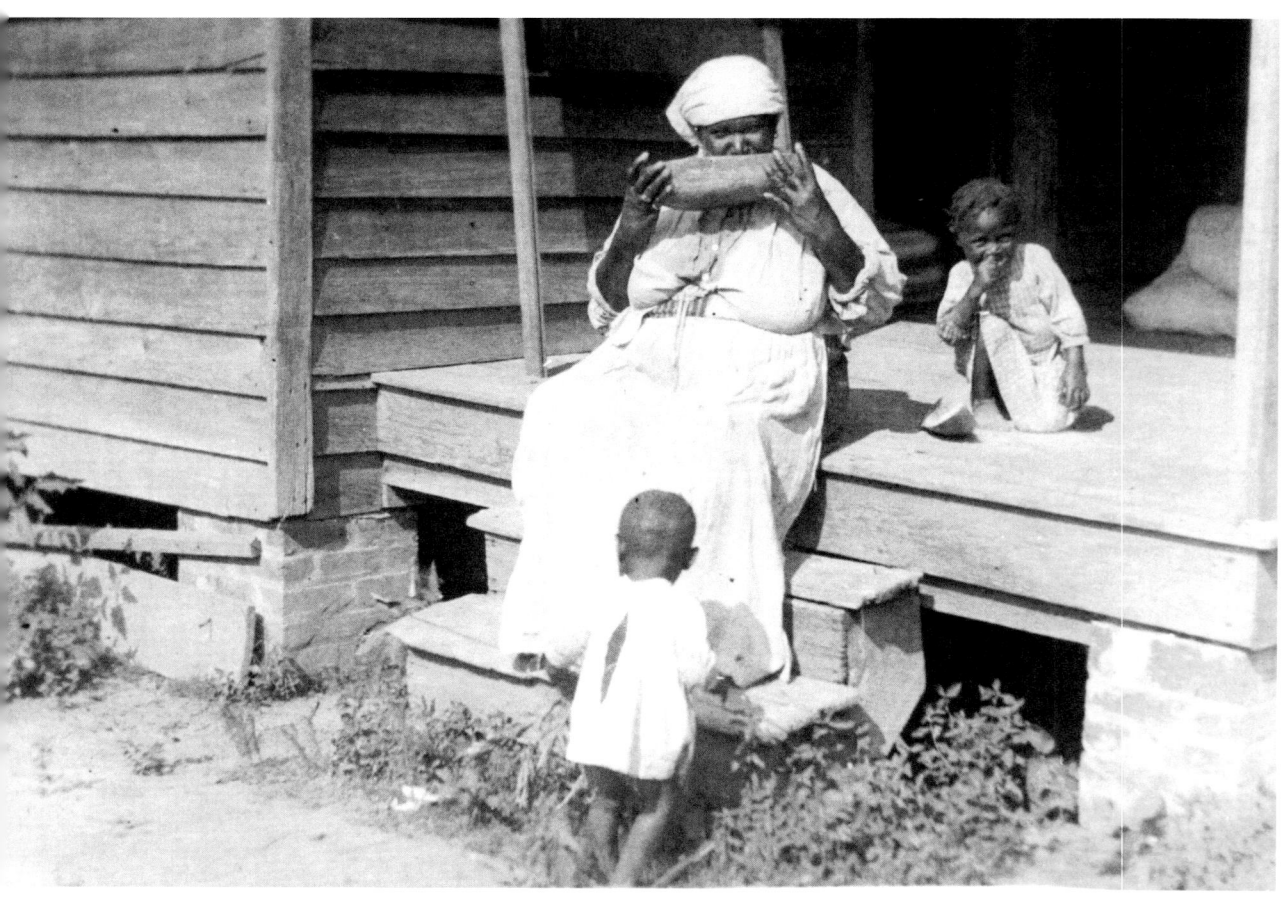

Plate 98.

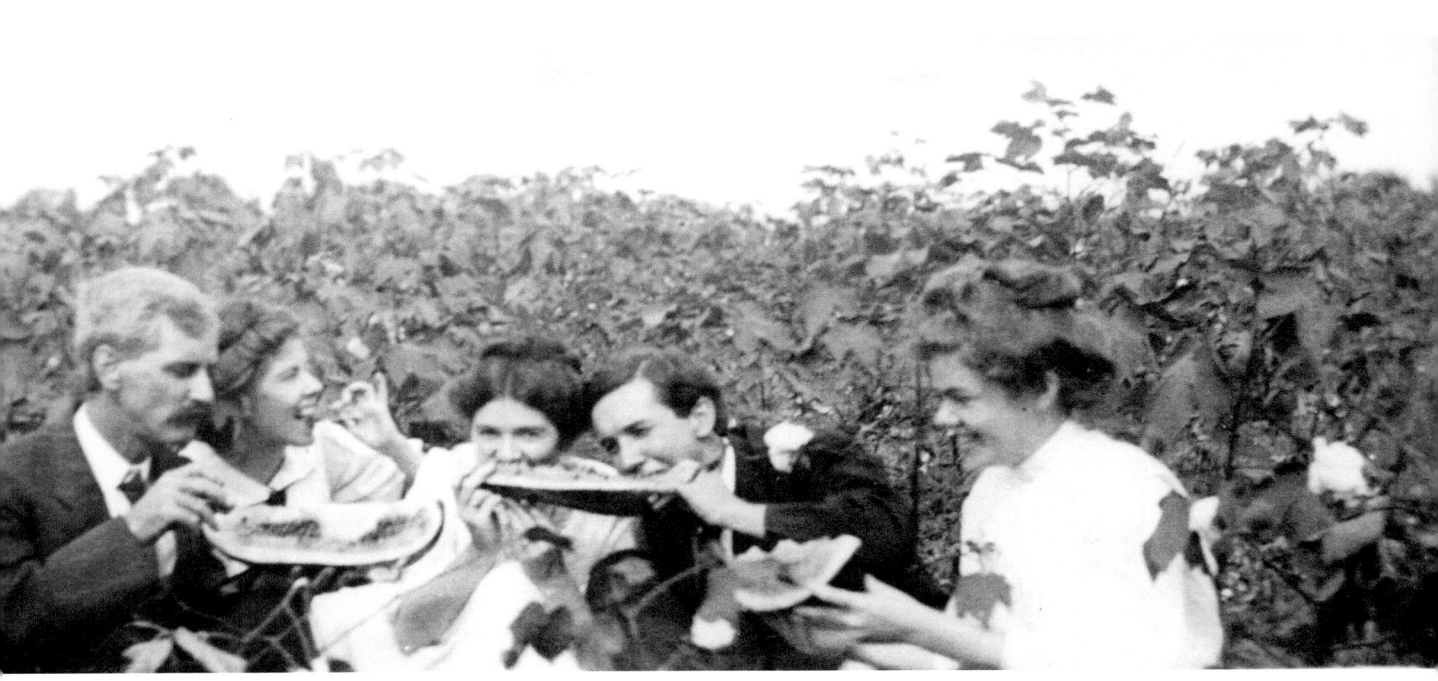

Plate 99.

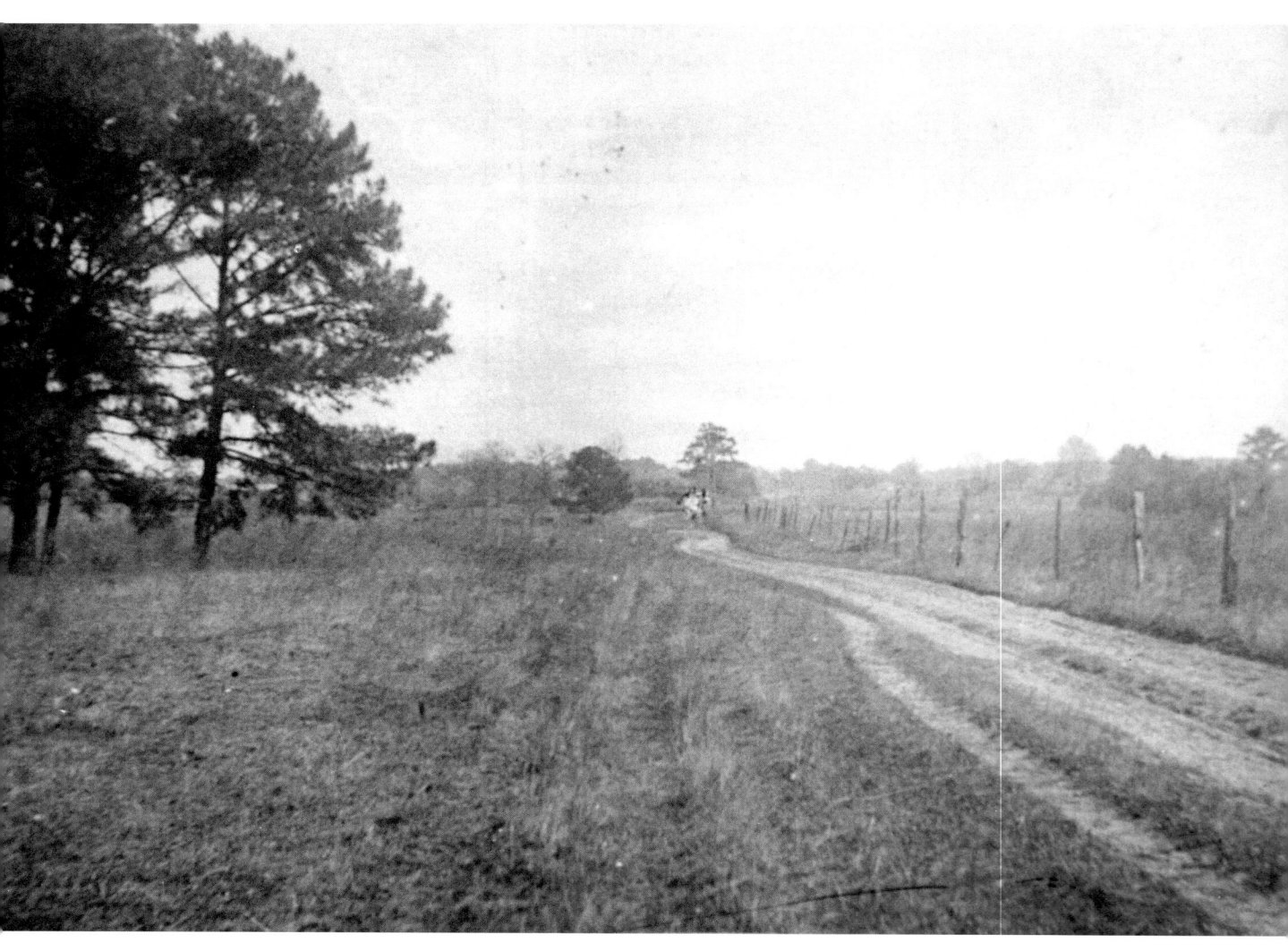

Above, Plate 100. Opposite, Plate 101.

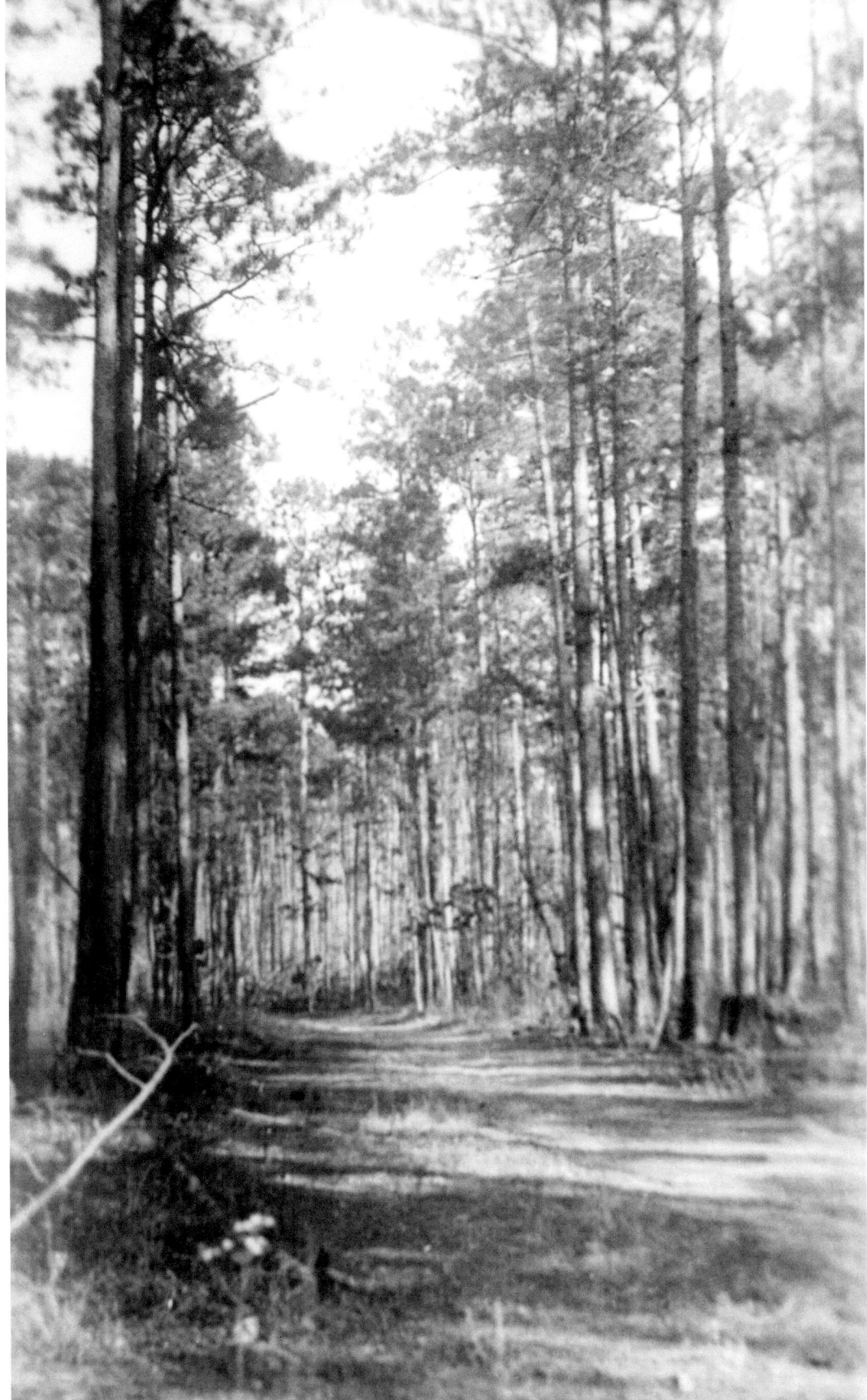

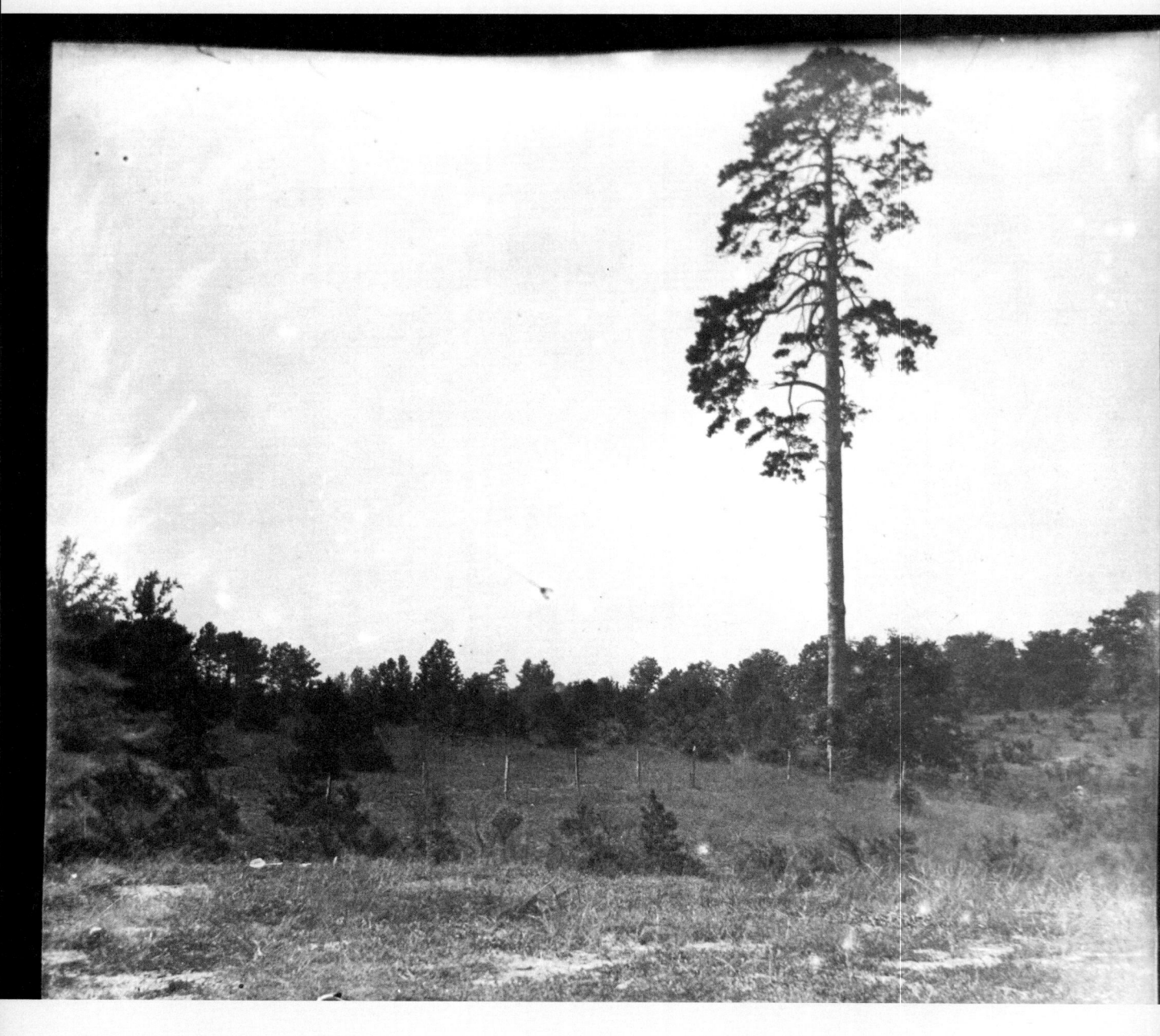

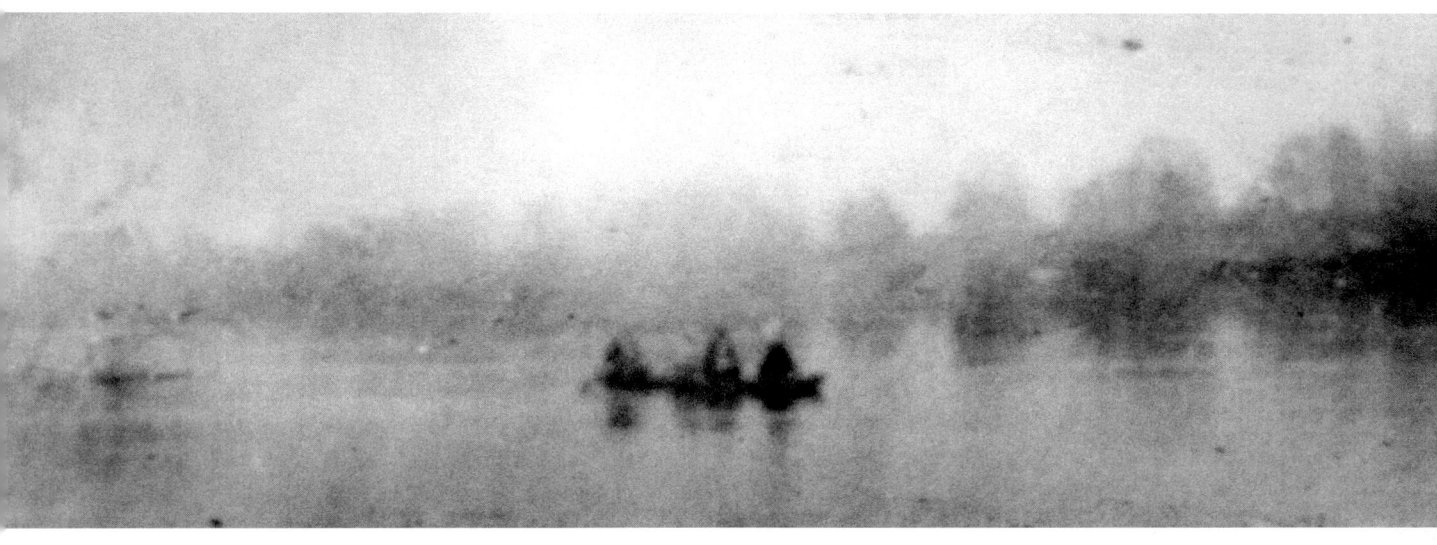

Opposite, Plate 102. Above, Plate 103.

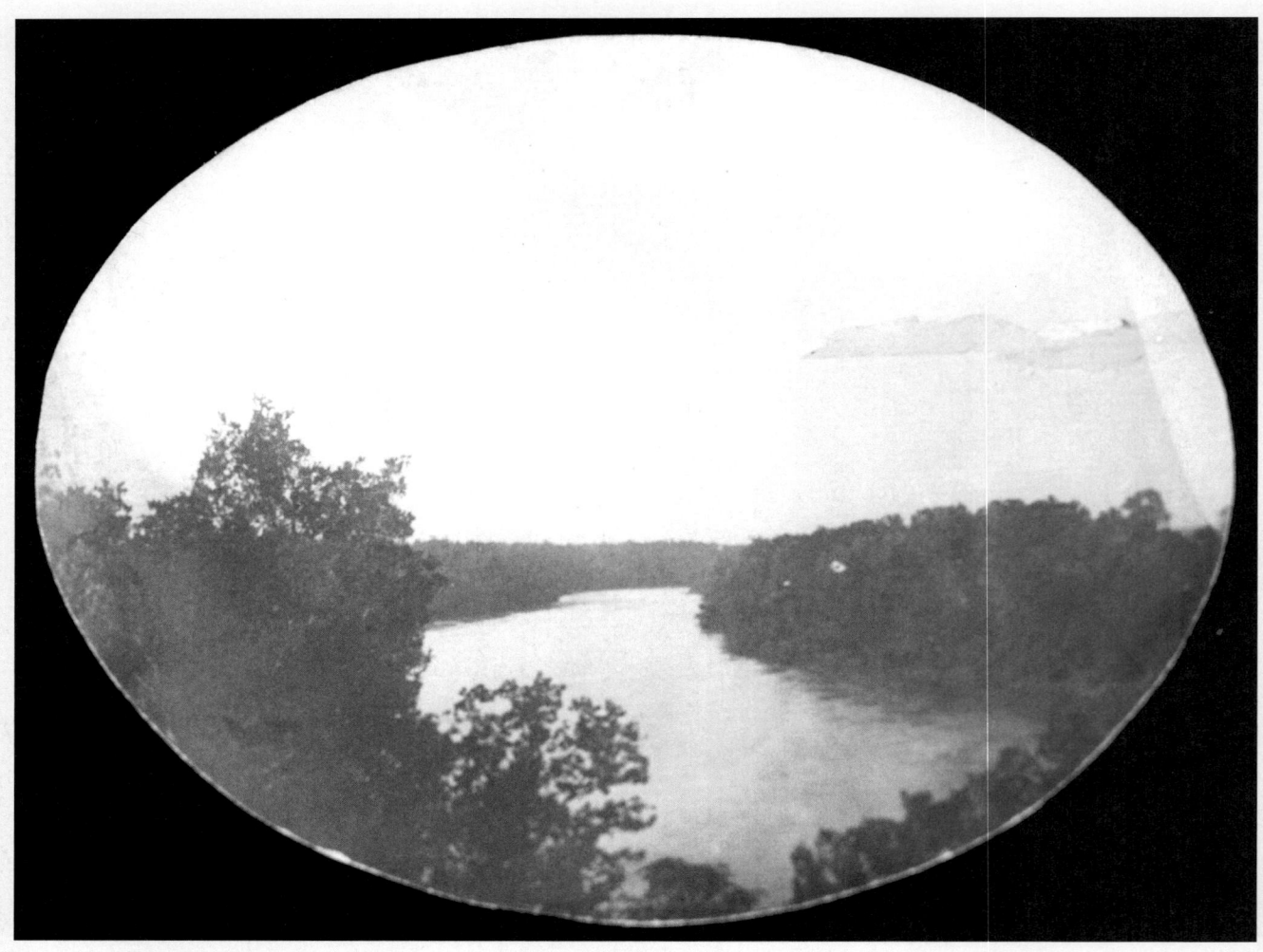

Plate 104.

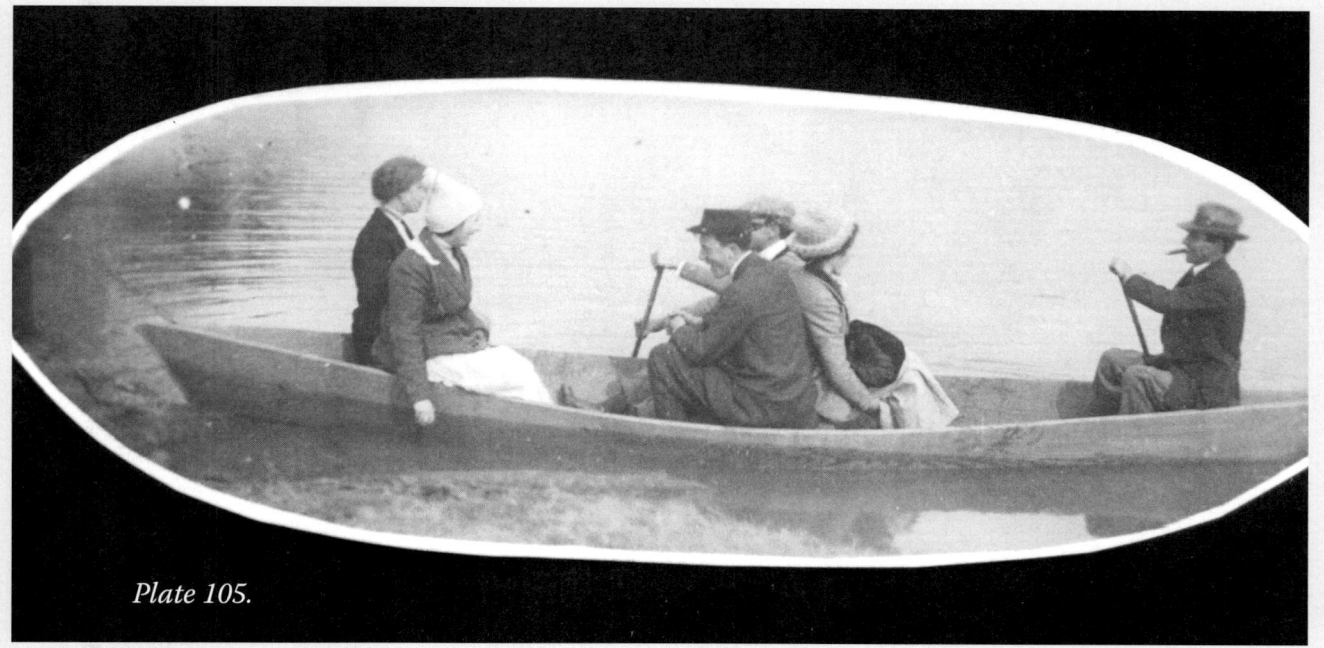

Plate 105.

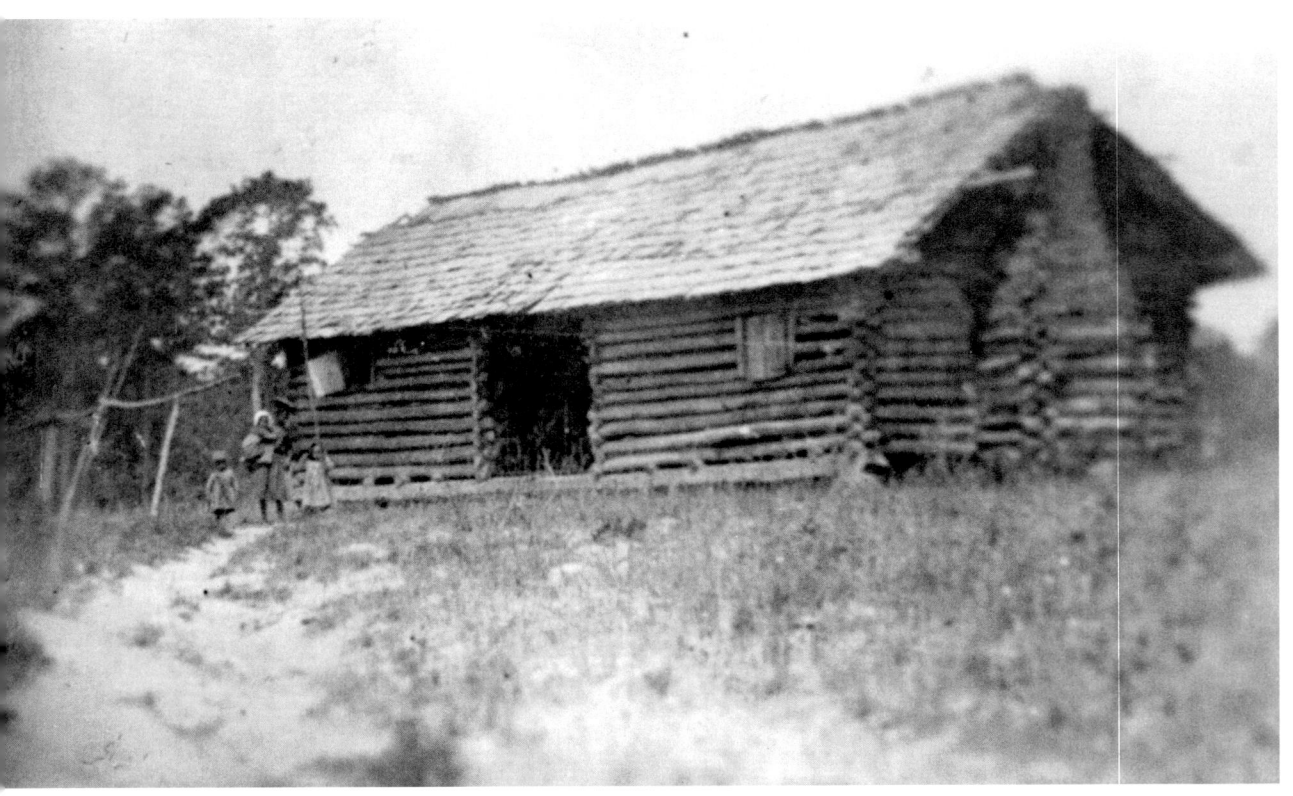

Plate 106.

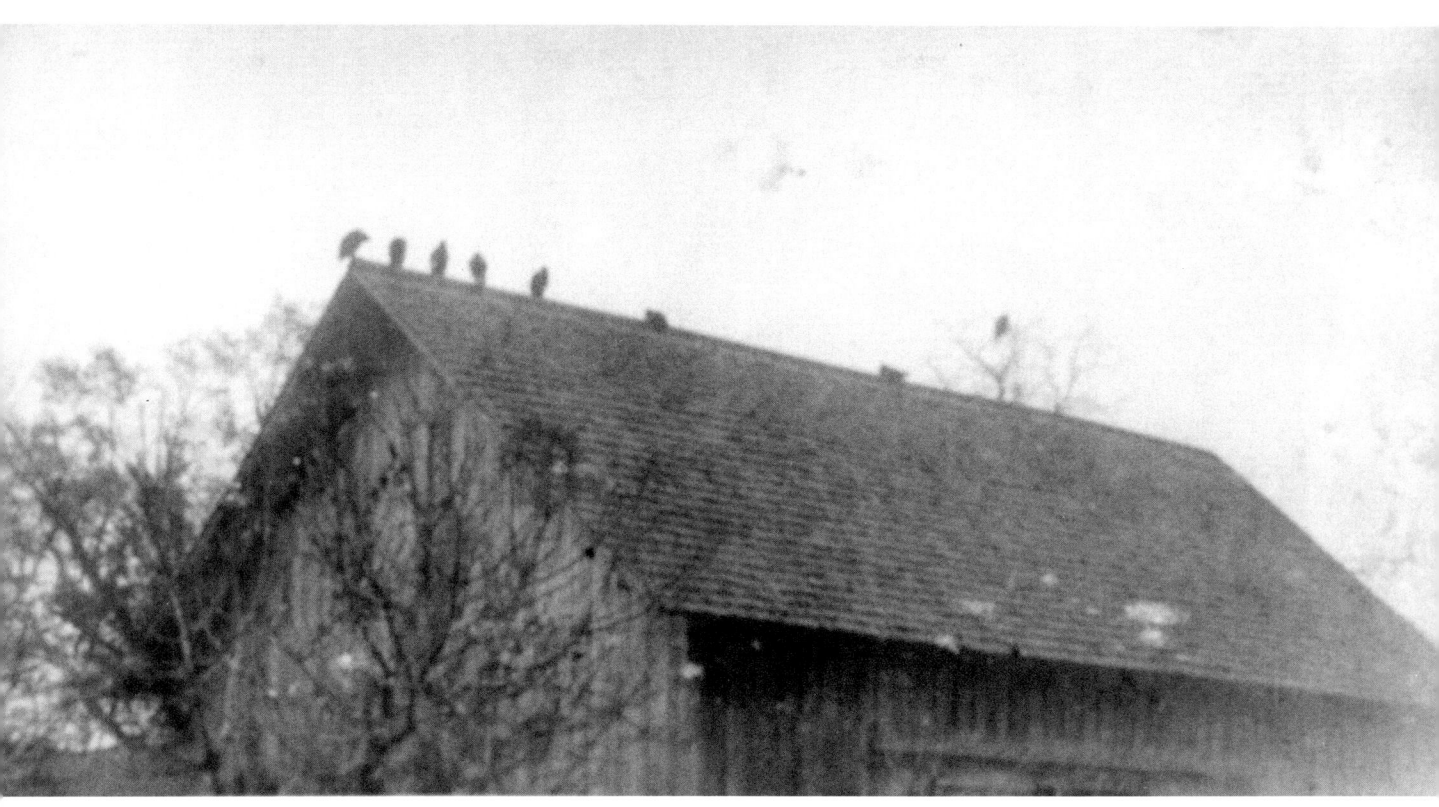

Plate 107.

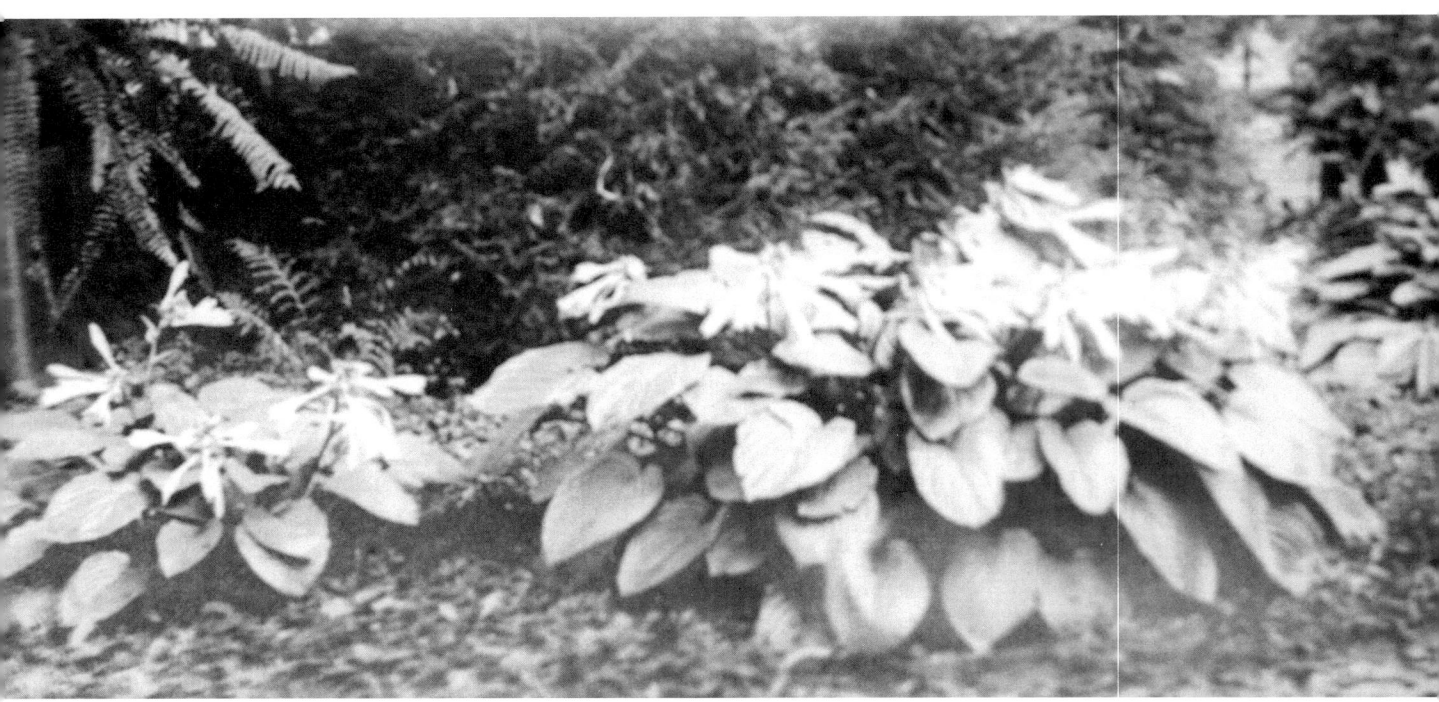

Plate 108.

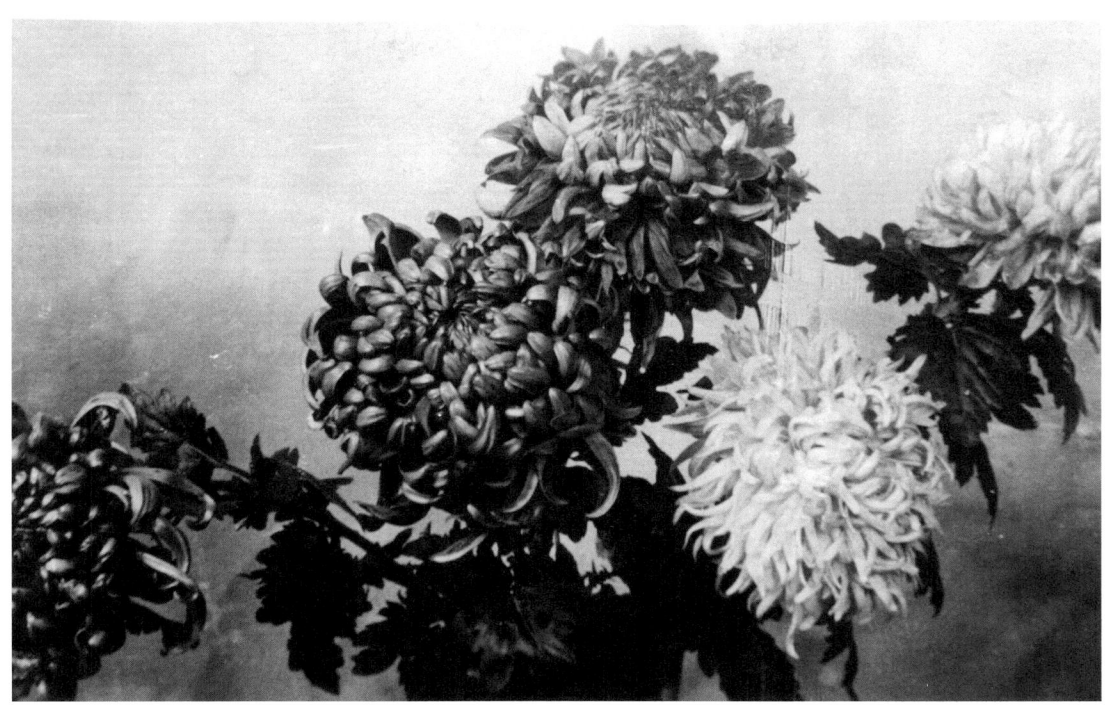

Plate 109.

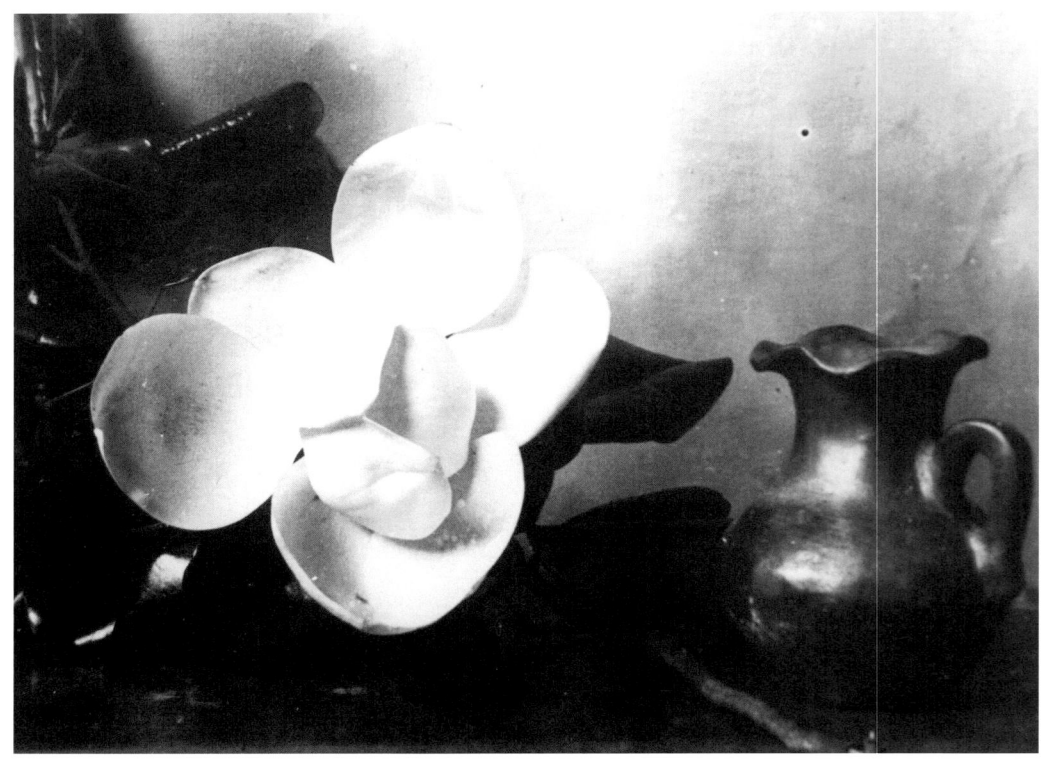

Plate 110.

Index

A

African Americans ix, 15, 18, 19, 21, 23, 24, 25, 26, 28, 29, 30–33, 34–36
Alabama
    constitutions, conventions viii, 4, 18
    flush times of 6
    legislature 4, 5, 18
Alabama Fever 7
Alabama River vii, 6, 7, 8, 10, 34, 118
Alabama-Tombigbee Regional Commission xiii
Alford, George xiii
Allen, Frances Stebbins 27, 28
Allen, Mary Electa 27, 28
Armstrong, Samuel Chapman 32
Art Institute of Chicago. *See* School of the Art Institute of Chicago

B

Barbizon School 27
Ben-Yusuf, Zaida 27, 30
Bible classes ix, 12
Birmingham 22
Black Belt of Alabama vii, viii, ix, 3, 5, 6, 7, 13, 15, 16, 21, 32, 33, 34
Black Belt Treasures xiii
Boiling Springs, Alabama 5, 18
boll weevils 7
Boykin, Annie Brice Miller 49
Boykin, Mary Riley 23
Bromberg, Frederick George 19

Brownell, Elizabeth B. 27, 29

C

Camden Academy 23
Camden, Alabama vii–x, 3–9, 15–16, 17–26
Camden Cemetery 25
Camera Notes 28
Camera Work 36
carpetbaggers viii, ix, x, xii, 3, 4, 9, 12, 18, 20
Chapin, Emma 5, 21
Chautauqua County, New York viii, 3, 17
Chicago, Illinois 3, 4, 10, 24, 46
Civil War viii, 4, 5, 7, 9
Clifton Ferry Road 10
Columbia University 34
Compromise of 1877 19
Confederacy viii, 3, 4, 5
cooperationists 4
Cooper, Frederick 25
Cooper, Narcissa Mayo 25
cotton 4, 5, 6, 7, 15, 29, 33, 68
crop-lien system 6

D

Dallas County, Alabama vii, 32
Daughters of the American Revolution 22
Democrats ix, 5, 18, 19
Dream Children 29

E

Eastman, George 32

F

Farm Security Administration 26, 34

Farnsworth, Emma Justine 27, 28

First Presbyterian Church 8, 9, 22

Fort Oglethorpe, Georgia 23

freedmen 4, 6

Freedmen's Bureau 4

French, William Marchant Richardson 23

Frissell, Hollis Burke 32

Furman, Jade Miller xiii

Furman, Marian Perdue xi–xiii

G

Gee's Bend, Alabama 8, 34, 35

genre works 26, 28–29

Great Britain 5

Great Depression 26, 33

Great Migration 6

Greenback Party 19

Gullett's Bluff, Alabama 24

H

Hampton Institute 31, 32

Haralson, Jeremiah 19

Harris, Nettie Floyd 25

Hayes, Rutherford B. 5, 19

Henderson, Fred 21

Hendersons x, xii, xiii, 9, 20

Henderson, William 18, 23

Hollinger, Martha "Mattie" Mobley 25

I

illiteracy 12–15

J

Jackson, Harvey xiii

James, Marcila 23

James, Wash 23

Johnston, Frances Benjamin 26–28, 29, 30, 31

Jones, Ellen Boykin 49

Jones, Jinnie 5

Jones, John C. 5

Jones, John C. and Jinnie 20

Jones, John Paul and Camilla Boykin 20

Jones, J. Paul 10

Jones, Minnie Miller 40, 49

K

Käsebier, Gertrude 27, 29

Keipp, Mary Morgan 32

L

Ladies' Home Journal 26, 27, 32

Law, Kristin xiii

Liddell, Glen David 11, 25, 49, 80, 81

Liddell, Helen Rickey 74

Liddell, John Russell 78

Liddell, John Russell, Jr. 18, 55, 80, 81, 83, 84

Liddell, John Russell, Sr. 80, 81

Liddell, Mary Helen Rickey 81

Liddell-Phillippi House vii, 11, 25, 40

Liddell, Roy Henderson 49, 78, 80, 81

Liddells x, xii, 9, 20, 25
Liddell, Viola Goode 20, 21, 22
Liddell, William Lithgow 28, 57, 58, 81
Logue, Narcissa 25
Logues x, xii, 9

M

Mason, Matt xii, xiii
McWilliams, Mary 25
McWilliams, Taylor 25
Miller, John 21
Miller's Ferry 21
Millet, Jean-Francois 27
Morgan, Agnes Josephine 24
Morgan, Albion LeBat viii, ix, 3–5,
    16–20, 25, 47, 50
Morgan, Benjamin, Jr. 17
Morgan, Edith 58, 70
    albums of xi–xii
    and religion 22
    as artist 23, 25
    as photographer ix–x, xi–xii, 15–16, 24–25,
        26–36
    as teacher ix, 11–12, 23, 25, 28
    background of viii, 16–25
    birth of viii, 20
    death of x, 12, 25
    education of ix, 8, 9–11, 21, 23–25
    family home of xi, 10, 20
Morgan, Frederick 17, 23
Morgan, Lydia Jones 4, 5, 17, 20, 22
Morgan, Minna. *See* Washburn, Minna
    Augusta Morgan

N

Nashville, Tennessee 22
Nesbit, Evelyn 29
New Deal 34
the "New Woman" 22
New York Times 34

O

Old South 3

P

Parker, Angelina 35
Parker, Mark 35
Phillippi, Janet Liddell 25
Phillippi, William Robertson 25
photography 16, 24, 26–36
"pickaninny" 35
Pictorialist movement 27
plantations viii, 15
Polk, Prentice Herman 32–33
Presbyterian Church 8, 9, 22

R

Radical Republicans viii, 4, 5, 18–19
Rapier, James Thomas 19
Reconstruction viii, 4, 5, 18, 19
Redeemers 5
Resettlement Administration 34
Riley, James Whitcomb 29
Roosevelt, Franklin Delano 33
Rothstein, Arthur 34
Roundtable Chautauqua Circle 22
Russell, Samuel and Robert 33

S

SAIC. *See* School of the Art Institute of Chicago

scalawags 4, 18

School of the Art Institute of Chicago ix, xi, 9, 23, 23–24, 28

Schütze, Martin 36

segregation ix

Selma, Alabama vii, 10, 13, 32

sharecroppers 6, 7, 15

Shelley, Charles Miller 19

slavery 6, 12, 15, 36

Social Darwinism 12

steel plow 6

stereotypes 21, 26, 35

"Storm" 36

Stryker, Roy E. 34

Sunday School Movement 12

T

tenant farming 6

Thompson, Samuel Ross 24

T. Lee Long Bridge 7

Tugwell, Rexford Guy 34

Tuskegee Institute 32

U

Unionists 4

U.S. Census 5, 9

W

Washburn, Charles C. 4, 22

Washburn, Minna Augusta Morgan 4, 11, 17, 20, 22, 25

Washington, Booker T. 32

watermelons 35

Watson, Eva Lawrence 27

Watson-Schütze, Eva 36

Weil, Mathilde 27, 28, 29

white supremacy ix, 21

Wilcox County, Alabama viii, 3–9, 15–16, 34–35

Wilcox County Courthouse 8

Wilcox Female Institute xiii, 8, 21

Wilcox Hotel 7

Wilson, Woodrow 19

Windham, Kathryn Tucker vii

Wolcott, Marion Post 34

Woodson, Oida xiii

Contributors

MARIAN PERDUE FURMAN was born and raised in the Black Belt of Alabama. She is a wife of fifty-nine years, a mother of ten, and a grandmother of twenty-seven. Marian and her husband, Herb, live in the home near Camden that her grandparents purchased in 1913 as newlyweds. Her love of photography and darkroom work began in her teen years. This interest, coupled with a passion for travel and adventure, propelled her on many trips with camera in hand. Her travels have included trekking in the Himalayas, following nomadic migrations in Iran, sailing in the British Virgin Islands, exploring Antarctica, and crossing Mongolia into the Gobi Desert, as well as conventional travel in eastern and western Europe. Furman's life has been nothing short of epic. Amazingly, despite the demands of raising a large family, she found time to work as a professional photographer. Her special interest in fine-art, black-and-white photography led her to appreciate and preserve the photographic legacy of Edith Morgan.

HARVEY H. (HARDY) JACKSON III grew up in Grove Hill, Alabama. He is a graduate of Marion Military Institute, and earned a B.A. at Birmingham-Southern College, an M.A. at the University of Alabama, and a Ph.D. at the University of Georgia. He taught at colleges and universities in Florida and Georgia, and until his recent retirement was Jacksonville State University Professor and Eminent Scholar in History. Jackson is the author, co-author, or co-editor of eleven books on various aspects of Southern history, including *Rivers of History: Life on the Coosa, Tallapoosa, Cahaba and Alabama* (1995); *Putting 'Loafing Streams' to Work: The Building of Lay, Mitchell, Martin, and Jordan Dams, 1910–1929* (1997); and *Inside Alabama: A Personal History of My State*

(2004), which won the Alabama Historical Association's C. J. Coley Award. He has also written numerous articles and reviews for popular and scholarly journals. Jackson serves on the editorial board of and writes for the *Anniston Star*, where his columns and commentary have won awards from the Alabama Press Association. He recently served as editor of Sports and Recreation in the 2010 edition of the *New Encyclopedia of Southern Culture*, University of North Carolina Press. His history of the northern coast of the Gulf of Mexico, titled *The Rise and Decline of the Redneck Riviera: An Insider's History of the Florida-Alabama Coast*, was published by the University of Georgia Press in 2012. He lives in Jacksonville, Alabama, with his wife, Suzanne. They have a son, Will, and a daughter, Anna.

MATTHEW DANIEL MASON is an archivist chiefly responsible for processing collections of photographs and other visual resources at the Beinecke Rare Book and Manuscript Library at Yale University. He is a co-author of the award-winning visual history of Native Americans in Wisconsin, *People of the Big Voice: Photographs of Ho-Chunk Families by Charles Van Schaick, 1879–1942*. Mason received a Ph.D. in history from the University of Memphis, as well as a Master of Arts in Library and Information Studies from the University of Wisconsin-Madison School of Library and Information Studies and a Bachelor of Arts from Humboldt State University. In addition to his archival work, Mason teaches courses in history and the history of photography at Quinnipiac University in Hamden, Connecticut. He also reviews works on photography, art, and architecture for several academic journals and presents professional papers on the history of photography and photographic archives.